FROM STEPNEY TO HELL AND BACK

Cliff Martin's journey from the East End to the Death Railway... and liberation

By Geoff Martin

Cover and book design by John Lister

Published by GM Management

GMmanagementLLP@outlook.com

Printed by Book Printing UK *www.bookprintinguk.com*
Remus House, Coltsfoot Drive, Peterborough, PE2 9BF

Printed in Great Britain

ISBN: 978-1-0369-1645-9

For Helen, Katie, Jo and Janette

Contents

Acknowledgements

I would never have embarked on the task of writing up our Dad's life story if I hadn't had the support, advice and encouragement of friends and family.

Firstly, I want to thank my sister Jan who went through Mum and Dad's things and dug deep into her own memory to help me fill in gaps and build up the timeline that has guided me throughout my research.

I'm not sure I would have got started on what I knew would be one of the toughest challenges of my life if it hadn't been for my old mates Chris Pearson and Rob Poacher sitting me down in a pub and telling me to get on with it. I owe you both a pint.

Keith Connor knew Dad well and read through some early draft chapters and gave me encouragement when I wasn't sure if I was on the right track. Thanks mate, I owe you one as well.

Author and pal Tim Rolls told me ages ago that I had a book or two in me and was also good enough to look at an early draft of the manuscript and offered time and advice freely as did Martin Knight from London Books and my old colleague Steve Silver who pointed me to important sources on Dad's early life. Sue Farley-Green looked into the family history and she and Dee Daley read through the manuscript and have been brilliant.

John Lister, who I worked with for donkey's years, shouldered the task of proofing and editing and offered precious advice on key sections. John also took on design and processing tasks to get the manuscript ready for print and really held the whole project together when I was way out of my depth.

Terry Manttan and Andrew Snow at the Thailand-Burma Railway Centre dug through both Dads records and those of some of his comrades and were generous and supportive with their time. They provide an incredible resource for anyone with an interest in Death Railway.

Likewise Ronnie Taylor and Glenda Godfrey and the rest of the community who exchange information on the COFEPOW Facebook forum - great people working hard to keep the flame burning in memory of our relatives who suffered so much.

The authors of all the books and reports that I've drawn on to illuminate Dad's journey and which I've listed as sources. I'm not an academic, I'm a journalist and I've tried to piece together my father's story through a journalist's eye and although I've not been able to trace his movements every step of the way the source material has allowed me to build as complete a picture as possible.

It's worth pointing out that the names of some of the many POW camps have various translations and interpretations by the prisoners and if there are any inconsistencies that is why. I have also avoided the use of the shorthand terms for the captors except where it is in direct quotation.

Finally, my wife Helen and our daughters Katie and Jo. This book is a labour of love for Dad, Mum and Jan but also for you as well. Dad's real triumph in the end was seeing the smiles on your faces. Say his name with pride.

Introduction

I had been planning to write up my father's life story for some years, initially I just thought it was important for my family that his extraordinary tale was put on the record and that it may be of interest to anyone researching the experience of Japanese prisoners of war or working class London history.

Once I got started I soon realised that what I originally thought would just be a long online essay would actually grow into a book, weaving together some of the most important events in 20th century history. I had no idea at the outset where this journey would take me.

There was always a good excuse for putting it off but having retired from full time work, and after a good cajoling from some of my mates, I fired up the keyboard, opened a file and set to work. I was also motivated by the death of a few friends, which reminded me that my time was finite and that if I didn't get a move on there would be no one left to piece the story together. I was reminded that I had missed the opportunity to sit Dad down in front of a tape recorder and get him to tell the story himself, I had been meaning to do that for some years but then, one day, it was too late. My prevarication had made this task a whole lot harder but I have no one to blame for that other than myself.

But as I got started it soon became clear that pulling

the timeline and the scattered facts together was forcing me to face up to my own demons. For a long time I had found it very difficult to read accounts of the Death Railway, the Hell Ships and the Japanese camps. I found it overwhelming and distressing at a level that is hard for me to explain. All I could ever think of was the battered, starved, exhausted and sick body of my father trying desperately to rest so tired in some stinking hell hole, knowing that this was his life day in and day out for year after endless year. His pain, loneliness and despair was, and still is, impossible for me to comprehend and bears no relationship to the gentle, kind and loving man that I was lucky enough to grow up with. I also know now that it's a cold, hard fact that if the atom bombs hadn't been dropped in the August of 1945 on Hiroshima and Nagasaki that Dad would have been shot and me, my sister and our kids wouldn't be here.

I realise now that I needed to confront those thoughts head on. In the early days of writing this book I met up with an old work friend and his partner. Over a pint I told them that I was working on this project and mentioned Intergenerational Trauma, something that I had only just come across. They went silent and then it emerged that my friend's partner had lost many of her family in the Holocaust, she was very familiar with Intergenerational Trauma and we talked about the feelings that it left you with; helplessness, anxiety, guilt and flashbacks to vivid and imagined images of your loved ones being tortured and traumatised.

I had packed all of that away and had never talked to anyone other than my wife about it before, I wish I had as it has helped me make sense of who I am and the shadow that my father's experiences still cast over me. It has also helped me to see the writing of this book as an opportunity to understand and also to process a huge backlog of feelings that were impacting my own health. I'm grateful to the friends who pushed me to crack on with it.

I never wanted this book to simply be about the incomprehensible brutality of Dad's three and a half years in captivity. It covers all of that, but his story is about so much more. It's about the unemployed and homeless orphan boy from the streets of Stepney who lied about his age to join the army and how his tough early life helped him in that battle to survive day after day when Lady Luck was looking down on him. But it's also about how hope was born out of those days of total despair, how something stopped him from succumbing when he was at his lowest ebb and how love eventually helped him conquer the tormentors that lived in his head and became the rock that he built a long, happy and successful life on. This story is as much about my Mum as it is about Dad. Without her I don't think he would have made it.

But despite all of that his war never ended. The nightmares that I remember so well as a kid may have become less frequent but they terrorised him until the day he died. He never forgot the friends and comrades he saw die on the battlefield or in the heat of the jungle camps and the hold of the Hell Ships. And he had the daily physical reminders: the ridge on the back of his skull from the day he was nearly beaten to death by a guard and which he would constantly run his hand over; the legacy of the many diseases and medical conditions that should have killed him; and the dance with death from self-medicating to alleviate the pain from the constant headaches. If he ever had the slightest inclination to forget what had happened he never would have been allowed to.

Dad's story is also one of betrayal. The betrayal of the incompetent military leadership throughout the battle and retreat all the way down the Malaysian peninsular, the cowardice, hubris and rank stupidity that led to the surrender at Singapore. The lasting betrayal of the "Forgotten Army" in the Far East that went on for years after the Japanese surrender and which was compounded by the failure of successive Governments to seek any sort of recognition and compensation for the years of suffering.

The final betrayal of my father came when he had to pick himself up and fight again: this time against the authorities for the War Pension that he so clearly deserved.

He never wanted to be pitied, and he never wanted his war time experiences to define him, but he was angry that right to end the system and the powers that be were prepared to try and turn their back on him.

On a personal level I am appalled at the lack of public knowledge of what happened to men like my Dad. Whilst anniversaries of the war in Europe still make headlines, Death Railway, the Hell Ships and the brutal Japanese slave labour camps like Mitsushima barely get a mention. At best people might have heard of the inaccurate and insulting Bridge on the River Kwai film but that's about it. If I can do anything, even on the smallest scale, to help address that imbalance I will consider it worthwhile and I know that my Dad would have been proud that I have at least tried to get his truth out there to a wider audience.

My father never considered himself to be anything special, he came from that generation where so many lived extraordinary lives but I think his story is a compelling testament to the sheer strength of the human spirit and the power of love and hope. He once told me that he thought he was the luckiest man alive and I can understand that but I consider myself to be dead lucky as well. I've never been called upon to uproot my life and fight in a war thousands of miles away and I've never had my freedom taken away and been condemned to years of hell in conditions where death stalked me day in and day out. Dad did all of that and more and although he never got to tell the world the truth I am proud to have the opportunity to do it for him.

CHAPTER ONE

Kilkenny to Mile End

My father, Cliff Martin, was born on the 16th of December 1919 at 94 Duckett Street in Stepney with his birth registered at Mile End Old Town on the 5th of January 1920. He was an East Ender to his tiny pink toes. He was the eighth and final child of George and Caroline Martin.

He used to tell us that he was a big bouncing baby of ten pounds and that his older sister, Auntie May, was fond of telling everyone that he "nearly killed his bleeding mother." He needed to be strong as he was born into abject poverty. My grandfather George claimed on Dad's birth certificate that he was a wardrobe dealer, that means second hand clothes, and on other documents either general dealer or just dealer. He was a totter. He scrounged, collected and sold anything that he could make a few pennies on. There was an old East End saying – "born a totter, die a totter". That was my grandad's life, it was in his blood.

My father told me that as a young child he would be loaded up in a hand cart and trundled off with his old man down to Brick Lane or other East End street markets to pick up any bits of vegetables that had been chucked away and old broken crates and packing cases. Grandad George broke these up and sold them in bundles of kindling, and he straightened out and sold on the nails as well. By the time Dad was born George was around fifty years old. His age is approximate as he was something of an enigma with a background that has proved impossible to penetrate.

Luckily, I talked with my Dad about him quite a lot as I grew up as I found him a fascinating character and his story helped fill gaps in my own quest for identity, I never met him of course but I felt a powerful connection. Although he claimed on the 1911 census that he had been born in Whitechapel it was simply not true. It was all part of a false identity that he had built around himself. He was actually born in Kilkenny in the south of Ireland. He spoke in a broad Irish accent, sang rebel songs about Bold Robert Emmet, a Protestant Fenian leader, around the pubs of Mile End and claimed to have once been one of the Kilkenny Cats - the nickname of the great, local hurling team. He wore a green tie at Easter to celebrate the uprising in Dublin. My father remembered all of these things fondly.

So why the mystery and the false trail? He would have travelled across to Liverpool on the boat around 1890 and at that time it wasn't unusual for Irishmen to change their names and create new identities as they headed across the sea to find work. Anti-Irish racism was rife. This was certainly common for those emigrating to America, the O or the Mac was dropped to anglicise the name and make it easier to find work or housing. Was he aiming to make that journey across the ocean to New York or Boston like so many before him but had a change of plan? Perhaps he was only able to raise the fare to England and so his voyage ended there.

I have asked friends who are experts on ancestry to try and trace George Martin but they have drawn a blank. There's certainly no record of him being born in Whitechapel and Irish records from that era are scant. It's also nigh on impossible to trace someone who has adopted a false or modified name. One other intriguing possibility begs another question, was he on the run? Whilst such an idea sends my imagination running wild, I've been forced to draw the conclusion that I will never know.

But Grandad George's back story is even more complicated. He was a Protestant, Church of Ireland, and although he was a Fenian and a United Irishman many records held by the Protestant church were destroyed during the Civil War. My Dad told me that when his father was a boy the Catholic kids would throw stones at them. Assuming he was born around 1869 he would have been a ten year old at the time of the last famine in Ireland. The brutal economics of the Long Depression forced him across the water to seek his fortune. With contacts in the strong and established Irish community in the East End, after landing on the Liverpool shore it's logical he would have headed south. If he was looking to seek his fortune on streets paved with gold he was soon confronted by a harsh reality and I doubt that he ever saw his family back in Ireland again.

The East London he arrived in was a centre of poverty, slum housing, infant mortality and grim, hard and short lives. It was also the East London of Jack the Ripper, Grandad would have first trod those dark streets as the fear of the Ripper, and the manhunt to find him, was at fever pitch. The two big waves of immigration into the East End had been the Irish in the late 1840s and 1850s and east European Jews from 1881 until 1905 - the Irish fleeing famine and the Jews fleeing the pogroms and growing antisemitism sweeping Europe.

Stepney and Mile End were massively overcrowded but more immigrants like my grandfather continued to arrive. The legendary Booth's Survey of London completed around that time scores Mile End Old Town, where I believe my Grandad sought out digs with family members who had already made the journey across over the water, as right off the scale – it's an area of Booth's "black streets" the poorest and most deprived of the lot, marked down as vicious and semi-criminal. In fact Mile End Old Town was specifically created around 1857 as a designated Poor Law Hamlet, and was dominated by the Work House built in the late 1850s. The records show that there were a lot of

Martins on the manor.

Although this was some decades before the infamous *No Blacks, No Irish, No Dogs* signs began appearing in boarding house windows, anti-Irish racism would certainly have confronted George in the world of employment opportunities and although he may have changed his name he had made no effort to disguise his accent. *No Irish Need Apply* was such an established thing in 1800's London that music hall songs were written about it. I can imagine my Grandad, who fancied himself as a singer, giving that one a blast down the pub alongside his traditional rebel songs. Buying, selling and dealing was up there with the rag trade and the docks as the top means of making a living in Stepney at this time and weighing his limited options Grandad decided that was the route for him. It's quite possible he had little choice, but it's also quite possible that he brought that small trader gut instinct with him from Ireland. The East End of this era is often depicted as lawless and beyond redemption, as one contemporary commentator put it:

> *"A shabby man from Paddington, St. Marylebone or Battersea might pass muster as one of the respectable poor. But the same man coming from Bethnal Green, Shadwell or Wapping was an 'East Ender'; the box of Keating's bug powder must be reached for, and the spoons locked up... it became a concentrated reminder to the public conscience that nothing to be found in the East End should be tolerated in a Christian country."*

Harsh words, but while this corner of London was undoubtedly riven with crime, disease and appalling overcrowding and poverty there was also an indomitable spirit that gave East Enders like my grandparents a sense of purpose. They were fighting for survival and were grafters prepared to put in the hard hours to put food on the table and pay the rent, thinking on their feet and prepared to be imaginative and entrepreneurial in the battle to make ends meet. I'm proud of them and I'm proud of their spirit and readiness to fight against the odds. They must have had hope that if they kept going there would be a chance of something better round the next corner. It was that hope that sent my Grandad across the Irish Sea as an economic migrant and I believe it was also somehow instilled in my father and would stand him in good stead in the years ahead. It was embedded in his DNA.

Sometime around the mid 1890's my grandfather met my grandmother, Caroline Gaffee. Grandma had been born in Bethnal Green in 1875 and her family was rooted in the East End - Shoreditch, Hackney, Stepney and Spitalfields. By 1897 they had had a son, my uncle George, the first of their eight kids with my father being the last. The 1901 census shows them living at 103 Roswell Street in Mile End, around the time that American author Jack London wrote this of the poor in London in his book *People of the Abyss:*

> *"The air he breathes, and from which he never escapes, is sufficient to weaken him mentally and physically, so that he becomes unable to compete with the fresh virile life from the country hastening on to London Town.....it is incontrovertible that the children grow up into rotten adults, without virility or stamina, a weak-kneed, narrow chested, listless breed that crumples up and goes down in the brute struggle for life with the invading hordes of the country."*

Whilst not downplaying the horrendous conditions in which my grandparents began their life together they were clearly made of strong stuff, and after George the family grew on an almost annual basis and these were tough and healthy babies born to survive the odds that had been loaded against them by class and geography. Most social coverage of the area at that time was slanted towards the arguments of the campaigners fighting for improved conditions.

There's nothing wrong with that in principle but the danger is that it lumps everyone together into the broad-brush description of Jack London and ignores the poor East Enders who weren't a "weak-kneed, narrow chested, listless breed that crumples up and goes down in the brute struggle for life." For my family nothing could have been further from the truth - in that brute struggle for life they were determined to not only survive but to come out on top.

My Dad developed a lifelong dislike of people, particularly politicians and commentators, who pictured the working class through their own ideology rather than through any lived experience. He would see right through them for the frauds that they are whether they came from right or left. That instinctive distrust of politicians, borne from the streets of Stepney, would be confirmed and escalated in the years to come.

CHAPTER TWO

Born into Poverty

By 1911, and now with six kids in tow, five sons and my Auntie May, the family had moved the short distance to 16 Lomas Buildings on Mile End Road and the final address we have for them is 94 Duckett Street, where my father was born in 1919. My grandparents didn't marry until 1917. As well as looking after eight children my grandmother also had to work to help keep the family afloat. She was a "sewer by machinery", a seamstress. I remember my father telling me that she used to wheel an old pram on foot up to the posher parts of North London to take in linen for washing and repairs, and then wheel it back.

It must have been gruelling work for a very small return, but it was that or watch your kids starve. Sometimes she would take my Dad with her on these expeditions to the leafier parts of the city and on one occasion he recalled the housekeeper giving him a bowl of tinned peaches and cream while his Mum sorted out her business. He had never tasted anything like it and even the thought of it would put a smile on his face. We often used to have tinned peaches and cream with our Sunday dinner, and it always brought back that memory for him.

At Duckett Street the whole family were rammed into a couple of rooms on one floor of the tenement block with a shared tap on the landing and an outside toilet. Occasionally enough coppers would be scraped together for a slipper bath down at Mile End, otherwise it was a wash down with cold water from a tin bucket. Pictures of the street at the time show that it was made up of narrow three story, brick built terraces. My grandmother would have had to find space within those confines to carry out her home-based seamstress work.

I never talked much with my father about these living conditions but I do know that he shared a bed with a couple of his brothers and that the winters were cold and hard in the old and draughty terraces and they'd wrap themselves up in old overcoats and anything they could find to try and keep warm. Old sacks were laid on the floor as carpets to try and stop drafts coming up through the boards. Finding wood to light a fire was a mission but the connection to the nearby docks would help. Lighting in the dark days of winters was primitive as the nights closed in and would have been by candle, paraffin lamp or gas if you were lucky.

Stepney was massively overcrowded. A comparison can be made with the City of Plymouth at that time which had roughly the same population but five times the total area. There was little outside space for recreation as unplanned housing development in the 18th and 19th centuries had swallowed up most of the available land. There were just 45 acres of open recreational space, whereas under the LCC plan 376 acres would have been needed, according to the *Living In Stepney* pamphlet produced by *The Stepney Reconstruction Group at Toynbee Hall* in 1945 which looked back at the years between the wars, arguing the case for post war change.

The pamphlet paints a stark picture of the impact of the overcrowding and housing conditions that my father was born into. Comparing Stepney with another working class London Borough, Lewisham, on the key indicator of infant mortality there were eighty deaths per thousand births in Stepney compared with fifty in Lewisham and the report, which was setting out the case for reducing population density and rebuilding the Borough, lays the blame firmly at overcrowding and poor quality housing.

The development of the docks had driven the population growth since the early 19th century. It peaked around the time of the 1911 census and would only start to decline as the Borough Council and the London County Council came under Labour control and began to take steps to tackle the housing crisis and reduce the population count. It was the combination of that political policy and the mass bombing of the East End in WW2 that started and then later accelerated the great cockney diaspora.

The East End in those pre-war days was chock full of pubs. If you look at a map it's just stunning how many there were and the area around the Martin family tenement was no exception. The Prince of Wales was a few doors down at 108 Duckett Street, and the Anchor and Hope, almost next door at number 90, was a traditional Watney's two bar, backstreet London boozer. The landlady Mrs Jane Palmer had a fierce reputation but she would have needed it to keep her punters in order. My Dad would get himself ready by the front window at closing time on a Saturday night to clock the punch ups out in the street, entertainment for a young lad but also a measure of the tough world he was growing up in.

As soon as he was old enough he had signed up at the local boxing club, same as every other East End boy, and had learned how to defend himself and throw a punch. I know he boxed in tournaments for the club but sadly any records have long gone. The importance of boxing in working class cockney culture cannot be overestimated, a conveyor belt of British champions emerged from clubs within the sound of Bow Bells and it gave lads like my Dad a sense of discipline and purpose as well as hardening them up and teaching them about physical fitness. He later went on to box in the army and as an old man he would still do exercises learnt as a boy at the boxing club.

Before my Dad's tenth birthday his own father had died. My grandmother was now heavily reliant on her children to help make the rent and put food on the table and that would have included young Cliff. The family still lived under the fearful shadow of the workhouse:

although the big one at Mile End was closed in 1926 the system itself wasn't abolished until 1930, and the actual dismantling took some years. The terror that the threat of the workhouse instilled was very real, and must have worried my widowed grandmother sick. One job my Dad took on to earn a few coppers was putting out the chairs for the boxing and wrestling at York Hall Bethnal Green. When we used to watch the wrestling together on World of Sport on a Saturday afternoon he would tell me that even when he was a kid the wrestlers used to practice their moves and choreography before a bout while the kids sorting the chairs looked on, getting a free show as well as a bit of extra cash.

As the youngest of a string of boys, Dad was last in line for the hand-me-down clothes and boots that were passed along the line from his older brothers and his clobber would have been worn and battered but carefully repaired by his Mum as best as possible. All the other kids he knocked about were in the same boat, the idea of buying new clothes was a fantasy world. I remember him telling me that if the old boots he inherited were too big they would be stuffed with newspaper until he grew into them. I think his pride in his appearance in later life came from both these early experiences and his years in the army. Long before the mods came along working class blokes like my Dad were following that ethos of looking sharp in difficult circumstances and buying the best gear you could afford. It was an ethos born out of those hard times in the East End.

My grandmother died in 1932, leaving my father orphaned at the age of 12. The death of his parents when he was so young would go on to have a lasting impact on him in many ways and would shape events that would map out the rest of his life. He was a bright kid. So bright that he sat tests and was offered a scholarship to the grammar school and the opportunity to extend his education and get into a trade or a profession. But although the scholarship paid the school fees it didn't cover the cost of the uniform and the other kit he needed to take up the place, and with the family skint he had no chance and had to turn down the offer.

He left school at 14. If he had been able to scrape together the funding to take up the grammar school offer he wouldn't have left school until he was sixteen, denying his family two years of potential income to support the household budget. Now they were orphaned there was no way his brothers and sisters could have made that work, although my father was the youngest his older siblings had their own financial pressures to deal with and some of them were starting their own families, there was no prospect of them carrying him for two years of further education and Dad understood that. In the end it was class and the harsh economics of the Depression that decided his future at every turn, and he never forgot that.

All he was able to find now was low paid manual work. If he was lucky. The Depression had seen unemployment rise to 2.5 million by 1933 - 25% of the workforce and the poor working class communities of East London found themselves hammered again . This was the world of work he now entered and he managed to land himself a labouring job at Charringtons Blue Anchor Brewery on the Mile End Road. Charringtons had been formed in Bethnal Green in the early 18th century and by the time my Dad joined the firm their Stepney headquarters was a huge and sprawling industrial site made up of vast brick built hop warehouses, production facilities, cooperages, stables and offices operating around the clock. It was the second biggest brewery in London covering some sixteen acres. Wages for a fourteen year old joining the firm as an unskilled labourer at that time of deep economic recession were low, around ten shillings a week, and the hours were long, with only one full day off on a Sunday. Dad learnt the hard way the importance of hard graft and the value of the money it put in your pocket.

In the 1930s the beer was transported in heavy wooden barrels and crates. My Dad would have joined the company as they were slowly automating their production from steam to electric and moving their distribution from horse-drawn drays to lorries. From what he told me his job was on the loading platform but occasionally he would get to go out on delivery. The sights and sounds and smells of the massive busy brewery must have been quite something for a fourteen year old lad and the heavy manual work would stand him in good stead for the future. By this time he was well and truly immersed in the unique culture of the East End. He could easily rattle off almost whole sentences in the Cockney rhyming slang that had grown out of the markets, the underworld and the docks, and to his dying day he would sing the tune 'My Old Dutch' to our Mum - the Old Dutch being the Duchess of Fife, rhyming slang for wife. I keep that tradition alive indoors today.

After he was orphaned at the age of twelve my Auntie May had taken on responsibility for my Dad, supported by his brothers. It was that, or he would have been sent off to the nearby Barnardo's Home until he was old enough to work. Dad was no stranger to Barnardo's though, he told me that poor kids from the area could get a cup of sweet tea and a sticky bun at the headquarters in Stepney Causeway on a Friday evening. He would also avail himself of a similar deal at the Salvation Army and a local Sunday school, possibly at the large Wesleyan Chapel. In a battle for survival he was tuned in to every charitable hand out on offer and in Stepney in the 20's and 30's there were a range of philanthropists and charities well established in the area, some of which, like Dr Barnardo's, could trace their origins to the manor.

The Methodist Mission on Commercial Road ran a cinema called the Penny Pictures for the poor kids of the area who couldn't afford the prices at the Troxy, the Rex or the Olympia. It drew huge queues, and for two and half hours they could escape the grim reality of life and laugh along with the likes of Laurel and Hardy and Charlie Chaplin and immerse themselves in the adventures of Tarzan and The Pirate of Panama. Once the doors were thrown open at the end it was back to the grinding poverty of the dark streets of Stepney: but that two and half hours of release in the warmth of the cinema must have been something to really look forward to.

As well as the boxing club the Stepney kids would fashion a football out of a bundle of rags and in the summer cricket stumps were chalked onto a wall, a bat carved out of a piece of packing case and an old ball found from somewhere. Dad told me that the first football match he ever went to was at Millwall, taken by a couple of his brothers who worked on the docks. That involved a trip over the water as the club had moved off the Isle of Dogs to The Den in 1910.

Although he always looked out for their results, he never became a Millwall supporter, dodging another whole world of misery and disappointment. There were no holidays of course: the best he could hope for was a day out in Southend and a trip to the legendary Kursaal, saving up a few pennies to take a trip on the massive wooden roller coaster and the sideshows.

When I was a kid he loved taking me and my sister to the funfair: I realise now it was because when he was a boy that was the absolute tops for him and he never forgot it.

CHAPTER THREE

Fascists on Duckett Street

Politics in Stepney in the 1930s were lively to say the least. At the time my father was born Clement Attlee, the future post-war prime minister, was the Labour mayor of the Borough and the party had established itself as a real force locally and across the London County Council area. The Representation of the People Act in 1918 widened the franchise and opened the door to the election of the first Labour MP in the area in 1923, John Scurr. But Labour wouldn't really establish itself as the dominant political force in the area until the 1930s. At a by-election in Mile End in 1926 the wonderfully named Johnnie Dodge, running on an *"anti-socialist"* ticket, won the Mile End seat on the London County Council. This was at the time of the General Strike, a tumultuous event on the streets and in the workplaces of the East End and particularly the docks, events that my father as a boy would have been witness to. As Labour consolidated its position in the Stepney Borough and across London it began introducing progressive policies but with advances hindered by the economic backdrop of the Depression.

The Communist Party was also laying down firm community roots, to a large extent through local tenant organisations and campaigns but also in challenging the growing threat of fascism, their local organiser Phil Piritin would go on to become the MP in 1945. The British Union of Fascists had been formed by Oswald Mosley in 1932 and from the off they saw the East End of London, with its large and well established Jewish community, as fertile territory for their politics of hate, division and scapegoating.

But Mosley had a real problem with Stepney. The Jewish and Irish communities were well integrated and solidarity from their Jewish neighbours to the Irish dockers during their two month-long strike in 1912 had built on a bond forged during the 1889 tailors strike when the mainly Jewish garment workers were financially supported by the Irish-led dockers union. As the employers tried to starve the dockers back to work Jewish families opened their doors to their kids and fed and sustained them. Those community links count for a lot when fascists hit your streets peddling their poison. As a result local branches of the Stevedores Union and the Transport and General Workers in Stepney took decisive action to expel BUF members from their ranks and frustrate their efforts to gain a toehold in the organised working class.

However, the fascists were making some advances and my father and his family lived right at the centre of one of the poorest and most deprived parts of Stepney where the BUF were cynically concentrating their activities as the book *East London for Mosley* explains:

> *"Population and housing shortages invariably contributed to high levels of deprivation. At the beginning of the decade. 15.5 per cent of Stepney's population were judged to be living in poverty. Stepney's infant mortality rate of between 77 and 80 deaths per 1,000 infants during the period 1927 to 1936 was regularly in excess of the London average. Among the most significant concentration of poverty were the dockland areas, Gill Street in the Limehouse area, Cable Street and the neighbourhood centred on Duckett Street in Mile End. It was this latter neighbourhood, around Duckett Street, that was to become the BUF's principal recruitment centre in Stepney during this period."*

Squads of BUF members, dressed in the blackshirt uniform, would head in from their strongholds in Bow, Whitechapel and Bethnal Green to join up with local members. and one of their pitches for trying to flog the *Action* newspaper and to hold street meetings was on the corner of Duckett Street and Ben Johnson Road, a stones throw from where my father's family lived, and that's where it got personal for the Martins.

One of my Dad's brothers, my uncle Gus, was seeing a Jewish girl who he later married, and that was bound to attract the attention of the fascists who gave him a hard time. I remember my father telling me that it was "sorted out" – I have always assumed that the other brothers and their mates stepped in and dumped the BUF on their backsides. That's "sorting it out", but despite that local hostility there were others in Duckett Street who were not only receptive to the fascists but were prepared to sign up to the party:

> *"In July 1936 the BUF opened its first official District Headquarters in the Borough of Stepney, in large converted stables at 29 Essian Street and Dongola Road in the Mile End division.......In July 1936 BUF speakers addressed a large, orderly and appreciative audience in Duckett Street, a locality which, as stated, would henceforth become their major centre of operations in Stepney."*
>
> *(East End for Mosley)*

BUF records show that a number of their leading members lived in Duckett Street, including a W. Betts who owned the bakery shop at number 73. However, it was organised labour that effectively put the block on their advances although their terminal decline wouldn't happen until global events took over and by then my father had left the area. Mosley and his propagandists had been astute in using the Spanish Civil War as a lever to pull with the East End Irish catholic community, painting a lurid picture of Republican persecution of nuns and priests and anti-clerical violence, but they failed to gain any traction with the influential local clergy. And leading figures like Canon Reardon, the Parish Priest of Wapping and Monsignor Canon Ring of the Church of SS Mary and Michael in Commercial Road were particularly vocal in their denunciation of the fascists with Canon Ring proclaiming that:

> *".....it was an outrage on the Catholic Church to associate it with the repulsive 'isms' of fanatic champions or to imply it has any sympathy for race hatred."*
>
> *East London Observer June 1937*

So it was that combination of public opposition from the pulpit and outright hostility from the trade union movement that limited Mosley's ambitions as Joe Jacobs, the former branch secretary of the Stepney Communist Party explained in his book *Out Of The Ghetto*:

> *"....the defeat of Mosley started way back when he failed to gain a foothold in Shadwell and Wapping, where lived the dockers of Irish descent with a strong Catholic background and a long history of working class struggle behind them."*

But one set piece event would catapult the area under the spotlight of national and global media. In the midst of the BUF's early recruitment push into Stepney the date that looms large in East End and anti-fascist history is the 4th October 1936 - the day of the Battle of Cable Street. Mosley had been frustrated at a tailing off in support after big rallies, including a show of strength at Olympia, had descended into violence and confrontation with a growing campaign of opposition. He decided to try and drive a set-piece march straight through the heart of Jewish East London in a deliberate act of grand-standing and provocation.

But the local community got themselves organised and Irish dockers stood together with their Jewish neighbours and led by communists, socialists and trade unionists blocked attempts to clear a path for Mosley through Cable Street. My father wasn't there: he was 16 years old at the time, but I know that at least two of his brothers were. Cable Street certainly wasn't the end of the fascists in Stepney though, not by a long chalk. In fact they recruited heavily after the event and were strengthening their organisation and the heart of their activities and recruiting remained in and around Duckett Street, where my family lived. Mosley himself spoke on the pavement on at least one occasion and drew large crowds.

One report for the London County Council from the height of the BUF's strength after Cable Street suggests that Duckett Street was "95% fascist" and although I suspect this was a major exaggeration there's no doubt that the careful exploitation of a number of local and international issues had enabled them to gain a significant foothold. A week after Cable Street a gang of BUF youths mobbed up on Mile End Road and ran down the street smashing the windows of Jewish-owned businesses in what became known as the Mile End Pogrom. My father as a teenager was not only a first hand witness to these turbulent times but he lived bang smack in the middle of it and although he never joined any political organisation the experience would stay with him.

In the middle of the winter of 1936 my Dad was laid off from his job at Charringtons, the impact of the Great Depression was still reaching deep into the economy of East London. One day you'd be working, and the next you would be out on the cobbles. These were desperate times for him, I know he tried to get work on the docks but they were gripped by the economic crisis and he would have knocked on every door and tried every avenue to try and get a job of any kind. In those days the casual employment practices on the docks were barbaric, straight out of On the Waterfront, with men walking miles to arrive at Tower Hill at dawn in the hope of getting a days graft. Most were sent away hungry, tired and disappointed and told to try again tomorrow. The juvenile employment exchange was at Toynbee Hall but hundreds of lads would have been chasing a handful of vacancies and it was a hopeless struggle. They were left hanging around on street corners cursing their luck, these were the grim conditions that Mosley and the BUF sought to exploit. Some of the lads turned to crime and the organised criminal gangs of the East End grew strong in the years of the Depression. Mob boss Jack "Spot" Comer, a Jewish Mile End boy and an active anti-fascist as well as a gangster, cut his teeth on the same streets as my Dad and found no shortage of recruits to his rackets and as soldiers for his battles with other London crime firms led by the likes of Darby Sabini and Billy Hill.

My Auntie May and her husband, who'd been looking after my father since he was orphaned, had been on the waiting list for one of the houses on the new London County Council estates in Becontree, St Helier and Mottingham where so many from Stepney would relocate to as the Labour authority stepped up their slum clearance plans in the East End. There would have been no space for him even if he had been offered the opportunity to join them. It was Becontree they eventually headed to, out of the slums and into one of the 27,000 brand new brick built houses that had risen out of the fields around Barking and Dagenham.

By the time he was laid off from his job my father was almost certainly relying on one of his older brothers to put a roof over his head and would have been dossing down wherever he could. For six months he had no income and was living on his wits and with no permanent home. The strict rules and means testing for the dole were loaded against young single men. He spent a lot of time walking, often into central London, looking for wherever opportunities might come his way, I have a strong feeling that at this point my father felt cut adrift and very much on his own at the tender age of 17. It was one of those long walks that paid off and offered him a future and a purpose and which would also turn his world upside down.

CHAPTER FOUR

Escape to the Army

On the 21st June 1937 my father enlisted in the British Army. From one of the interviews he recorded for his old regimental archive he tells the story in his own words;

> *"I joined in 1937 in the height of the depression. I had been out of work for over six months and I was going round Whitehall and there was a place there called the Central London Recruiting Office, and I was standing outside looking at all the pictures of various regiments and a Guard Sergeant came up with his hat pulled down and said, "Would you like to join the Army, son?". I was only 17 but I said "Yes". So he took me in, I passed all the various tests, I went in front of the Colonel that said, "Well, you've passed all your tests and that", he said, "Which Regiment would you like to join?" I said, "I'd like to join the Argyll and Sutherland Highlanders", and he just laughed at me and said, "It'll take you two years to understand what they're talking about, join an old cockney mob".*
>
> *I said, "I'll join the Royal Fusiliers", he said, "Sorry, but we've just finished a squad of those, but what we are recruiting for are the East Surreys". It was the first time,*

I must say, I'd ever heard of the East Surrey Regiment. That's how I came to join the East Surrey Regiment. When I went to Kingston it was the first time I'd ever been to Surrey. I lived in Stepney in London, I used to go the other side, Essex side, Southend, for my days out and that sort of thing, or for holidays and things, never had a holiday anyway, but that's how I came to join the Regiment."

My father had lied about his age to get in. His army record will forever show his date of birth as 16-12-18. He was actually born exactly a year later. It's worth reminding ourselves of the hard facts of life that were driving him at this stage. He had lost his job as a labourer at the brewery, there was no work for a young lad in the East End and he was struggling for somewhere to live.

His elder sister who had brought him up since their parents died had been offered and quickly accepted a house on the new LCC estate in Becontree where there was no room for my father He had to do something, the last thing he would have wanted to do was sponge off members of his family who had their own daily pressures to deal with.

The army must have seemed like a perfect solution at that time of deep, gloomy and unrelenting economic recession. As a new recruit he was offered two shillings a day on top of the free bed and board - it must have felt like riches indeed compared to the grinding monotony of being skint back in Stepney with zero prospects.

The enlistment and recruitment register for the 2nd Battalion East Surreys shows Dad signed up in that summer of 1937 with a number of other lads and notes scribbled onto the two pages I have, later and in red ink, show that many of them never made it back home.

As well as the Regimental register I have also managed to get hold of Army Form B271 - the questionnaire and declaration filled in at the recruitment office at Old Scotland Yard on the 21st June 1937 in my father's own hand and it was the point that he really did seal his own fate, committing to seven years in the colours and five in the reserve.

There was no turning back now. Knocking that year off his age I wonder if he felt any nerves as he read the bold and capped up words:

> **"YOU ARE HEREBY WARNED THAT IF AFTER ENLISTMENT IT IS FOUND THAT YOU HAVE GIVEN A WILFULLY FALSE ANSWER TO ANY OF THE FOLLOWING EIGHT QUESTIONS, YOU WILL BE LIABLE TO A PUNISHMENT OF TWO YEARS IMPRISONMENT WITH HARD LABOUR."**

The form was signed off by the magistrate and that was that. Dad would have known very well that joining the army may have been a route out of the grinding poverty of the East End but also that it was no ticket to the easy life, but what he couldn't have known was just how fate would stack the odds against him in the years that lay ahead and how much courage, resilience, strength and pure luck he would need to ever see London again.

After initial induction at the regimental HQ in Kingston, with Dad passing his Army Certificate of Education Second Class in August 1937, the new recruits were sent to Cochester for training as a machine gun battalion at Goojerat barracks but in early 1938 they were ordered to change back to a rifle battalion and to prepare for foreign service. Later in his life I took my father to be tested for a hearing aid and I remember him telling the audiologist that his ear drums had probably been damaged from firing machine guns in corrugated iron sheds out in Essex as a young man.

I have Dad's service and pay book from this period and it's clear that he threw himself into army life, taking driving tests, swimming tests and pretty much anything that was on offer to broaden his experience and education. Passing the test to drive an army truck round the barracks meant that like many men of his generation he would never have to take a driving test when he eventually returned to civilian life. He actually found it quite amusing that people had to buy L plates and take lessons and tests to get a licence when he had been given his for chucking a three and a half ton Leyland truck around some muddy tracks.

You can only imagine how a lad who had barely left the East End before felt on the 1st of September 1938 as he and his battalion marched the half mile from their camp to St Bodolph's railway station to catch the train before they sailed from Southampton on HT Lancashire for Shanghai calling at Port Sudan and Aden en route. I have a newspaper clipping from the day of departure at Southampton docks with young soldiers and ratings packed on the decks beaming away for the camera, it must have seemed to these boys like they were embarking on one hell of an adventure. It would be more than seven years before my father eventually returned to Britain and he could not have had the slightest idea what lay in store for him. It has been estimated that around three quarters of the young troops who left that day would never return, either killed in battle or dying in captivity.

Heading through the Suez Canal for the stop off at Port Sudan to pick up a group of men and officers from 1st Battalion East Surreys to bring their numbers up to strength, and after a refuelling stop at Aden, the troops had a two day stop off at Colombo, the capital of Ceylon, which gave them a brief chance to stretch their legs and grab a bit of R&R. Back on the ship they headed across the Bay of Bengal and through the Straits of Malacca arriving in Singapore's Keppel Harbour on the 29th September.

Due to the deteriorating situation in Europe, the battalion joined the garrison at Tanglin Barracks in Singapore for two weeks, with rumours rife that with the crisis growing at home they might just be turned around and sent back. But after Chamberlain returned from his "peace in our time" meeting with Hitler the journey continued on the submarine depot ship HMS Medway as far as Hong Kong, where the battalion were given a warm welcome by the Royal Scots lads they were replacing and spent nearly four weeks in camp at Mount Nicholson.

Pre-war Hong Kong must have been another real eye-opener for my father and the Surreys enjoyed the hospitality and entertainment at venues like the Cheerio Club before they packed up and completed their long journey on the British India boat, the SS Santhia. They arrived in Shanghai on the 17th November to take up their duties as part of the League of Nations protectorate. This final leg was undoubtedly the worst part of their trip so far, because the Santhia was a repurposed cattle boat, still stank of animal shit, and the men had to sleep on straw mattresses on the metal decks. The food was also dreadful, the weather stormy and the lads were glad to disembark.

Shanghai at this time was a global melting pot, a commercial port full of bars, brothels and bustling shops and restaurants but was also a city on edge with the Japanese aggression towards the Chinese. Money went a long way and the off duty young British troops must have had the time of their lives blissfully unaware of where this first international trip would eventually lead them.

The East Surreys were based in what was known as the Bad Lands area - home to gangsters and where murder, kidnap and robbery were rife. It was also one of the homes of the Japanese puppet leader, the collaborator Wang Jingwei, of the alternative Chinese Government in Nanking. It was a place straight out of a grainy black and white movie - treading a narrow line between gangsterism, political intrigue and war. By the time the Battalion arrived the Japanese had taken over most of Greater Shanghai.

The thronging neon-lit pavements of what was known as Cabaret Street or "Blood Alley," due to the regular fights between soldiers and sailors out on the lash, would have been a sight to behold for a lad from Stepney who'd never been further than a day trip to Southend before joining the army. Just over a year before he had been skint - unemployed, no fixed address, and with the soles out of his boots and his clothes tattered and worn. Now he had a few bob in his pocket, a clean bunk to sleep in, decent grub and freshly pressed and laundered clobber. The guard duties may have been long and tedious but there was the down time to look forward to, and a whole new world to explore.

Off-duty soldiers were permitted to be out of the barracks between 4pm until 12.20am but before being allowed out they had to be inspected by the guard commander. Assuming they passed muster they were issued with a box of condoms and sent on their way. Not surprisingly Shanghai at this time was rife with Venereal Disease and the Army Medical Corps established special centres in the hot spots around the town.

After the war, my father wrote some wonderful words about this first adventure overseas with his Battalion for his regimental comrades:

> *"We left England in'38 for Shanghai. What visions of the mystic East that name conjures up for you old 2nd Bn wallahs! How many of you remember "Ginger" Hefferman borrowing a steam roller and running it over his KD shorts in order to press them. Those heavy duties! Numerous guards! Inlying Picquets [squads of soldiers on alert to deal with internal disorder] and those seven to ten day sojourns on the Perimeter and later our first contact with the Japanese. Although the duties were heavy, such was the spirit of comradeship in the Bn that life was quite bearable and even exciting. But what made Shanghai so appealing was its cheapness and the variety of entertainment that it offered, all within the reach of the lowest paid private. Remember Blood Alley!, the Canidrome!, Nanking Lee!, and the numerous Bars and Dance Halls - Happy Days! Knowing what was to come no one can begrudge our fling in Shanghai."*

The boys were clearly having the time of their lives, and for my Dad it was all a far cry from the grinding poverty and bleak outlook of Depression East London that he had sought to escape. But he is right, no one could have begrudged these young soldiers the days of their lives in the bars and clubs of Shanghai knowing what fate had in store for them down the line.

To try and keep the lads occupied, and possibly away from the neon lights of the fleshpots, sport was encouraged and the East Surreys football team competed successfully in the Shanghai League.

My father was a good all round sportsman. Like most

East End boys boxing was in his blood and he was also a decent cricket and hockey player. He fancied himself as a pacy left winger on the football field, and I've no doubt he would have thrown himself into any activities being organised by the regiment. The Shanghai YMCA was a popular destination for men who loved their sport and looking to burn off energy with its swimming pools, gymnasium, snooker hall and restaurants.

There was just a wire fence that separated the International Settlement from the Japanese occupied territories of Greater Shanghai, and the League of Nations guards effectively stood cheek by jowl with the Japanese on the other side of the wire. The soldiers had to pass through each other's lines to access different parts of the city and the Japanese would often take pleasure in making that process as slow and convoluted as possible in deliberate acts of provocation. This was a taste of what was to come.

My father had a common blood group that was readily comparable, and he told my sister of a sick Chinese child who required a transfusion while he was on duty in Shanghai. My father stepped forward without hesitation and with the blood pumped across directly from his veins the child's life was saved.

American, French and Italian troops, along with another Battalion of the British Army, the Seaforth Highlanders, were also engaged in the policing duties. With the declaration of war the presence of French and Italian soldiers became problematic with the local French Commandant declaring support for the Vichy Regime and the Italians entering the conflict on the side of the Germans. New demarcation areas had to be laid down to keep the troops apart and the glamorously named French Concession was placed out of bounds. The Germans themselves had a presence and proudly flew the swastika over the German club. To be billeted right at the heart of this extraordinary global interface as the world teetered on the brink must have been mad, scary and exciting in equal measure.

With the outbreak of World War 2 the battalion remained in Shanghai, albeit on a war footing, and in

December 1939 my father was part of a group that was moved to Tientsin. To combat the freezing cold weather the troops were issued with special winter clothing and I have a picture of him on guard duty wearing a Russian style fur hat. I remember him telling me that he couldn't believe how "bloody cold" it was. It was Siberian levels of cold.

That picture also shows Dad sporting the two stripes of a corporal that he had been awarded on the 19th January 1940. His natural ability as a leader had already been recognised and a couple of years into his service he had already had two promotions and was now at a rank of non-commissioned officer where he could issue orders and would be put in charge of a group of men, no mean achievement for a lad just turned twenty.

Tensions with the Japanese were now rising and there was a growing threat that they would mount a takeover bid for the whole of Shanghai with the British military position pretty much impossible. Contingency plans were made to agree to the internment of the entire British garrison by either the Americans or the French - a desperate move which would have been a major military embarrassment for the Government leaving the troops banged up indefinitely in neutral hands.

With other British assets being withdrawn to Singapore, including almost all the warships, it was time to pack up and get ready to clear out sharpish. A secret order issued to the Commanding Officer, Lieutenant Colonel Swinton, could hardly have been more blunt:

You are now of little military value

The Japanese are out to force a quarrel leading to hostilities

Failure to withdraw now might lead to an ultimate withdrawal in humiliating circumstances.

CHAPTER FIVE

Shanghai to Singapore

In August 1940 all British troops were recalled from China. Part of the battalion was shipped from Shanghai to Singapore on the 21st August with the Tientsin group joining them on the 3rd September reuniting the 2nd battalion of the East Surreys.

The local paper the Straits Times ran a piece welcoming their arrival:

> *"The most pleasant memories that the East Surrey Regiment brings back from its 21 months tour in Shanghai, Tientsin and Peking is the very close liaison with the United States Marines.*
>
> *It is very appreciative of the honour that the Marines paid the regiment when it "trooped" it out of Shanghai, its band heading the battalion as it made its farewell march through the International Settlement and into the Japanese concession to the docks for embarkation to Singapore."*

The band played "*Will ye ne'er come back again.*" The poingananacy would have been lost on the men of the East Surreys at that time, but I suspect that they would remember it only too well in the long years ahead. After living under canvas for a few weeks the Battalion was found a permanent base at the Chinese High School on Bukit Timah Road where they would remain for the rest of their stay.

In Singapore the battalion was trained to operate machine guns and searchlights for six months in the Pasir Panjang sector on the South East Coast before being sent to Tanjou Pau, near Jitra, in the extreme north of Malaya on the 20th February 1941. The time spent in Singapore would have been the last chance that the men would have had to enjoy the real vibrancy of life for many years as they spent their off duty hours in the bars, clubs and restaurants of this global and cosmopolitan city and had a chance to practise their sports in the many green spaces that surrounded the urban sprawl.

From February to August 1941 the battalion was kept busy training and preparing defences alongside the 6th Indian infantry brigade, battalions of the Punjab Regimen and the 1st Leicesters and it was during this period that my father passed out first class in the rifle shooting class and on the 12th March 1941 he was promoted again by his commanding officer from corporal to the rank of lance sergeant - senior enlisted soldier within his platoon carrying enormous responsibility for the men under his command.

The numbers were brought up to strength with the arrival of around 200 men, mainly fresh conscripts, on the Empress of Japan which shipped out from Glasgow as part of a huge convoy. An important task for the newly-swelled ranks was the construction of the Jitra defensive lines. This crucial work would never be completed and was a marker for the poor decision making and planning by the military high command that would come back to haunt my father and his comrades.

A military plan, Operation Matador, had been drawn up to confront and push back any Japanese assault on Thailand and Northern Malaya. The weakness of Malaya's defences, and by definition the overland route to Singapore, had been identified as far back as 1937. With forethought that would later turn out to be spot on Major General William Dobbie, Officer Commanding Malaya 1935-1939, identified potential invasion landing points at Songkhla and Pattani in Thailand and Kota Bharu in Malaya. He called for large military reinforcements to be installed. His predictions turned out to be correct but his recommendations were ignored.

In August 1941, the Commander in Chief of Far East Command Air Chief Marshall Robert Brooke-Popham produced the Matador plan which again correctly identified the expected landing points for an invasion and the route for a push south. Matador planned to intercept the invading forces just over the Thai border and hold them up long enough for main forces to regroup and counter attack. The resources required to make the plan work had once again been delayed but Matador itself remained in place, ready to be actioned when an invasion appeared imminent.

On Saturday the 6th of December, two Australian airforce reconnaissance planes spotted a Japanese convoy of transport ships, supported by cruisers, heading towards the Gulf of Thailand. The transport convoy was moving more than 26,000 troops of General Yamashita's 25th Army - spearheaded by the 5th Division, ruthless hardcore veterans of the China campaign who had taken part in the infamous Rape of Nanking.

Also in this formidable force of experienced soldiers were members of the crack Imperial Guards Division. Interestingly my father and his East Surrey comrades would have seen the Japanese Imperial Guards as they were also on duty in Shanghai. Since then they had been trained specifically for the Malayan campaign.

Backing up this manpower Yamashita also had the support of 230 light and medium tanks and 534 modern aircraft - compared to the 158 old and slow planes on the allied side.

The British Combined Intelligence Bureau now had all the information it needed to confirm that a Japanese invasion was well under way. It could not have been more obvious and you would have thought that the Matador plan would have been immediately swung into action. But you would be wrong and a catalogue of ineptitude that would have massive implications for my father and his fellow soldiers, blissfully unaware of what was going on at General Headquarters, was starting to unfold.

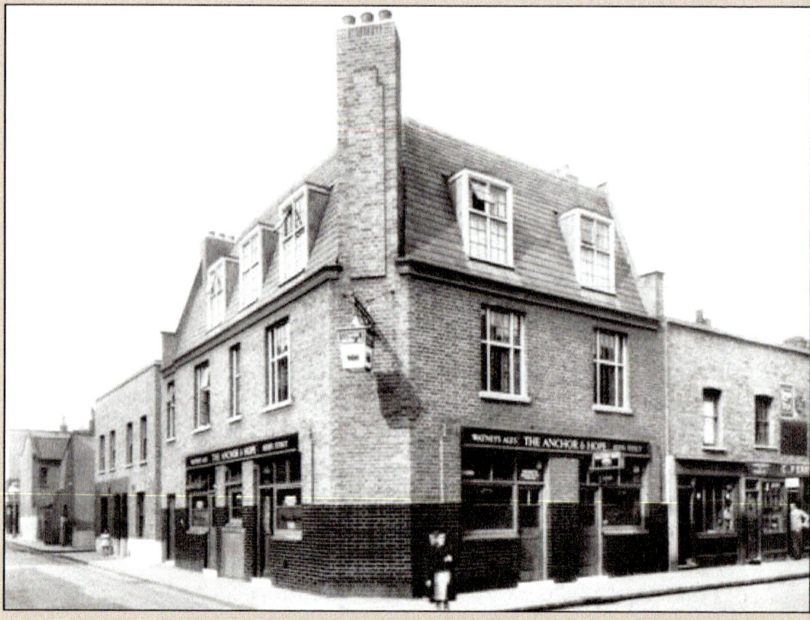

The Anchor and Hope pub in Duckett Street. Cliff was born a couple of doors down.

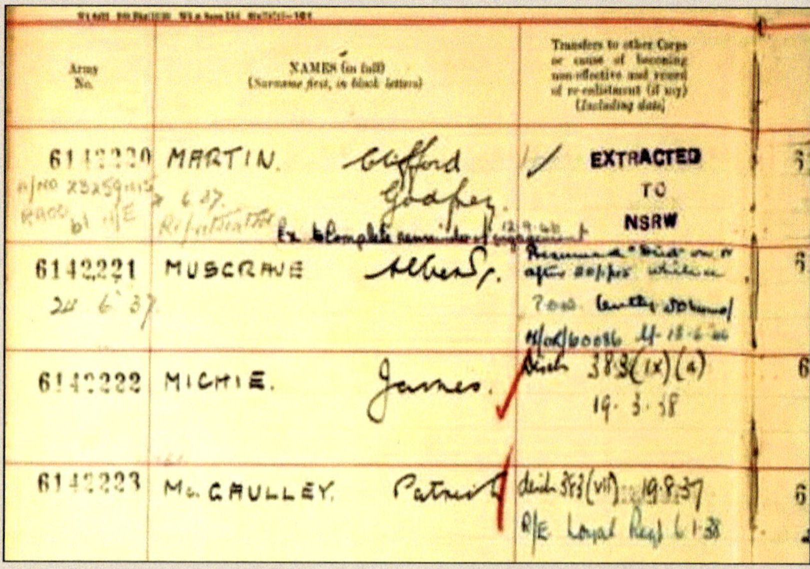

Army No.	NAMES (in full) (Surname first, in block letters)	Transfers to other Corps or cause of becoming non-effective and record of re-enlistment (if any) (Including date)
6142220	MARTIN. Clifford Godfrey	EXTRACTED TO NSRW
6142221	MUSGRAVE Albert	
6142222	MICHIE. James.	Disch 383 (ix) (a) 19. 3. 38
6142223	Mc. CAULLEY. Patrick	disch 383 (vii) 19.8.37 R/E Loyal Regt 6.1.38

The Whitehall recruitment register showing Dad enlisting June 1937

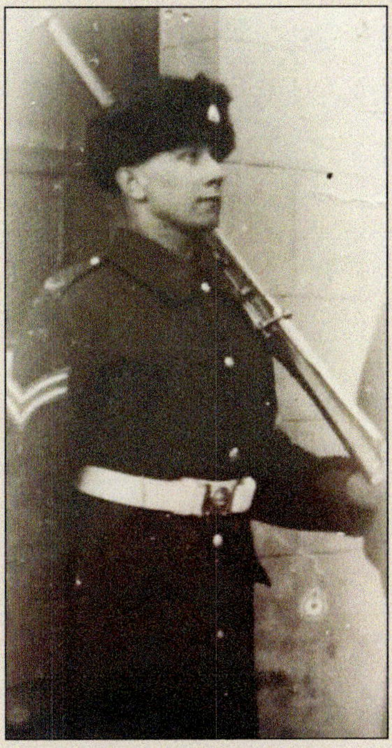

Cliff on guard duty, Shanghai deployment 1939

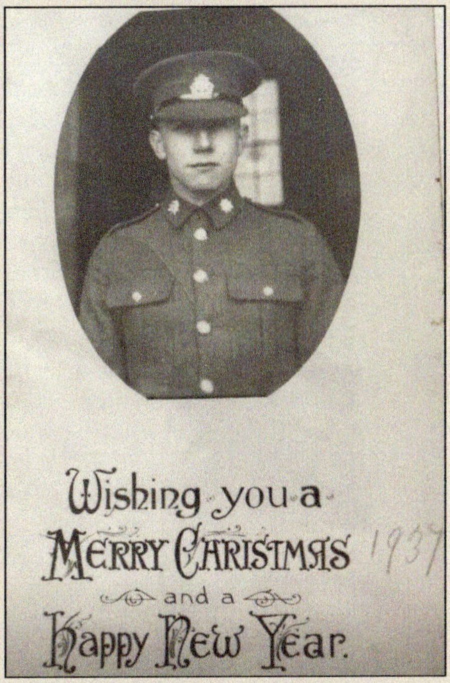

Cliff's first Christmas card home as a squaddie. 1937

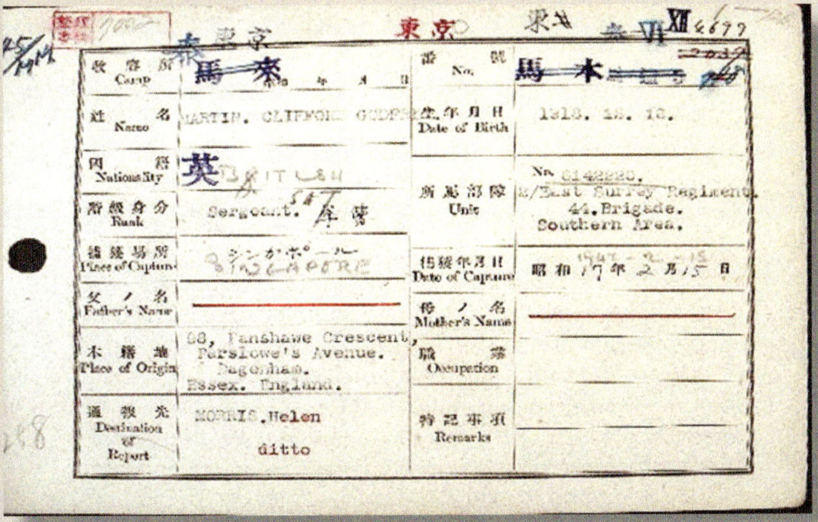

東京

收容所 Camp	馬來	番號 No.	馬來
姓名 Name	MARTIN. CLIFFORD GODFR	生年月日 Date of Birth	1918. 12. 12.
國籍 Nationality	英 BRITISH	所屬部隊 Unit	No. 6142220. 2/East Surrey Regiment. 44. Brigade. Southern Area.
階級身分 Rank	Sergeant. SGT		
捕獲場所 Place of Capture	シンガポール SINGAPORE	捕獲年月日 Date of Capture	昭和17年2月15日 1942-2-15
父ノ名 Father's Name		母ノ名 Mother's Name	
本籍地 Place of Origin	58, Fanshawe Crescent, Parslowe's Avenue. Dagenham. Essex. England.	職業 Occupation	
通報先 Destination of Report	MORRIS. Helen ditto	特記事項 Remarks	

Dad's Japanese POW index card

Sir Robert Brooke-Popham was given the intelligence on the convoy at 2pm on the 6th December at GHQ. He had time to order his troops to move up to meet the threat head on in Southern Thailand as his own Matador plan set out, but he bottled it. It appears he was afraid to be the man who effectively declared war on Japan, and so he played for time, saying that the evidence in front of his own eyes was insufficient and calling for more reconnaissance flights to shadow the Japanese movements.

Brooke-Popham had had the necessary authority from the War Cabinet to put Matador into action the day before but the Foreign Office were wary of upsetting diplomatic relations in Thailand and Churchill himself was wary of upsetting the Americans. The 2nd Battalion of the East Surreys, still working on the defences at Jitra, were caught in the middle of a grotesque exercise in prevarication, buck-passing and politicking.

Arthur Percival, the General Officer Commanding (GOC) Malaya returned to Singapore expecting Brooke-Popham to have put Matador into action. He hadn't. Nor had he activated a second associated plan, Operation Krohcol, which would have moved troops up to a key strategic position known as The Ledge in advance of a Japanese landing at Patani.

The move would have made all the difference to the defence of Jitra. Meanwhile, time was running out, and failures that would kick off a chain of events that would both reverberate around the world and turn my father's world upside down were being cast in stone.

Further reconnaissance on the morning of the 7th December revealed that the Japanese convoy was now steaming full pelt towards Patani and Kota Bahru, landing points either side of the Thai/Malaya border, expected to arrive around midnight. The Japanese shooting down one of the allied reconnaissance planes and opening fire on another were the first acts of war in Malaya, and should have triggered Matador. Instead Percival now concluded that the operation was unsound. The way the British top brass had dragged their heels now meant that they wouldn't be able to get troops in position to confront the invasion until at least two hours too late. Those troops had been mobilised and been left hanging around in the pouring rain awaiting the order to move into Thailand. That order never came, presenting the Japanese with a head start of at least ten hours. The repeated delays now caused serious problems for the move back to the incomplete defences at Jitra.

One of my father's East Surrey comrades, John Wyatt, sums up the position the men now found themselves in in his book *'No Mercy From the Japanese'*:

> *"At 1300 hrs orders came through for us to return to our defensive positions at Jitra and as we made our way back, thick clouds of black smoke rising high in the sky further to the south were clearly visible. For over a week I had geared myself up for a push into Thailand and as we neared our defensive positions I was further demoralised to find the trenches filled with water.*
>
> *Time was short and we sweated and toiled trying to get our defence lines finalised. For three days we dug weapon pits, laid telephone cables, planted over 1,500 Land and Anti-Tank mines and cleared fields of fire, all in heavy monsoon rains. With tracks just thick muddy morasses our vehicles had great difficulty moving around so we had to haul ammunition and stores by hand. Trenches had to be re-dug as they quickly filled with water and the sides often caved in under the constant deluge.*
>
> *We had little or no protection from the elements and nights were spent in our rain soaked uniforms huddled under capes, ready to spring into action at the first sign of an attack. Sentries were posted and patrols were sent out regularly to probe for any sign of enemy infiltration. Our nerves were stretched to the limit as we knew that the Japanese were likely to attack at any moment.*
>
> *As I sat waiting with the rest of the regiment, news began to filter through that the Japanese had attacked Pearl Harbour….."*

CHAPTER SIX

Betrayal in Malaysia

On that pivotal day in our modern history, the 7th December 1941, with the 2nd Battalion East Surreys soaked, filthy, tired and having already been forced into retreat before a shot was fired and doing their best to set defensive lines, the Japanese entered the war with the attack on Pearl Harbour and attacks on Shanghai, Manila, Thailand (then commonly known as Siam) and Hong Kong.

The same night Japanese troops invaded Thailand close to the Malayan frontier and the east coast of Malaya itself sweeping south towards Jitra - landing seventy minutes before the bombs were dropped on the American fleet at Pearl Harbor. The attacks were supposed to have been synchronised, but nobody thought to warn the Americans in Manila that war had now been declared.

Intercepts by operators at the Kranji listening post in Singapore meant that for nearly two months they had known the name of every Japanese ship in the Gulf fleet and the destination of Kota Bahru. GHQ Far East could hardly have been better briefed, making their failure even more of a betrayal of the men that would soon be thrown in front of the marauding invasion force.

The Japanese did land in exactly the locations identified in Operation Matador, but the state of chaos in the British top command meant that they could crack on unopposed and get some important momentum going.

In the appalling conditions of the monsoon work was immediately stepped up by my father's battalion to strengthen the incomplete fixed defences at Jitra, which weren't originally scheduled to be ready until February 1942, and which weren't in an ideal defensive location anyway. It was all too little, too late and a case of more poor planning and preparation.

Writing after the war, Lt-General Sir Lewis Heath, Commander of the Indian Corps, wrote;

> *"I find it impossible to excuse General Percival for permitting Air Chief Marshal Sir Robert Brooke- Popham not to arrive at a decision on the 7th December when everything pointed to the certainty of Japan initiating the war in Malaya." (Imperial War Museum)*

Add into this toxic brew of rank incompetence the fact that the order ***"Matador off, man Jitra"*** was delayed by two hours due to an inexplicable comms breakdown. The 11th Division troops, who had been expecting to go on the offensive over the Thai border were now sent, tired and soaked, back to the unfinished and waterlogged defensive lines at Jitra, so you can see why their morale would have been so badly damaged.

These brave men, including my father's battalion, who were held back at Jitra, would now go into battle hampered and compromised by poor and weak leadership at the very top. In the much-used First World War term they were truly "lions led by donkeys". We can't be sure how much of this would have filtered back to the lines, but I suspect that they would have known enough to have an inkling that something had gone wrong. Hardly the best preparation for soldiers about to get their first taste of actual battle.

Back home the propaganda machine was in full swing. The Evening News of the 8th December, reporting the invasion, ran the headline:

> *JAPANESE ROUTED IN MALAYA: TROOPS LEFT ON BEACHES*

Nothing of course could have been further from the

truth. Whilst I understand how media works during war, that old adage of the first casualty being truth is ringing in my ears, this was also the first stage of building in a narrative that would wind up with the blokes now hastily digging in at Jitra, as the Japanese poured men and equipment forward, being effectively shoved out of the public eye all together. One minute being hailed, wrongly as it turned out, as heroes who had "routed" the opposition and then, as reality became too hard to spin, written out of the headlines all together. It must have been incredibly confusing for friends and relatives back home hoping for positive news of their loved ones engaged in the battle.

On the 11th December the Japanese, who by this point must have felt they were well and truly on a roll, launched a well-planned attack. The East Surreys lines weren't directly engaged at this stage but first casualties were sustained from heavy shelling. By 1600 hours that day the Leicesters were being withdrawn from their forward positions after taking heavy losses. And my father's D Company was heavily involved in the fighting.

The invading Japanese troops who had landed on the Malay Peninsula were issued with a pamphlet called "Read This Alone - and the War Can be One". It was a blueprint for not only the jungle warfare they were now engaged in but also how they should view their opposition in line with the "Bushido" code tracing back to the Samurai warriors of the Middle Ages and indoctrinated into the ranks. They were told to see themselves as:

> *"…an avenger come at last face to face with his father's murderer…..Here at last is the man whose death will lighten your heart of it's brooding anger. If you fail to destroy him you can never rest in peace."*
>
> Stanley Sander, *World War II in the Pacific*.

The pamphlet also drilled home that surrender and capture was the ultimate disgrace, an instruction that would hang heavy over my father and his mates in the months and years ahead.

The following day the Japanese troops broke through the Jitra defences and the East Surreys fell back to protect bridges over retreat lines. The battle of Jitra decimated the allied forces with massive losses. During the retreat, men had been cut off and left behind and important equipment, including eight Bren gun carriers, had also been abandoned. The situation could only be described as chaotic with defensive positions being taken up and quickly evacuated. D Company dug in on the south side of the Bata River near Kampong Budi, trying to hold the area as what remained of the battered troops looked to regroup at Anak Bukit: but within half an hour they were off again, on foot, to the totally unprepared Alor Star. These were southernly retreats covering several miles of ground each down the West Coast of Malaya through difficult terrain as the Japanese consolidated and advanced down the peninsula.

Jitra, supposedly the first line of defence against the Japanese invasion, had been a disaster. Despite the brave efforts of my father and his fellow troops it was entirely predictable. There hadn't been enough time or priority given to strengthening the defensive lines, and there was no air support from the RAF because the Japanese had raided the allied airfields at Kepala Batas and Butterworth - an RAF base established in 1939 on the coast opposite the island of Penang which was supposed to be central to the defence of Malaya but which was poorly equipped and fell into Japanese hands on the 20th December.

The British anti-aircraft gun batteries were simply inadequate, and the high flying Mitsubishi bombers flew with almost impunity. The consequences of abandoning Operation Matador, and the failure to take key decisions when they could have made a difference, were now being felt by the weary, battered and soaked troops as they moved from slit trench to slit trench down the Malaysian Peninsular.

I remember my father telling me just how badly the military command had underestimated the experienced Japanese troops, who had previously fought in the testing conditions of the jungle. Manning an observation point early in the battle, he saw Japanese soldiers with bicycles. But when he reported this back to the officers they dismissed what he had seen with his own eyes as a fantasy, telling him that no one fought in the jungle on a bicycle. They were wrong of course, and Dad was right: the mobility, swift movement and cunning of the enemy would be decisive as the battle unfolded.

The Japanese had also mastered the use of tanks in the hostile jungle terrain and the battlefield advantage that would give them would also prove crucial. Their air force had already achieved superiority, flying out of seized air bases in Southern Thailand and taking out allied capacity at will. The clapped out and inferior allied planes were no match for the Japanese, and Percival later conceded that:

> *"....the success of the enemy's attack on our northern aerodromes would considerably handicap our own air action and that this in turn would unfavourably prejudice our fortunes in the fighting on land."*

"Unfavourably prejudice"! What an understatement that would prove to be for my Dad and his platoon as they did their best to take cover in rain-filled ditches, wondering if the next aerial bombardment would be the one that took them out. My father must have been showing exceptional leadership skills prior to the battle for Malaya commencing, because he had been promoted again to the rank of paid acting sergeant out there in the field on the 5th of September. From then on he would forever be known in the war records as Sergeant Clifford Martin and now a couple of months later here he was leading his men through day after day of gruelling and brutal jungle warfare. It was a hell of a responsibility for a young man of 22 years old experiencing his first taste of battle but one that he shouldered with courage, pride and determination.

If that courage, leadership and gut instinct for the fight forged on the impoverished streets of the East End had been matched by the top military command it's possible that the front line troops might not have found themselves defending their positions in such impossible conditions.

The East Surreys and the other allied defensive forces had already been fighting for days without sleep in terrible conditions. Soaking them to the skin, the monsoon rains also washed off their insect repellent. Socks had rotted away, and their feet were sore and full or blisters. Uniforms were caked in mud, with no time to either wash or rest.

Two days later the troops retreated and blew the bridge and headed off again towards new positions in the jungle north of Gurun. The tired men had to withdraw at night from their positions to the south of Jitra and head to Gurun some thirty miles away in a hellish journey through muddy rice fields.

Another East Surrey Dennis Gavin, part of a mortar team that had been held back, summarises the chaos at this point in the battle in his book *Quiet Jungle Angry Sea*:

> *"Most of our Brigade was still intact, but the remainder of the Division had been badly cut up at Jitra, many of the survivors being forced to take off into the jungle to save their lives. The few that were left had been collected together south of Gurun to act as a reserve, while we and the 1/8th Pujabis flanked the main road to the north in an attempt to hold back the Japanese long enough for the formation of a defence line further back.*
>
> *The rearguard action we were on was supposed, I believe, to make the enemy pause long enough for the formation of a defence line to the south.*
>
> *Always blasted defence!"*

As the Japanese advances continued the allied troops found themselves split up and fragmented even further and were in full retreat. On the 14th December my father and his comrades were ordered to withdraw to the Kedah Peak area with D Company under Captain Cater. The Japanese broke through and the Company was ordered to retreat further to the Penang coast area to try and join up with the rest of the battalion.

The East Surreys' John Wyatt explains why they never stood a chance at Gurun as the retreat continued:

> *"Gurun was supposed to be one of the best natural defence positions in Malaya; it could have been, had the necessary preparation work been done in advance by a fresh division with good reserves, but this certainly didn't apply to us as we were all exhausted. There was no respite however as*

we were ordered to immediately start digging again.

Gurun would have been a strong defensive position had we had the time or the energy to prepare it properly, but we were all totally exhausted. My feet were also in a very bad state after marching for miles in soaked and mud-coated boots."

So, on the 17th December after a gruelling three day march through hills and jungle to reach the coast, boats were commandeered to row across to Penang Island. It sounds like some kind of Boys Own adventure but it was nothing of the sort, with my Dad taking the lead the men were quite literally fleeing for their lives. If they had been caught it's almost certain that they would have been shot and left to rot in the heat.

In another of my father's interviews he tells the story of his platoon's escape and rescue:

'We were trained as soldiers and we had to try and fight them and hold them back, but they were very clever, they were very experienced troops. We weren't at all......they just slaughtered us when they first caught us. I managed to escape from them, or rather my platoon, and we had to get to the coast of Malaysia and commandeer some row boats and rowed across towards Penang.

'On our way we were picked up by a British Navy mine-sweeper because we were rowing across and a tropical storm blew up and we were baling out and then all of a sudden somebody said, "Look Sarge, there's a ship over there", and we looked and there was a ship with no flag, we didn't know if it was Japanese or English. Then the click of the tannoy came on and a very cold British voice said, "I say would you chaps like a lift?"

After several days at sea they were taken back to the mainland. They were lucky. A group of 1st Leicesters, who had also been isolated during the battle had commandeered boats to get across to Penang and made it -- only to find it already in Japanese hands. They ended up being sheltered and fed by local Chinese for nearly three years. After being grassed up by an informer they were eventually rounded up, tortured and shot.

Others in the East Surrey D Company group hadn't been picked up in the stormy seas on the way to Penang, and having also made it across to the now surrendered island had to think quickly to make good their escape. As Captain Carter explained:

> *"...with Captain Howard, the Adjutant, and the 8 Punjab company commander, we commandeered a Malayan junk. We had raided a civilian house and put on plain clothes to avoid detection. This was lucky, because as we sailed the junk out of harbour we hid under the huge sails, and the Japanese landing parties passed us in a fleet of motor boats.*
>
> *We sailed south with the help of the old Chinese junk owner, heading for Malacca..."*

They say that a cat has nine lives. My father and his Company of the 2nd Battalion were already well on the way to using up theirs. These escapades read like a film script but for the men involved they were a matter of life and death. The Chinese junk owner was also risking everything to help them to get away back to the mainland.

CHAPTER SEVEN

The British Battalion

There wouldn't have been much of a Christmas for these weary men, and on Boxing Day 1941, having journeyed across to Kampar, an inland position in central Malaya, the platoon was reunited with the rest of the Battalion which had now merged with the Leicesters to form the British Battalion which had been created at Ipoh a week earlier to harness and organise what was left of their manpower. The East Surreys had been reduced to just 270 officers and men.

Sergeant Cliff Martin again:

> *"Came back up later on through various camps, found that because we were in the same division as the Leicestershire Regiment, two British Battalions had got knocked about so much by the Japanese there were was only about half a Battalion each left and they joined them together and amalgamated them and called them the British Battalion for want of a better title, there were so many Indian troops out there, and of course we've been very proud of that title because the first action we had was the battle of Kampar in Malaysia."*

The newly formed Battalion had settled into the Anglo-Chinese school at Kampar and had managed to rearrange the wooden desks into beds of a sort. After a brief rest and reorganisation preparations continued to be made for further defensive lines around Kampar. Six Vickers heavy machine guns had been manoeuvred into position and the Companies of the British Battalion were moved up to locations behind the strategically important Green Ridge.

New Year's Eve was marked by strafing and bombing of the British Battalion by Japanese planes and from noon onwards the Japanese artillery opened up as they laid the ground for the next phase in the battle for Malaya.

On New Year's day 1942 the Japanese attacked the Kampar positions, leading to a massive battle, in which the British Battalion held firm and launched a counter attack at Thompsons Ridge. But the Japanese strengthened their positions and attacked again. After hand to hand fighting the allies were forced to prepare a further retreat, and there followed twelve days of fighting on the retreat down through Kuala Lumpur.

Despite being heavily outgunned and outnumbered by the crack 41st and 42nd Japanese infantry battalions the British Battalion inflicted heavy losses on the opposition. The well-trained Japanese Infantry group was over 5000 strong and were held back by the brave and resolute action of less than 1500 combined troops from the British Battalion and the Indian regiments who had already, in my father's beautifully understated words been "badly knocked about" since the invasion of Malaya began. The Japanese Chief of Staff Col Masonobu Tsuji commended their bravery.

It's too easy to define the British Battalion by the long retreat down the Malaysian Peninsular and their eventual surrender at the fall of Singapore without recognising their courage and bravery in extremely difficult conditions made with their ranks seriously depleted.

After the war my father wrote these words about the Malayan campaign for his regiment:

".....Malaya and our all too short period in action. Jitra!

Our first position. Gurun! Where the Bn was literally cut to pieces. Such were our losses we were amalgamated with the 1st Leicesters and designated The British Bn. How proud we were of that title. I'll always remember the beginning of a poem I read whilst a POW. It went like this

"It was a day in late December and Gurun had drawn to a close,

When the Surreys met the Leicesters and the British Bn arose.".

But we never forgot we were Surreys, and I think that says a lot for the spirit of the Bn that we got on so well with the Leicesters.

Kampar! Where Johnny Craggs won his D.C.M. He is now the Drum Major of the last Bn. If you're listening John, I would like to say Hello and I feel sure you don't mind me mentioning you like this."

Sergeant Craggs, along with Captain Vickers and Private Graves, received his award for gallantry after an extraordinary fight to rescue a group of men from the Leicesters who had been cut off, and hold a position for hours under heavy fire with a brave counter-attack against the enemy at the battle of Kampar. They were comrades of my Dad and he was rightly proud of them. There were so many brave men putting themselves on the line during that battle who deserved to be honoured that their level of courage and gallantry must have been quite exceptional.

The definitive account of the campaign '*The British Battalion Malaya 1941-1942*' is a detailed record published in honour of the men involved and to those who lost their lives. Written by a Malaysian teacher, Chye Kooi Loong, the book stands as a tribute to:

"... these brave men. Hardship and confusion did not weaken their resolution and their discipline never faltered.

"In the Battle of Kampar (30th December 1941 - 2nd January 1942) the men of the 1st Leicesters and the 2nd East Surreys fighting together for the first time as the British Battalion have won their finest glory on Thompsons and Green Ridge of Kampar. They have conducted themselves

in the grim struggle with consummate bravery and exemplary discipline under the most trying conditions..."

In 1996 my father, along with my mother, met the author who presented him with a copy of the book with a personal tribute...

"With best regards to my friends Mr and Mrs Cliff Martin of the 2nd Btn East Surrey Regiment and the British Battalion.

In memory of the gallantry in the Battle of Kampar 30th December 1941 to 2nd January 1942.

It is my honour to meet someone who fought in the unique British Battalion."

A glossary at the end of the book jumped out at me as I skipped through it. One table lists all of the soldiers on the Roll of Honour of the British Battalion on the 20th December 1941 comprising the men of the East Surreys. My father had carefully marked in pencil five names, men who I assume were his closest friends. I can think of no other reason why he would have singled their names out.

Of the five, four never made it back. Lance Corporal Dave Booker and Private R.W. Abrahams both died in captivity and were buried in war graves at Kanchanaburi and Chungkai. Lance Corporal E Samuels died at the battle of Batang Berjuntai and Private J.M. McLeary in the final battle for Singapore. Neither of these men have known graves.

One other man, Private Michael Lyons, did make it back. Like my father Michael had enlisted with the East Surreys before the war, in his case in 1938. In all likelihood they would have been together as young soldiers all the way from the pre-war duties in Shanghai until Dad was selected for the transport to Japan. It appears from his records that Michael probably spent the whole of his captivity in Thailand.

Intriguingly Michael Lyons was an Irishman. On his liberation questionnaire he lists Bonham Street in Dublin as his address. So how did he end up in the East Surreys? He lists his trade as a labourer, the same as my father, had he travelled to London like so many other young Irishman to find work but with the tough economic times made the same decision to travel to the recruitment office in Whitehall and sign up? It all seems very possible, and with my Dad being London Irish, with his father coming from Kilkenny, they would have had other common ground on which to build a friendship. I'm not aware that they were still in contact by the time I came along, or how long Michael survived after repatriation, but the fact my father marked his name out of the hundreds of others on the East Surrey Roll of Honour reflects a strong bond cemented by their years of common struggle.

If you imagine you are in a close friendship group of six, in your early twenties, and not only do you witness the deaths of four of that group but you are there when two of them are killed in action and you witness two others fading away sick and starving before your eyes, it puts into the sharpest possible focus what happened to those young men of the East Surreys in the Far East. And then you carry the experience of those deaths, along with many others, into the years after your liberation. Another huge burden. Do you shoulder that as a sense of guilt that you survived while your closest friends perished? Or do you try to live a good and fruitful life in honour of their memory? I never talked to my father about coping with that, and as with so much else I dearly wish that I had.

Having endured more miles of hard marching south on the 6th January the battered and tired men of the battalion had regrouped at Batang Berjuntai north of Kuala Lumpur and the troops counterattacked the next day to try and capture strategic positions. But by the 9th of January the thinned out lines had been forced into further retreat, and the Indian Battalions are reported as being "cut to pieces." The retreat continued to Labu, south of Kuala Lumpur some seventy miles of ground had been covered since the battle at Kampar.

By the 13th of January the battalion had reached Kluang but plans for a much-needed rest in the cool labour quarters of the Coronation Rubber Estate were abandoned as the Japanese landed further troops on the coast to the West. At 9.30 am on the 16th January the British Battalion was given just one hour notice to ship out and to pick up motor transport for the journey to Batu Pahat some eighty miles south west . They were joined by much-needed reinforcements from the 2nd Cambridgeshires and the British Battalion managed to grab a day's rest at Kluang before the Japanese attacked again down the West Coast.

Around this time my father contracted Malaria for the first time but was still able to write his final letter home to his sister before captivity, on Australian Red Cross paper from his hospital bed. Here are some extracts:

"Dear May and George,

At last I have a chance to write since war was declared out here. There is such a lot to write about but I only have one sheet of paper so I have to cut it short.

Well, after all the waiting something did happen and although it was sudden we were really prepared for it. Within a few days we were in action against the Japanese and although we held them up for a few days we were forced to withdraw owing to their great numbers and the fact that they were infiltrating through us and that's how it's been going ever since…..

In the action following the time we were cut off our Battalion lost a lot ….killed, wounded and missing and had to reform, amalgamated with another British Battalion but eventually we found that a lot of the missing trickled through the Japanese lines.

I could tell you a lot more including things about being cut off by the Japanese and about a bayonet charge we done the other day, but I haven't room.

At the time I writing from hospital….just got over a dose of Malaria…..have not a letter from you for a long time but I heard a lot of mail was lost.

Let everyone at home know that I am alright and I will write again soon as I get some more paper. Well I must close now. I hope that you and all at home are safe and well.

Your loving brother, Cliff."

His determination to reassure his family and to put a brave and positive face on his situation rings through in his words and is a measure of his courage and selflessness. But his sense of isolation from having no contact with home also cries out. That feeling would only grow in the long years ahead.

The memory of the bayonet charges and the close hand to hand fighting would stay with him. He told me of plunging his bayonet into the guts of a Japanese soldier and the screams and his contorted face as he drew his last breath.

He wasn't proud of himself, but it was kill or be killed and he was a professional soldier. He was telling this story because the sounds and image would live with him forever. The screams and bulging eyes would come back as one of the repeating nightmares that would haunt him till the day he died. The battles of Malaysia never ended for him.

With a planned counter attack on the 20th January held back by the dense jungle, two days later orders were received to defend Batu Pahat at all costs. However, on the 25th January, with the seriousness of the situation now clear, orders were received to evacuate the mainland and retreat to Singapore. The British Battalion were deployed to provide cover for the evacuation.

The next day the troops set off on foot for a nightmare retreat through mangrove swamps with exhausted men falling out through sheer exhaustion. On the 27th of January efforts to reach Benut for evacuation by an agreed time proved impossible, and the troops were marched five miles further south to Pongor where after dark they eventually boarded the gunboats Dragon Fly and Scorpion.

The evacuation of Pongor became known as the Malayan Dunkirk; but unlike that escape from the French beaches very few people have heard of it. The men of the 1st Leicesters and 2nd East Surreys were now battle-hardened soldiers and were commended for keeping the raw and inexperienced men of the 2nd Cambridgeshires and 5th and 6th Norfolks calm in the face of grave danger.

CHAPTER EIGHT

The Final Battle

On the 29th January the Battalion arrived in Singapore and on the 1st of February they were transported to the North of the island to take up defence positions. D Company were dug in on the beach awaiting the coming onslaught. The causeway that connected the island to the mainland had been blown up by the retreating troops.

One of my father's comrades from the British Battalion Pte Frank Farmer from the Leicesters described what they found in what was supposed to be a fortress and one of the jewels in the crown of the British Empire:

> *"We were terribly shocked to find our area to the east of the great Naval Base not prepared for any sort of defence at such a crucial period! Our British Battalion position faces the Straits of Johore and it is a bloody nasty area of creeks, tidal mudflats and mangrove swamps along the coast with a hinterland of rubber and coconut estates.*
>
> *The so-called fortress of Singapore was a myth and it was naked in the area where we had to work like mad to get some sort of defences ready to meet the invaders from the mainland.*
>
> *The much vaunted fortress of Singapore was no fortress except for its comprehensive southward coastal defences*

covering the approach to Singapore harbour! It was an undefended island and the enemy had found its undefended back door to capture the island."

The men had also been appalled to find that the great naval base itself, the pride of the Royal Navy, had been abandoned on the 28th December leaving behind millions of pounds worth of vital stores and supplies. The naval base could have played a crucial role in the defence of Singapore, and the men of the East Surreys and Leicesters were rightly angry to find that while they had been fighting like lions to defend their ground behind them, strategic decisions were being taken to pull the rug from under them. The Japanese couldn't believe their luck.

In my opinion the brave troops who fought their way right down the Malaysian peninsula, losing so many of their comrades in the process, had been betrayed by a combination of poor planning, hubris and a lack of basic intelligence and leadership from the very top. That must have just added to the burden of bitterness and anger that the survivors carried with them.

On what would prove to be a pivotal date in the fall of Singapore on the 8th of February the Japanese launched an assault on the North West shores of the island after days of bombing, initially engaging the 22nd Australian Infantry Division, who were thin on the ground,. The Japanese established several bridgeheads and began to move inland.

Nearly 13000 Japanese troops attacked by landing craft during the night of 9th February, with a further 10,000 arriving at dawn. The whole of Singapore was now covered with a thick cloud of acrid black smoke and dust from the constant bombardment by the advancing Japanese.

I remember my father telling me that during the battle for Singapore he found himself in a trench alongside an Australian soldier and on turning to speak to him realised he had been shot clean through the forehead. Dad's luck in the lottery of the battlefield had held again, it could easily have been him that took that bullet and he knew it. By now my father and his comrades who had been there from the initial invasion had been fighting flat out for two solid months with barely any time to grab a bit of sleep let alone have a proper rest. They were shattered, but somehow summoned up the energy to keep going.

Now they were sent into battle again to dig slit trenches and other defences while crowds of civilians, still believing the myth that Singapore was impregnable, despite the evidence all around them, continued to drink and party at high-end bars and hotels like Raffles. Frank Farmer said it "made him sick" and I suspect he spoke for the whole of the British Battalion. Reinforcements that had been called up arrived straight from England and with no experience of fighting in the conditions that now confronted them were thrown straight into battle. Frank described it as "suicide."

Over the two days of the 9th and 10th February the British battalion was moved from the coast to a defensive line on the Jurong Road, but the Japanese advance continued with the Battalion being heavily shelled and bombed. D Company was sent to defend the left flank but by now the forces were in disarray and the order was sent to make the difficult retreat three miles to the East to join up with other brigades. The 10th of February was a grim day with the East Surreys sustaining further heavy losses.

A planned counter attack on the 11th February was anticipated by the Japanese, and in the chaos comms broke down. With the Battalion in danger of being surrounded and an initial order to fight through to Bukit Timah proving impossible, they moved south east under heavy fire from the rear, the flanks and the air. This broke up the already depleted ranks to the point where the remains were placed under the command of the 22nd Australian brigade. Heavy attacks continued on what would turn out to be one of the worst days for the East Surreys.

On the 12th February the exhausted troops fell back again, and by the 13th February the British Battalion was so weak in terms of numbers it was no longer an effective fighting force and its remaining men were held in reserve as the Japanese tightened the net. On Black Friday, the

13th February 1942, the screech of Japanese planes filled the sky as the bombardment from both land and sea escalated. Oil tanks were set ablaze by retreating Dutch troops filling the air with yet more dense black smoke, and as the Japanese soldiers advanced they committed one of the worst atrocities of the campaign at the Queen Alexandra Military Hospital.

On the excuse that they had been fired at from within the hospital grounds, the Japanese Imperial Guards entered the hospital and unleashed a systematic massacre of all patients and staff on the ground and first floors, running them through with bayonets. One patient was murdered on the operating table. Off-duty staff were herded together before being marched off for mass execution.

One member of my father's regiment, Private Charles "Ches" Chessman survived the massacre, as he was on one of the upper floors at the hospital recovering from a gunshot wound. He wasn't the only one of the East Surreys to have a miraculous escape from the horrors at Alexandra Hospital.

John Wyatt, shipped back from the front line with a shrapnel wound to his shoulder, had also been sent upstairs at the hospital because he was one of the few admissions able to walk. It saved his life. He witnessed from his upper ward window the Japanese advance into the hospital grounds and then its building as they began the indiscriminate and systematic massacre and bayoneting of nurses, surgeons and patients alike. When the soldiers entered his ward of five, two patients nearest the door were bayoneted to death before an officer moved them on.

At the later War Crimes trials General Yamashita, the commander of the invading Japanese Army, was tried for his responsibility, found guilty and hanged in Singapore for ordering the cowardly murder of defenceless patients and staff.

It was later reported that the Japanese atrocities against the civilian population in Singapore were deliberate acts designed to pile pressure on Percival and the allies to surrender. These were the same Japanese troops responsible for the rape of Nanking. The message was if you don't agree to terms we will systematically wipe out non-combatant men, women and children until you do. One million civilians were now being kettled and trapped in the City as the Japanese advanced with ruthless efficiency.

With the exception of very few who made it onto ships, they had no means of escape. Those who did manage to board the last ships out risked being torpedoed and recaptured by the invaders navy. It was cynical and astute tactics to use the civilian population as pawns in this military exercise and it certainly played a part in the impending surrender that would seal the fate of my father and his comrades.

Among those caught in the last ditch defence of Singapore was war artist and cartoonist Ronald Searle:

> *"On Friday 13th the Japanese reached the outskirts of the town and everything came easily within shelling range. On the 14th they closed in, shelling, mortaring and strafing what was now a tightly-packed sardine tin".*

With only hours of freedom left, on what would become their last day of liberty, the British Battalion was moved for the last time taking up position on a hill just outside the town among the villas near the junction of Alexandra Road and Henderson Road.

The island of Singapore was now surrounded from sea, land and air. Ammunition was running out and it would have been impossible to bring in reinforcements. Water supplies were also running low and were estimated to last no more than 48 hours.

Dennis Gavin from the East Surreys sums up the chaos and sense of impending doom that now prevailed;

> *"This was Singapore in the last days of the siege. It had lasted only two weeks, one of apparent passive complacence and one of chaotic noise and movement. The noise was almost continuous, with Japanese aircraft always droning somewhere overhead, the whistling of artillery shells, and then later, as the battle came nearer, the violent eruption of mortar bombs.*

By Friday 13 February, 1942, it just had to be accepted that Singapore was doomed. The Japanese had encircled the entire suburbs at a radius of just five miles from the centre of the city; drinking water and water for fire fighting had practically disappeared, deserters and looters were roaming the streets of the town and general morale was at rock bottom. God knows how it happened, why our superior numbers had not swamped the Japanese army, or why we had spent the whole ten weeks of war on the run."

CHAPTER NINE

"The Worst Surrender"

Come the fateful day of the 15th February - bombed, shelled and mortared the East Surreys took further heavy losses as two slit trenches full of men were struck by direct hits. A planned counter attack by the Surreys across the golf course opposite their position was cancelled. Rumours that a surrender was imminent proved to be true and at 8.40 in the evening the order came to stack arms and wait for further instructions from the victors. During that long Sunday afternoon while the huge numbers of soldiers awaited their fate a strange and subdued silence was reported to have descended over Singapore. It is no surprise that men like my Dad who had given their all since the invasion felt a sense of deep anger and foreboding that it had come to this.

As the battered remnants of the British Battalion awaited instructions on Mount Echo the final command that eventually came through from the GOC Malaya was stark:

> *"It has been necessary to give up the struggle but I want the reason explained to all ranks. The forward troops continue to hold their ground but the essentials of war have run short. In a few days we shall have neither petrol nor food.*
>
> *Many types of ammunition are short and the water supply, upon which the vast civil population and many of the fighting troops are dependent threatens to fail. This situa-*

tion has been brought about partly by being driven off our dumps and partly by hostile air and artillery action.

Without these sinews of war we cannot fight on.

I thank all ranks for their efforts throughout this campaign."

And that was that. The order would condemn my father and the rest of the surrendered troops on the Island to a living hell for more than three and half years, a living hell that many wouldn't survive. The civilian population would be subjected to similar horrors. My father's military records simply list him as 'MISSING' from that date of the 15th February 1942

Major Tony Ferrier, 5th Battalion Royal Norfolk Regiment, summed up the scene at the point of surrender in an interview with Peter Thompson in his definitive book *'The Battle for Singapore'*:

"All around I could see the oil tanks burning and great palls of smoke. The whole island seemed to be in complete desolation and I could hear firing going on all around. When I got back to my company, I had to tell my platoon commanders the bad news. I felt extremely emotional that we had to lay down our arms and surrender....I was almost in tears at the very thought of it. But those were the orders and they had to be obeyed."

And Stan Henderson, a Communist Party member who was there with the Bedfordshire and Hertfordshire Regiment, put an interesting take on it:

"I just couldn't believe it, like others of my generation I had been brought up and educated in the prose and poetry of British imperialism. 'Whatever happened to that thin red line of Imperialism?" I asked myself. Then I had to smile as the thought occurred to me that I, as a communist, had really believed that the thin red line would hold out. Was there no public schoolboy here to rally the ranks with the cry, 'Play up, play up and play the game'?

My father wasn't a communist, although he came from a part of London where the communists were a strong local force before the war. He could never have followed rigid party ideology and his own brand of socialism was much more of the old school Labour style but when I gave him a copy of Stan's booklet he told me that discussion of communism and socialism was popular amongst the troops when they had the time and the energy. But he also said that they would discuss just about anything, with food and what they would do if they ever made it home ranking way above politics. However, he certainly would have concurred with Stan's view that it was the failures of the class system that dominated the military and the British establishment that had failed him and the rest of the ranks on an unprecedented scale.

Unknown to the soldiers, preliminary talks on a surrender had been going on for some time. It was to become one of the biggest defeats in British military history with 85,000 allied troops surrendering to 30,000 Japanese. The seeds of the defeat had been sown long before the surrender, both before the war and in the abject failure to prepare for the Japanese invasion of Malaya and to action the plans to confront it at the outset. The men now piling up their arms and ammunition in the battle-scarred streets were about to reap the whirlwind.

Singapore was the most important British military and economic base in South East Asia and had been regarded as an impregnable fortress. But those who planned its defences had made a massive mistake. Large fixed gun emplacements faced towards the sea but were useless come the Japanese advance down the peninsula to the north. The final defence was made by brave soldiers who were let down by poor communication and leadership from the very top.

Churchill had said that Singapore should be defended to the last man. It was a pledge abandoned before the ink was barely dry on the paper. When the biggest surrender in British history became a reality it was hushed up so as not to further damage public morale back home. Whilst that may be understandable, it meant that the men caught behind the wire were effectively cut adrift. The forgotten army. That sense of abandonment and betrayal would last with many of those men who survived long after they were released from captivity. The post war failure to secure any kind of meaningful compensation and the battle for war pensions the men were forced to mount into their later years was a bitter and constant reminder.

Churchill later called the fall of Singapore 'the worst disaster and largest capitulation in British history." Not only was that a statement of the bleeding obvious, but it also emerged after the war that the whole Japanese assault on Singapore had been a massive bluff that the British military establishment fell for. Writing in his war diaries the General Officer Commanding of the Japanese invasion forces Lieutenant-General Tomoyuki Yamashita makes it clear:

> *"My attack on Singapore was a bluff: a bluff that worked. I had 30,000 men and was outnumbered more than three to one. I knew that if I had to fight long for Singapore I would be beaten. That is why the surrender had to be done at once. I was very frightened all the time that the British would discover our numerical weakness and lack of supplies and force me into disastrous street fighting."*

More than eighty years later those words fill me with anger and contempt. Anger at the failure of military intelligence to assess the strengths of the enemy forces and contempt for those who took the fateful decisions that would unleash a long chain of horrific consequences. Of course, a house by house street fight for Singapore would have been grim for the civilian population, but so was surrender.

Lieutenant General Arthur Percival has been rightly held up for much of the blame for the disaster in Singapore but the lack of strategic planning and intelligence on the enemy goes much wider. Percival said that he had no option but to agree to surrender as the Japanese shut down the water supply and launched continuous bombing raids on civilian and military targets.

My father believed that they should have fought on, not least because they knew enough about the Japanese to have some idea what to expect in captivity. I think he also felt that they owed it to the hundreds of his comrades who had already been killed. It's easy to understand the bitterness that after fighting so hard for so long, in an almost permanent state of retreat, and having seen your mates shot and blown apart in front of your eyes you were now giving in to an enemy you outnumbered and who could not believe their good fortune.

But it couldn't be clearer that the poor decisions that led to the humiliating capitulation of Singapore had been made much earlier in a sequence of failures: they had failed to build proper defences instead of the symbolic big guns facing out to sea; failed to recognise the capacity of the enemy prior to the invasion of the Malaya and to equip and prepare for it; and panic decisions like the evacuation of the naval base while the ground troops were still bravely fighting up country.

The vulnerability of the water supply, which was key to the surrender, should also have been recognised earlier, and measures put in place to either defend it or prepare an alternative. I could go on: there was the lack of air cover, giving the Japanese air superiority, and the lack of mobile heavy arms while the enemy proved that they could bring tanks into the jungle battles. But for the men stacking arms it was all too late, and they were to be left to their fate and the PR disaster and military humiliation would pile on the anguish as the Forgotten Army was airbrushed out of the picture for propaganda purposes. Nor was this to be the final kick in the teeth for soldiers who had given everything, far from it: but they were now viewed by the establishment as little more than an embarrassment to be pushed to the back of the public's mind.

When the British Battalion had been formed on the 20th December from the already heavily reduced ranks of the Surreys and the Leicesters its strength was 786 men. By the time of surrender on Mount Echo on the 15th February it had been reduced to a total of just 265. Those 521 lost men had left England like my Dad, full of determination and pride that they were sailing overseas to do a job as soldiers. Many of their corpses now lay rotting in shallow graves along the long trail of the eventual defeat, never to be recovered and long forgotten. Many of their surviving captured comrades would join them on the lengthening death roll in the years that lay ahead.

In just over two months since the Japanese invasion my father and his last remaining comrades had retreated from Jitra in the north all the way down the Malayan peninsula to Singapore at the southern tip abandoning position after position, commandeering boats and surviving repeated bombardment on little or no sleep in the most treacherous jungle conditions. There were points along the way where they had had a chance to take the fight bravely to the invading forces but that counted for little now. It was a journey of over 500 miles zig-zagging through the hostile terrain, further than Glasgow to Dover, and most of it had been covered on aching and blistered feet battling through mud, torrential rain and dense vegetation under heavy enemy fire. They were shattered in every sense of the word.

CHAPTER TEN

Into Captivity

So on the 16th February the remaining East Surreys men were amongst the tens of thousands of captured troops left awaiting instructions. There were chaotic scenes as they took whatever action they could to secure a share of the dwindling supplies still available on the island, and there would have been discussions late into the night about what fate had in store for them.

Denis Gavin paints a vivid picture:

> *"....as we journeyed through the town, the full picture of chaos and devastation unfolded and a sense of desolation swept over us. Everywhere was rubble and wreckage, and we got the impression that Singapore was indeed destroyed. There were broken wires, leaning telegraph poles, shattered cars and trucks, many of them still burning, and piles of rubble everywhere."*

But despite the feelings of desolation and trepidation for many of the men, like my father, it was the first chance to get a decent night's sleep since the invasion of Malaya ten weeks earlier. They bedded down wherever they could in various deserted buildings. For the East Surreys who had first docked in Singapore in September 1938 on their way to Shanghai the contrast couldn't have been starker. Then it had been a bustling, glamorous and vibrant city, now it was a battered, boarded up and burnt out shell shrouded in smoke and fear as the enormity of what had happened began to sink in.

On the morning of the 17th February the order was received to march the 22 miles to Changi on the North East corner of the island the following day in blistering heat. Some supplies and kit were transported by road.

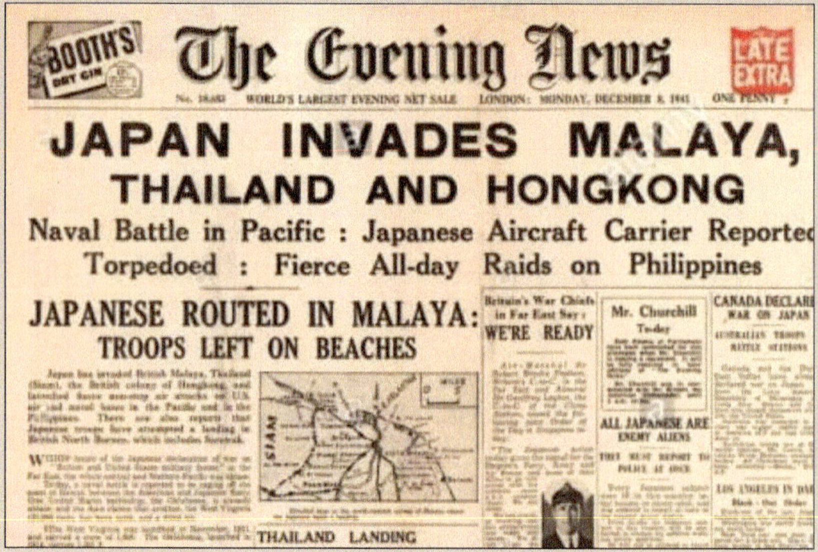

BOOTH'S DRY GIN

The Evening News

LATE EXTRA

WORLD'S LARGEST EVENING NET SALE · LONDON: MONDAY, DECEMBER 8, 1941 · ONE PENNY

JAPAN INVADES MALAYA, THAILAND AND HONGKONG

Naval Battle in Pacific : Japanese Aircraft Carrier Reported Torpedoed : Fierce All-day Raids on Philippines

JAPANESE ROUTED IN MALAYA: TROOPS LEFT ON BEACHES

Britain's War Chiefs in Far East Say: WE'RE READY

Mr. Churchill To-day

CANADA DECLARES WAR ON JAPAN

ALL JAPANESE ARE ENEMY ALIENS

THAILAND LANDING

News of the Malayan invasion. The Japanese were anything but routed.

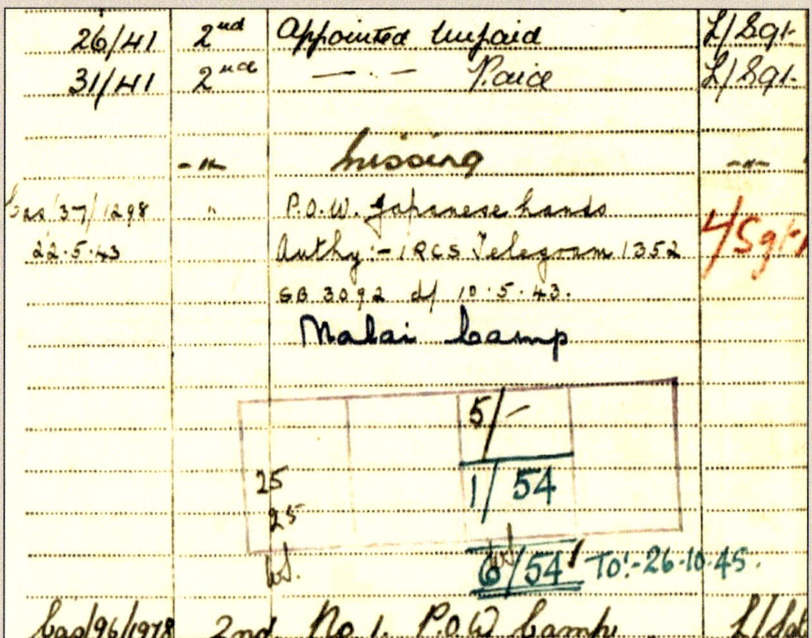

26/41	2nd	Appointed unpaid	L/Sgt.
31/41	2nd	— " — Paid	L/Sgt.
	— "	Missing	— " —
Cas 37/1298	"	P.O.W. Japanese hands	L/Sgt.
22.5.43		Authy:- IRCS Telegram 1352	
		GB 3092 d/ 10.5.43.	
		Malai Camp	
	25	5/-	
	25	1/54	
	W.	6/54 To:- 26.10.45.	
Cas/96/1978	2nd	No. 1. P.O.W. Camp	L/Sgt.
d/31.1.45.		Thailand. Letter from	

Military records listing Dad as missing after the fall of Singapore

Captured troops were forced to endure the humiliation of lining the roads to be inspected by victorious officers of the Japanese army and navy. They also witnessed the aftermath of atrocities against the local civilian population with bodies piled up and severed heads rammed on the spikes of ornate railings, an ominous insight into what they were now dealing with as prisoners. Mentally and physically broken they trudged off, carrying as much kit as they could manage although much was left behind and lost. That night they slept as best they could by the side of the road continuing their journey at dawn the next morning.

It may have been surprise at the speed of their victory, and surprise at the Allied capitulation, but the Japanese didn't appear to have any logistical plan for dealing with the tens of thousands of prisoners now in their hands. However, their attitude to the prisoners was baked into their Bushido code, they were to be despised. Their rights should have been protected by the 1929 International Convention on the Treatment of Prisoners of War, the Geneva Convention, but although Japan signed up to it they claimed they had never ratified it and in subsequent war crimes trials the Army Minister, General Tojo, claimed that Japan had the right to revise the principles of international conventions to meet the demands of the "immediate situation" and Japanese domestic laws.

Arriving at Changi the men were billeted in overcrowded Tamil huts and initially, when their trucks of supplies turned up and despite the overall lack of food, the conditions were as good as could be expected and the Japanese allowed them to get on with it and manage themselves to a large degree with the British officers maintaining discipline. But it was to prove a false dawn and would be the best of conditions the prisoners would experience throughout their captivity as the shadow of sickness, hunger and brutality spread across their world.

During March and April 1942 a camp housing the remaining East Surreys was established in Changi Village and restrictions were gradually tightened. By now the food supplies they had brought with them at the point of capture were dwindling and the stocks of remaining army rations and medical supplies were running out. The first wave of dysentery had also broken out, overrunning the limited hospital facilities that had been hastily established in the camp. My father is recorded as being in the hospital hut with Malaria in April 1942.

Although work at this point was mainly around organising and building camp facilities the men were growing weak on their diet of boiled rice and a thin, watery stew. Combined with the increasing problems of disease, sanitation, water supplies and wounds from the battles of the months before their situation was grim even before the Japanese began the process of putting the men to work.

At the crack of dawn on the 14th May 1942 a working party of 600 men including the East Surreys were lined up to leave Changi to march to the River Valley Road Camp. The men were weak from starvation and disease and, with only limited transport, were weighed down with their heavy packs. They were also forced to take thirty hospital cases with them including eight dysentery patients. It was a nineteen mile march under the blistering tropical sun and with their feet bleeding, little or no food and water running out a number failed to make it with some being picked up later by truck. Others would have died at the roadside where they fell.

In the evening the men arrived at River Valley Road but were sent on a bit further to the new Havelock Road Camp. A canal separated the two camps, and was crossed by a bridge. The troops at Havelock Road were put to work in two different groups - a Transport Battalion and a hand cart battalion. At this early stage in captivity the men were still responsible for organising and running the camp themselves and although it's a low bar the conditions would still be some of the best they would experience as POWs. The camp even had a chapel and a small library with books looted from nearby houses.

In late May 1942 work on building the camp from scrap materials continued along with the digging of roads and drains and the food rations were a slight improvement on Changi but the men were still surviving on a diet of boiled rice, thin vegetable stew and some supplies bought from outside from the 15 cents a day paid to the men for their transport work. Dad never smoked, but for those men who did, obtaining cigarettes or something to spark up had become an obsession. As time went on in the camps some prisoners would trade their food rations for a few smokes and would fight over dog ends stubbed out in the dirt by the guards. Cigarettes had become hard currency and it must have been a relief to my father that he never had that craving as he witnessed the desperation of his mates.

Some of the boredom and monotony of life at Havelock Road was relieved when a prisoner called Johnny Sherwood, a former professional footballer with Reading, Aldershot, Middlesbrough and Crystal Palace, was given permission along with another group of men to get a football pitch together. Sherwood tells the story in his book about his life as a Japanese POW and beyond, *'Lucky Johnny'*;

> *".....I had a dozen light-sick men (ill but mobile) allotted to work with me every day, and within a couple of weeks we had completed our task, and made goalposts as well. The fittest men now started to play football in the evenings.....It felt amazing to be playing again and I enjoyed sorting out who should play and in what position, giving everyone what they wanted in return."*

Games were organised against the nearby River Valley camp and amongst the many prisoners there were some great sportsmen including at least one other professional footballer, the brilliantly named Albert Hall who had played for Spurs before the war. The football matches must have come as a welcome relief for both those playing and the men watching. But the grim reality of life in the camp would soon put an end to the football matches as Johnny Sherwood explains:

> *"We were getting no extra food coming into the camp now and we had precious little nourishment from our daily rations of watery stew which had almost nothing in it, and*

the lowest grade of rice. We were all malnourished and beginning to suffer from a number of complaints through vitamin deficiencies. Nearly everyone in the camp now had beriberi…..

"The boys at River Valley camp were just the same and our games became slower as we grew weaker every match and had to have lots of rest in between. The medical officers at both camps were increasingly concerned about our health. In fact, our doc came to see me after the match was over one day. He looked me up and down with a stern expression….

"'…..You're not in a fit state to play football for more than a few minutes at a time and if you continue like this, malnourished and riddled with beriberi, you are in effect committing suicide. We have no medicines to help you now, so I'm sorry, but I must order you to stop playing football.'"

It was a grim indicator of the lives that the men were now being condemned to but they still did what they could to make the best of their situation and maintain discipline. By June 1942 the dire sanitation and washing situation had improved slightly with some showers rigged up. The lack of medical supplies and equipment was serious but other than more dysentery and beriberi cases as the impact of malnourishment deepened there had not yet been major outbreaks of disease as the prisoners did their best to maintain hygiene standards.

That's not to minimise the impact that the poor diet and malnutrition was already having on the men. Vitamin deficiency manifested itself in many ways and scrotal dermatitis, given the name 'Changi balls' by the prisoners as the scrotum became inflamed and painful keeping you awake at night, was increasingly commonplace. Wet beriberi could effectively drown a man within his own body as water accumulated in the tissues of the extremities and the heart didn't have enough strength to pump blood through the muscles to collect waste to be passed as urine. I don't remember Dad ever talking about surviving these waves of sickness.

Clothes that the men arrived with had gradually been reduced to rags and a third had no boots and were now forced to go barefoot. There was no contact with the outside world and the relentlessly grim conditions that the prisoners would be subject to for the next three years or more were starting to be defined, the early days at Changi were now just a memory.

The men were now allocated to forced working parties and were engaged in building 'go downs' -- sheds for the transport trucks. Two thousand men were involved in this project. It is hard work carting bricks and other materials by hand on a starvation diet and often barefoot. The prisoners were given their first standard postcard to send home. These were pre-written affairs that allowed the men to just strike out a few words and add very few of their own. My father sent a few of these home to his sister but none of them actually reached her until after the war.

CHAPTER ELEVEN

The Inhumanity Escalates

While being held in Singapore four men, two Australians and two British, including one from the East Surreys, Private Waters, escaped and were recaptured, badly beaten and shot as a warning to the rest. I believe that Private Harry Waters was a regular soldier at the outbreak of the war and would have been with my father right the way through from the battalion's first duty in Shanghai in 1938. He was so sick at the time of his execution that he was dragged from his hospital bed, propped up in a chair and hadn't been allowed to get dressed to at least grant him some basic dignity.

The men were taken to Changi Beach and ordered to dig their own graves before being shot by firing squad. Before they were executed one of the Australians, Corporal Breavington said that he alone was responsible for the escape and the others should be spared. He was ignored and the men were forced to stand to attention and salute their commanding officers, Colonels Holmes and Gallegan, who had been ordered by the Japanese to witness their men being murdered. It must have been a horrific experience for the East Surreys and the other men and was a measure of the sheer brutality they knew that they could now expect. The Japanese officer Fukuye who ordered the beating and execution of the men was found guilty at the war crimes trials and was hanged in Singapore.

When I was a kid I remember asking my father why he had never tried to escape, I had been fed a diet of Colditz, the Great Escape and other war films. He said it was simply impossible but it was only later I realised just how trapped the men were. Getting out wouldn't be a problem, but hundreds of miles of dense, hostile jungle was a better barrier than any barbed wire fence and the guards knew it. But it didn't stop a few brave and desperate men from trying against impossible odds.

I know of five other private soldiers from the East Surreys who gave it their best shot. Privates Cleaver, Croker, Richardson and Dorval had hatched a plan with the support of their senior officer Lieutenant Colonel Toosey. They slipped away on a march from Ban Pong to Chunkai and aimed to either steal a boat or swim across the river, but they were betrayed by some Thai villagers and handed over to the Japanese for the bounty money on the head of escapees. After they were captured they were tortured and shot and are now buried in the military cemetery at Kanchanaburi. It was intended that they should be executed in front of the other prisoners as an example but after representation from Toosey they were shot in semi-secrecy with bugler Arthur Lane playing the Last Post. The man who ordered their deaths, Major General Sasa Akiro, was later tried for these crimes, found guilty and hanged.

Joe Holland, a fellow East Ender who Dad would have known, was the last of the Surreys to attempt an escape with the help of Chinese resistance men who were making raids on Japanese camps along the railway, but he was recaptured after three weeks. Although badly beaten and stuck in a tiny hut in solitary for several weeks he somehow dodged the expected death penalty, and was released back into the camp. He miraculously survived the rest of the war and made it back to Bow after his repatriation. Although my Dad was sold the East Surreys on the basis that it was a "Good Old Cockney Mob" there were very few Cockneys in the ranks and Joe Holland's is a truly incredible story of survival amongst many extraordinary stories of men living on their wits. Battered and covered in his own blood and filth, he was left standing on the parade ground and every passing guard gave him another whack but somehow they never broke him. There's a lot of baloney talked about so-called East End hard men but Joe was the real deal, it would take brains, courage and nerves of steel to try and pull off a one man escape like he did. However, I'm not surprised the vast majority of prisoners viewed the whole idea of escaping as totally futile.

In August rumours began circulating of a move to Thailand, once the building work was completed, to work on a new transport project but details were sketchy. Food rations had deteriorated further and the prisoners were now banned from buying food outside the camp, the one chance that they had of supplementing their starvation diet. By the following month the rumours of an impending move had now grown as the 'go downs' had been finished and work was drying up. On the 2nd September members of the East Surreys were moved into the Selarang Barracks, the former home of the 1st Battalion Gordon Highlanders, which had been built to house 900 men but now had more than 15,000 British and Australian prisoners are rammed into it.

Seralang, part of the Changi garrison, was the site of an important, but ultimately unsuccessful, act of resistance by the POWs. Following the earlier failed escape attempt, the Japanese demanded that the prisoners sign a pledge not to escape from captivity. The men refused and as result the guards herded them into the open air around the barracks where they remained for nearly five days with little food and water. Even the slaughter of their four comrades captured after the escape attempt didn't break their spirits but by the third day the first prisoner collapsed and died as sickness, particularly dysentery and diphtheria, began to spread.

The Japanese commander Fukuye warned the men that if they continued to refuse to sign then the seriously sick men housed in Roberts Hospital would be moved out and forced to join them. With hundreds of lives now at risk the allied officers decided that enough was enough and advised the men to sign under duress. There was little or no choice but to comply as the officers were in no doubt that the Japanese would have stood by and watched on as many of the POWs faded and died before their eyes. It was a measure of the brutal levels of control the captors were prepared to resort to and sent a message that would stay with the men throughout their captivity: a heavy price would be paid for any form of resistance.

CHAPTER TWELVE

Marched to Death Railway

On the 9th of October 1942 my father was one of 42 East Surrey men shipped overland to Thailand. They were marched to Singapore station in the late afternoon heat and entrained in covered trucks with 32 men per carriage. A total of 650 men were on board under the command of Lt. Col. Richard Alexander Owen Clarke of the 5th Searchlight Regiment. The trucks were seriously overcrowded with barely room for the men to sit let alone lie down as they began an 800 mile journey that would take four days and four nights. The trucks were steel - furnaces during the day and freezing cold at night. Very little food was supplied en route other than the occasional watery stew with rice and rotten dried fish.

Luckily the men had been issued with some very limited Red Cross rations before they left but these soon ran out. There were no washing or toilet facilities. Prisoners needing to empty their bowels were held out of the open train door of the moving carriage but for many with dysentery or diarrhoea it wasn't an option, and they were left in their own filth for the duration. Before long the burning hot trucks were stinking with the bodily waste of sick men and if they were lucky there would be one main stop a day to fill their single water bottles, grab whatever meagre food rations were available and stretch their legs.

The men had been fed the lie that the transfer would be to specially constructed camps where better food supplies and medical support would be readily available. This was also the point at which what remained of the East Surreys who had first fought together at Jitra would be split up and that must have been tough in itself. My father would have had to say goodbye to one his great mates, Sergeant Dave Boorer, as he got ready to leave. I'm not sure if he ever saw Dave again during the years ahead in the various camps. Dave was transported north up to Thailand and the railway camps a bit later in March 1943 and their paths may have crossed, but by some miracle he also survived captivity and after liberation they were reunited and both became leading lights in the East Surreys regimental association and the FEPOW organisation.

After a hellish four days travel on the 13th October they arrived in Ban Pong, Thailand. After leaving the train they were paraded outside the station and given a lecture by the Japanese Commander 'Colonel Ishie' who told the men that they had been shipped to Thailand to build a railway and that if they worked hard and obeyed orders they would be well looked after and that if they didn't they would be severely treated. After this warning the exhausted men were marched another three miles to the transit camp.

The monsoon rains had left the camp underwater and conditions were appalling. The latrines had flooded and the camp was awash in filth, a thirty acre sea of black, stinking mud. The 'hospital hut' was so bad that doctors and orderlies had to wade through a foot of stagnant, muddy water to attend the patients. It soon dawned on the men that they had been fed a big lie about improved conditions on this new work project. Before long they would look back on the time at Changi as the best of a bad bunch during their time in captivity, something I don't think they would have believed when they were under the cosh in Seralang barracks. Their first task on arrival was to bury their dead. The bamboo crosses marking the graves of those who had succumbed to sickness, starvation and injury would become a growing feature at this and all the other camps along the railway.

Ban Pong was the main base camp for all the prisoners heading up to the railway. The camp was made up of four long bamboo and leaf attap huts on low lying land, and was notorious for its poor and insanitary conditions even by the standards of Death Railway. The water supply was drawn from a single filthy well and one prisoner describes the food as being worse than that endured on the journey up from Singapore. Efforts to improve the latrines and sanitation by the men passing through were hampered by the refusal of the Japanese to issue even basic tools. The floors of the huts were flooded with a mixture of mud and the overspill from the latrines, the whole camp was the perfect breeding ground for disease.

Frank Davies, another POW who followed the same route up to Thailand, tells of the journey, the arrival at Ban Pong and the conditions at the camp.

> *"There were blokes with dysentery and we were huddled in this truck with nothing to lie on for five days....Our first camp was Ban Pong. It was a foot under water and the latrines had overflowed with faeces and maggots. As time went on, the camps got worse."*

Frank, in interviews for the Imperial War Museum North, also had an interesting take on why he may have survived captivity while others were dying all around him:

> *"I survived through pure luck. A lot of my mates were big tough lads and they were going first. A medic put it down to the fact that if you came from a rough area like Salford and were brought up in the gutters, you had a better immune system."*

If you substitute Salford for the streets of Stepney maybe the same theory could apply to my father. Colonel Toosey, the senior British officer on the Kwai, made a similar point that it was the former slum dwellers of Glasgow, Liverpool and London, who had fought all their lives and become used to deprivation, who stood up best to the conditions. Having a tough upbringing in a tough area may well give you some added strength and resilience but I think Frank Davies' opening line is probably more pertinent - you survived, in the main, through pure luck.

On the 16th October at dawn the men, now just 500 strong, were assembled for the next stage of their journey, a five day march through the jungle, carrying what was left of their kit, to Tha Sao camp. After the first morning marching in blistering heat a number of men had already collapsed. Some Chinese civilians along the route attempted to help with small amounts of food and water. After more than twelve hours marching at 7pm the column reached a transit camp which I believe was Tha Rua, the first of the river camps, which was set in a beautiful mountain location: but the tired and starving men would have had no time to enjoy the scenery. Stragglers were still arriving two hours later. After a meal of boiled rice and thin vegetables, and a hose down with a pipe the men turned in for the night, exhausted.

Assembling again at dawn the following day the march continued. Men who dropped from exhaustion were kicked and abused by guards as the hot sun rose in the sky, some were picked up and carried by their comrades but others just died where they fell. Meagre water supplies that had been brought for the march ran out at lunchtime, and only pails of water supplied along the trail by brave locals kept the men going. By 4pm another twenty miles had been covered by the starving, exhausted and dehydrated men. Feet were by now blistered, swollen and bleeding, and every step was excruciatingly painful. Few men still had boots of any sort by this stage. That evening they eventually reached Kanchanburi Camp. One man reportedly forced by the guards to keep moving died 200 yards from the camp entrance.

On the 18th of October there was at last a small period of respite on this horrific march. Pleas by the medical officers to the Japanese to allow a day's rest were initially ignored but on inspection of the condition of the men it was finally agreed. Even the guards realised that at this rate they would have no labour to work by the time they reached the destination. But after that brief rest the march continued, with depleted numbers on the next leg of the journey with even worse conditions lying ahead for this ragged and shattered group of men. Now the roads disappeared and the prisoners had to cross rice fields and plough on through heavy mud slowing progress even further.

The battalion held together as best it could, eking out their meagre water supplies in the sweltering heat. Some men resorted to drinking from the potentially dangerous jungle streams despite warnings that it could be laced with disease. The first break they had came at a location called Lat Ya.

After a long day of battling through the mud and undergrowth of the jungle, with the conditions even making it impossible to sit down when they were given a break, the tired, starving and soaked men had to try to sleep without any proper cover in a jungle clearing at Tha Dan. With all the available wood being soaked even boiling up their meagre rice rations was nearly impossible. The cooks were routinely expected to try to work miracles but the conditions confronting them on these forced marches were sometimes insurmountable.

The men prepared for the final stage of the journey to Kinsaiyok by boat, with everyone crammed into two small barges. Eventually they arrived at the new camp, Tha Sao, a large HQ facility, late in the evening where they were at least able to get their first taste of anything even resembling a meal in days. The boat journey would take another two days before they eventually reached Kinsaiyok, and although dangerously overcrowded in sweltering conditions it would at least come as some respite from the gruelling march.

Kinsaiyok was a big construction camp housing thousands of prisoners, mainly British, Australian and Dutch. It was located on flat ground close to the Menam Kwai Nor River and a short distance beyond Hellfire Pass. The next day work began on building more accommodation in the growing camp with huts constructed from bamboo and attap - large leaves - but the leaky and uncomfortable structures did little to address the severe overcrowding and the poor sanitation.

Being up river, even the usual meagre supplies were restricted even further, and the men were basically living on small portions of boiled rice with the occasional addition of dried vegetables and maggot infested fish. Trading with locals was possible for those able to raise funds, but by now very few men had anything left of any value to barter with. The officers had a job on their hands controlling some of the men who had resorted to theft and racketeering and it would be foolish to pretend that everyone was pulling together all the time. Some had decided that their best chance of survival was to go it alone.

A post-war report for the Australian Army says that the close proximity to the river at Kinsaiyok meant that a member of the Thai Resistance, Nai Boonpong Sirivejabhandu, was able to smuggle in money and some drugs: acts of incredible bravery. Men and women of the Thai resistance were also able to feed back information on the conditions and location of camps to British intelligence through a network set up by the Special Operations Executive. They knew that they risked torture and execution by the brutal Kempeitai, the military police of the Imperial Japanese Army.

Lieutenant Colonel "Weary" Dunlop, the Australian surgeon , explains the conditions at Kinsaiyok in his War Diaries:

> *"Things at Kinsaiyok are very much at sixes and sevens… Each group looks after its own sick, the hospital being run by a 'Soviet of captains', but no common policy, no common stores, no arrangements for diet or special segregation of disease….Sanitation poor, with only one big latrine for all…"*

CHAPTER THIRTEEN

The Horror of the Jungle

My father was now set to work on Death Railway. Ironically the project for a 250 mile rail line linking Bangkok and Rangoon had first been conceived by the British in 1929 but the costs and logistics involved in running a line through the terrain of dense jungle, rivers and ravines was regarded as totally unviable and the idea was dropped. But in 1942 the Japanese Imperial Army, with its supply lines stretched across its growing and expanding empire, revived the plan. Their engineers were skilled planners and they now had a crucial resource at their disposal, a huge pool of slave labour that they could work to death at the most minimal of cost. So my Dad and his pals were woken at dawn every morning and sent off to work with empty stomachs and only the most basic of hand tools, and forced through the threat of beating and death to build the railway for the Emperor.

In November 1942 the sickness rate in the camp was soaring as the effects of the starvation diet, hard physical work clearing the jungle and building roads with only primitive tools and the brutality of the guards combined to take effect. Captain Barnard reported that 64 men had dysentery and over two hundred were seriously weakened by malnutrition. The doctors had no drugs to treat the men. Malaria was breeding in the stagnant water around the camp and was now taking hold, my father, along with the other prisoners, suffered from repeated bouts of malaria with little treatment available to alleviate the symptoms. Men who survived captivity would later bring the legacy of Malaria back with them.

Meanwhile, more men arrived in the camp and rather than easing the pressure the Japanese introduced what they called "Speedo" - demanding more work from men who were starving, weak and sick and could barely stand. Barnard explained what the rations and daily routine for the men were like at this stage of captivity;

> *"We get up just before dawn and turn out to roll call.... Next comes breakfast of boiled rice and a pint of hot river water. Half an hour later, with officers as supervisors, the men go off to work for a long day in the jungle. They take lunch with them, which is usually some cold rice, and a little dried vegetable. They return worn out, about an hour before sunset. This leaves just time for a wash before the evening meal.... Which is another meagre ration of boiled rice and thin vegetable stew."*

The death rate and the brutality of the guards were both escalating, 'Speedo" had given the most sadistic of guards the green light to step up the beatings and punishments. In some areas 24 hour working was introduced to step up the pace, including at Hell Fire Pass, with the 12 hour night shift forced to work by flaming torch light and then try and sleep by day in their rotten huts and tents in the burning heat of the daylight hours.

Day shifts were increased to up to 18 hours giving the men no real time to try to rest before dragging themselves back to their backbreaking work, the combination of sheer exhaustion, starvation and disease claimed many lives during the Speedo period. A hospital hut was built at Kinsaiyok: but with no drugs and only minimal equipment its ability to cope was very limited although the dedication and ingenuity of the medical staff was extraordinary. Surgical instruments were fashioned out of old spoons and bits of tin cans and bandages were shredded from bits of blankets and boiled up in an attempt to keep them sterile.

My father had nothing but the utmost respect for the medical officers who worked themselves into the ground trying to keep prisoners alive against the odds. Their extraordinary efforts saved many who otherwise would have joined the growing numbers in the burial ground. It's almost impossible to believe that major surgery was carried out successfully in these appalling conditions, but it was.

In his book *'Faith, Hope and Rice'* my Dad's East Surrey comrade Fred Cox recounts the random nature of the beatings handed out during the 'Speedo' phase on the railway;

> *"Whichever working party we were on, we were constantly goaded by the guards. Often they would bark out orders to us in their own language, which we stood little chance of understanding and then, if we didn't immediately comply with what they had said, they would lash out with whatever weapon was the nearest, often a bamboo pole. Trying to reason with them simply made matters worse; there simply was no reasoning with these people. If one of us was getting a beating, it was a case of just letting him take it. If anyone tried to step in to help one of their pals, they would get a beating too, and things could, and sometimes did, quickly escalate to the point where the punishment meted out became one that was out of all proportion to the original so-called crime."*

Preventing men from being able to jump in and help a mate taking a kicking and a beating was part of the strategy to break their spirit and exert complete control. It must have been humiliating in the extreme to have to stand back as spectators while friends they had been through hell with were battered to a pulp. Comrades who did step in were given worse punishments as an example - beaten, tortured and put in the cage or box, or forced to stand at attention outside the guard hut day and night until they collapsed and often the outcome would be death. Every prisoner knew this only too well. My father developed a lifelong hatred of bullies, because that's what these guards were. He told me to get your retaliation in early, before they could exert control over you. That advice had come from the bitter and painful experiences he carried with him.

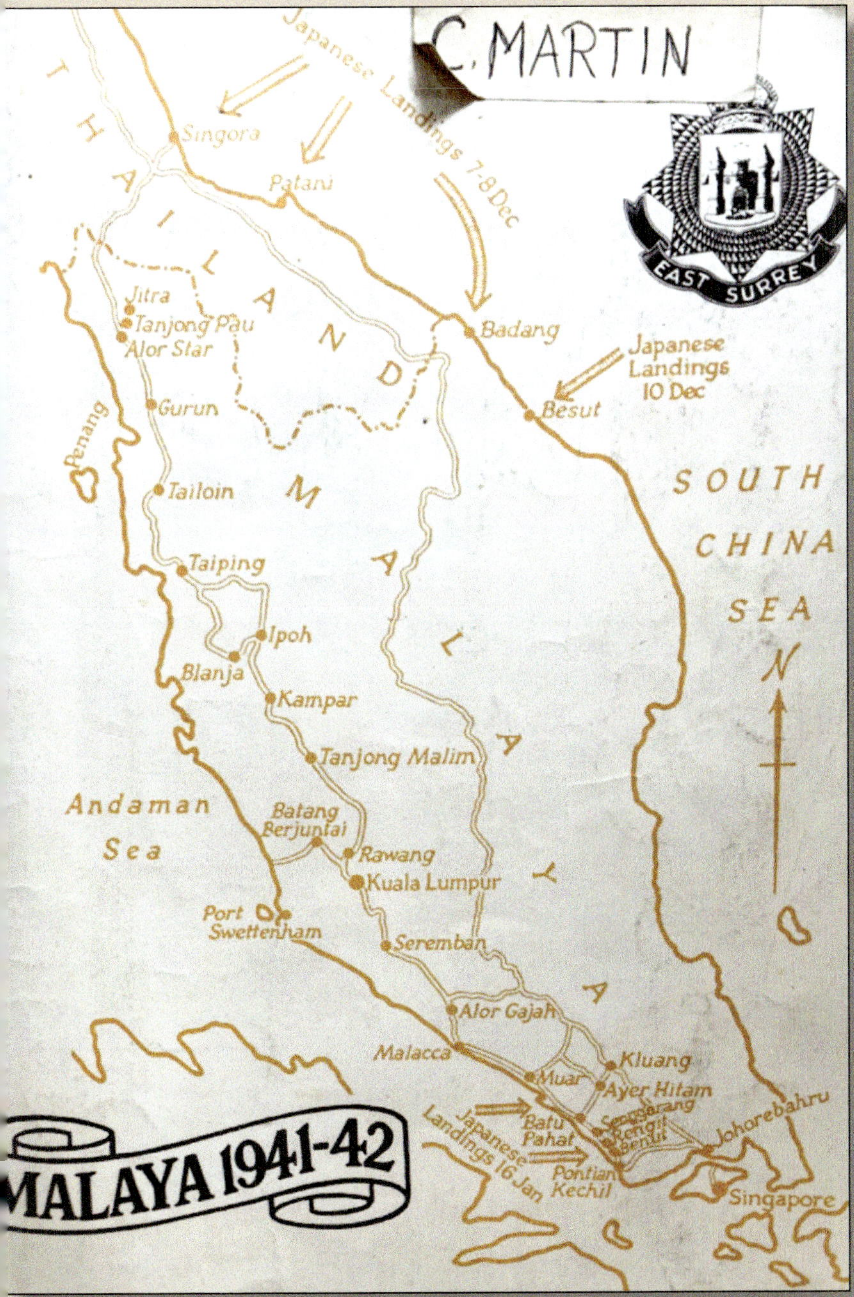

Dad's map of the battle and retreat down Malaysia.

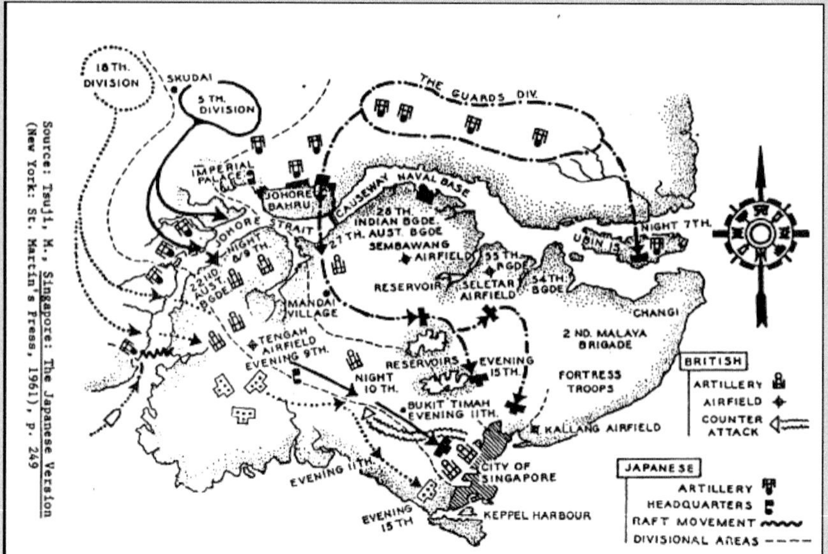

The capture of Singapore.

The invasion of Singapore

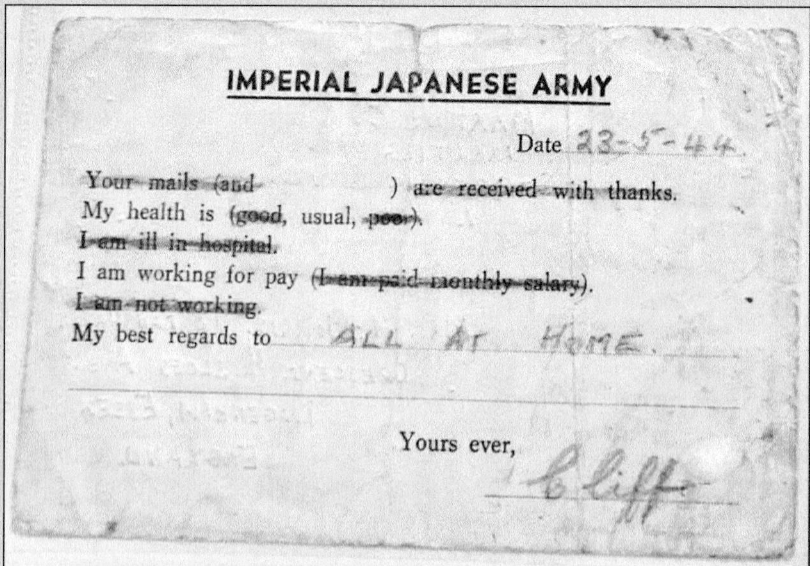

IMPERIAL JAPANESE ARMY

Date 23-5-44

~~Your mails (and~~) ~~are received with thanks.~~
My health is (~~good~~, usual, ~~poor~~).
~~I am ill in hospital.~~
I am working for pay (~~I am paid monthly salary~~).
~~I am not working.~~
My best regards to ALL AT HOME.

Yours ever,
Cliff

A card home that never made it until the war was over

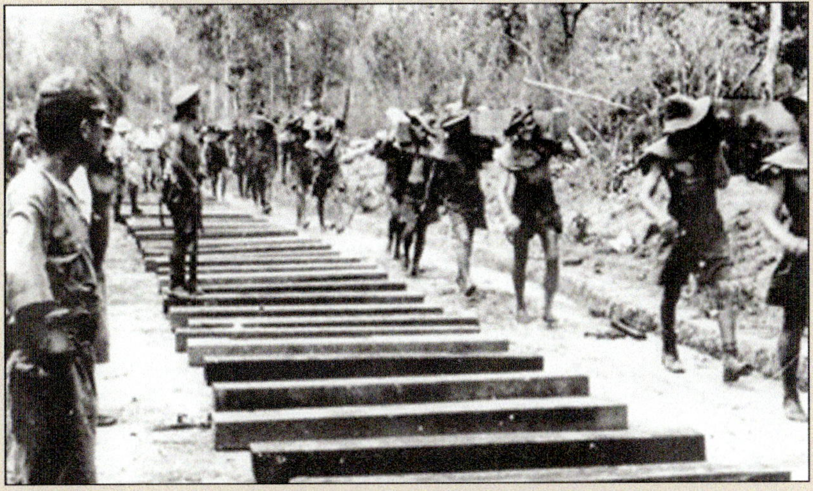

A work party on the Death Railway (from the Australian archives)

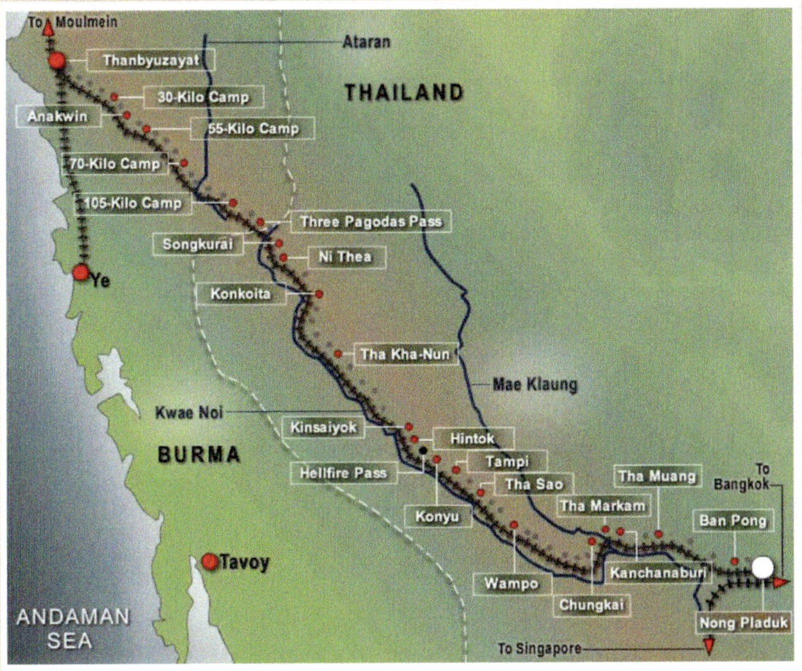

Map of the camps along Death Railway (from the ANZAC portal)

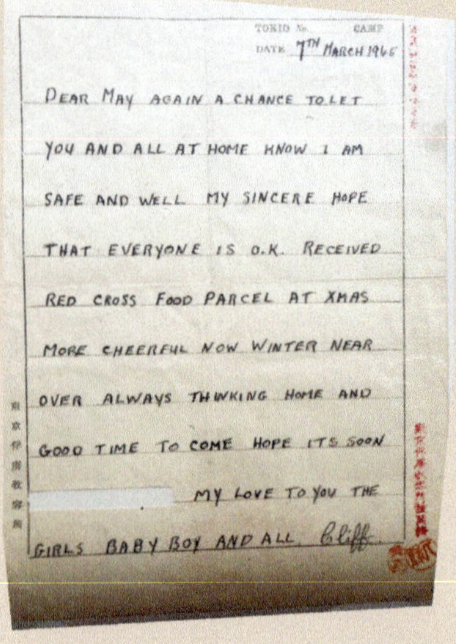

TOKIO No. CAMP
DATE 7TH MARCH 1945

DEAR MAY AGAIN A CHANCE TO LET YOU AND ALL AT HOME KNOW I AM SAFE AND WELL MY SINCERE HOPE THAT EVERYONE IS O.K. RECEIVED RED CROSS FOOD PARCEL AT XMAS MORE CHEERFUL NOW WINTER NEAR OVER ALWAYS THINKING HOME AND GOOD TIME TO COME HOPE ITS SOON MY LOVE TO YOU THE GIRLS BABY BOY AND ALL Cliff

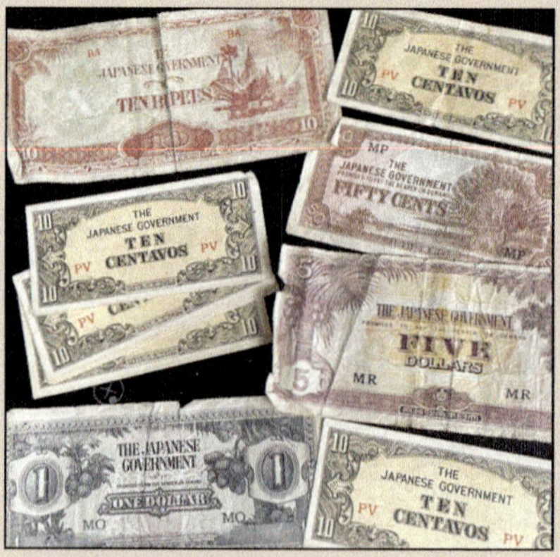

(Left) A censored letter home from Mitsushima that never made it.(Above) Prisoners' "pay" notes found in my father's things.

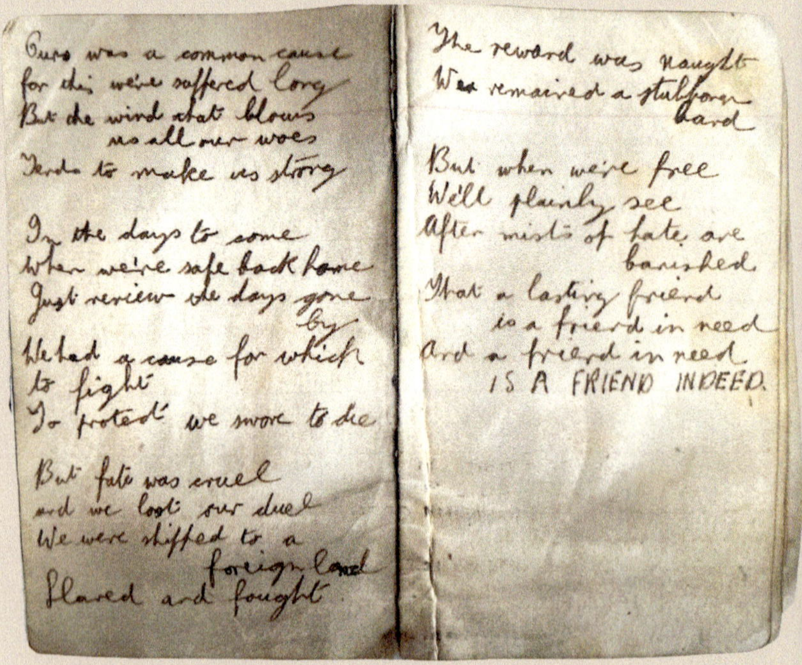

Ours was a common cause
For this we've suffered long
But the wind that blows
us all our woes
Tends to make us strong

In the days to come
When we're safe back home
Just review the days gone by
We had a cause for which
to fight
To protect we swore to die

But fate was cruel
and we lost our duel
We were shipped to a
foreign land
Slaved and fought
The reward was naught
We remained a stubborn band

But when we're free
We'll plainly see
After mists of fate are
banished
That a lasting friend
is a friend in need
And a friend in need
IS A FRIEND INDEED.

The poem Dad wrote towards the end of his captivity.)

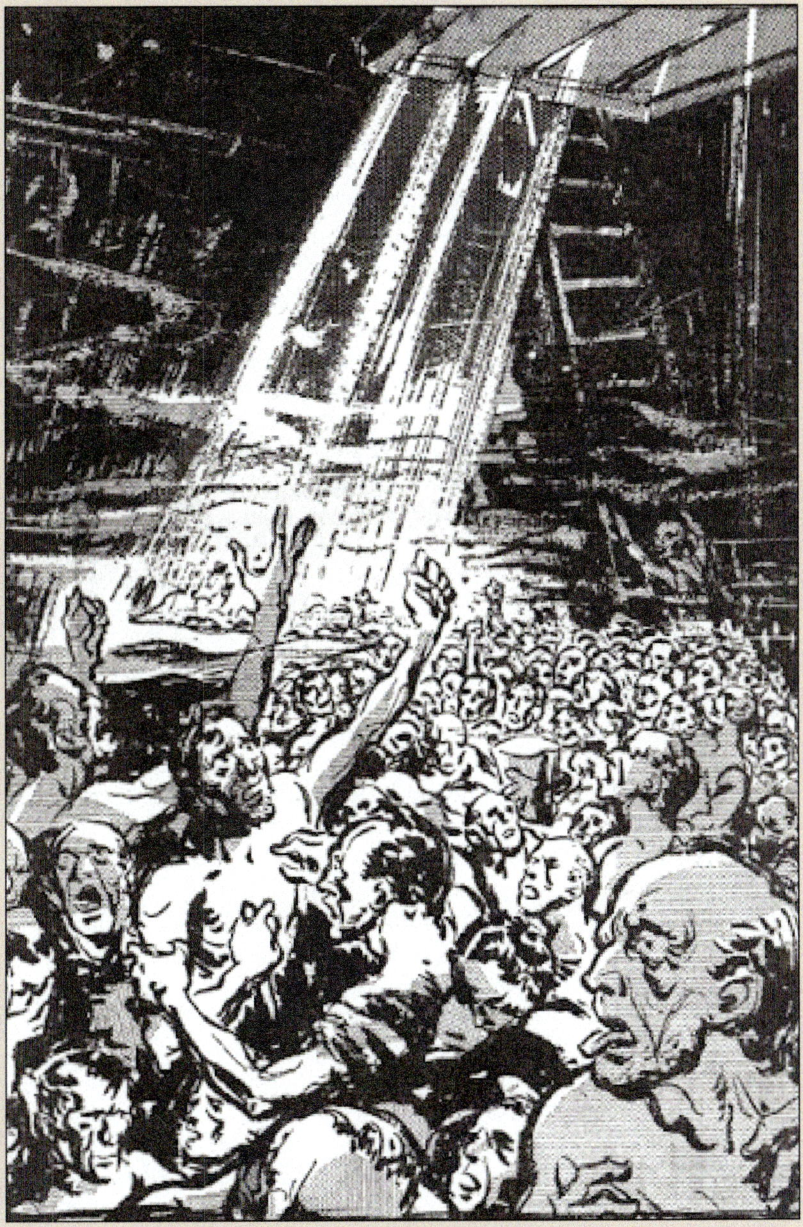

An illustration of the conditions in the hold of a Hell Ship (from the Chicago News, November 1945)

The men did the best they could to celebrate Christmas 1942 and were granted a day off but straight after they were back to work although two thirds of the camp were on the sick list with malaria, dysentery, beri beri, tropical ulcers and malnutrition. All conditions that would later feature in my father's battle to secure a war pension.

Into the New Year of 1943 conditions worsened further and in the morning roll call seriously ill prisoners were lined up in the morning by the guards and prodded like cattle and despite the protests of British doctors were sent off to a long day's hard labour in the jungle heat regardless. The guards knew exactly what they were doing, this was now systematic murder and for every sleeper laid on the rapidly developing railway a prisoner is said to have died. Many of the dead were buried in shallow graves in the hastily constructed camps as the track headed north, never to be recovered and giving their families no closure in a final insult to their memory.

In January 1943 a group of 150 men including my Dad were taken up river on a barge to a camp called Rin Tin to cut a road back to Kinsaiyok. Rations for the working party would soon run even shorter than usual. These working parties, hacking their ways through barren jungle miles from even the basic medical provisions of the base camp, and with only the food they could carry with them, had a terrible death and sickness rate. They were quite literally being worked to death.

Back at the main camp more Dutch prisoners arrived piling further pressure on the rations and the infrastructure. Some canteen barges were now able to get up the river and the prisoners were occasionally able to spend their "wages" on a couple of duck eggs or a scoop of sugar. These trades were not permitted by the guards but the starving men were prepared to risk a beating for a little extra food.

The officers were on higher wages than the ranks and were able to buy into a better diet as a result. Although it's clear that some officers donated their extra money and rations to the medics to support the sickest of men it still seems extraordinary to me that even in this grimmest of times the class-based hierarchy and preferential treatment of the army structure still held good. That was the world that regular soldiers like my Dad signed up to but it must have had a corrosive impact on morale as men starved to death.

Searches of the camp by Korean guards become routine and my father tells the story of why he never kept a diary during captivity;

> *"Well I had a very painful experience early on. I saw somebody who had been caught writing a diary and they literally beat him to death. We actually witnessed his beating by the Japanese because no diaries, and they were kicking and beating him, but he died a few days later. So I said, that's it, I'm not going to keep a diary or anything."*

This was typical. In some camps ingenious men were able to construct radios from parts smuggled in at huge personal risk and in a desperate attempt to pick up any news from the outside world. In Kanchanaburi, where my father would spend some time, four officers were discovered with a radio and were beaten and tortured and met a slow and lingering death as a warning to others. Other men kept notes, diaries, medical records and drawings buried in tins under their beds, some of which were left and recovered after the war and which were important in building a picture of the camps after eventual liberation. Without those notes and sketches we would have had nothing but the men's memories. Amongst the most important were the paintings of Ronald Searle, later the artist who produced the original St Trinians cartoons.

Sick from malaria, Searle had been so badly beaten with a pick axe for his inability to work on the railway that he had to be transferred all the way back to Changi. Using inks smuggled into the camp and a brush made from the hairs of a cat tail he painted hundreds of pictures capturing the life of the prisoners and forming one of the most important records. It's incredible that those paintings survived. I later bought a beautifully presented book of his works for my Dad, and as he looked through it there were tears in his eyes. It was the most graphic illustration of his life through those years. As Searle said later:

> *"We were so hungry in the Japanese camps that we ate cats, the tails were always saved to make my brushes."*

Johnny Sherwood, in his book '*Lucky Johnny*', also talks about the lengths men would go to find something to eat. His experiences are reinforced in conversations with my father, who told me in graphic detail about catching a monkey and cooking it whole in a pot. It's quite possible that Dads tough upbringing, where you ate what you were given or went hungry, had equipped him to some extent for what now confronted him but I know that the thought of the measures the men were reduced to in the jungle camps turned his stomach and he had a lifelong hatred of rats:

> *"....I shudder at some of the things we did eat - snakes, monkeys, lizards, stray dogs and cats, rats, mice, maggots, insects, boiled flies and once we even found a newly dead horse. Nearly all our men were so weak, ill and in constant pain by this time we often found ourselves thinking about how death would bring us peace. Yet, the will to survive is so strong that we took every chance to keep ourselves going, somehow."*

Throughout February and March 1943 the gruelling work schedule continued with the men engaged in building a large embankment with nothing but picks, shovels and baskets. The baskets were filled and dragged by hand up heights of thirty feet. The working day started at dawn, and the jungle insects soon found the men who were dripping in sweat but with much worse to come as the sun climbed high in the sky. A midday lunch of a couple of balls of boiled rice would do nothing to help as the men faced up to the worst part of the day. Men thought to be slacking would be beaten by a guard with a bamboo cane. A one pint water bottle had to be made to last the day.

Some elephants were made available to help with dragging the heavy teak logs out that are cut down and erected as part of the building process. The first time my father worked with the elephants he was badly beaten in an assault that would live with him the rest of his days with long term implications for his health. This is an extract of his statement to the war pensions tribunal;

> *"On the day of the incident I had been selected to work with the elephants. The job was to attach the chains to teak trees which had been felled so that the elephants could pull them out of the forest nearer to the line of the railway. It was the first time I had worked on this particular job and I had difficulty in attaching the chain properly and consequently when the tree met an obstruction the chain came off.*
>
> *The Japanese in charge became very angry, and after beating me demonstrated again how the chain should be attached. When we came back for the next log I attached the chain as I had been instructed but after pulling it a distance the log became detached.*
>
> *It was while I was kneeling to re-attach the chain that I felt a blow to the back of my head. I must have blacked out immediately as the next thing I remember was being brought round by my friend, Cpl David Booker. He explained that he was on his way back to collect another log when he saw the Japanese in charge approach me with a heavy branch in his hands which he swung at my head while I was kneeling.*
>
> *I had a splitting headache for quite a while and blurred vision for some days. I also had a large lump at the base of my skull, the ridge from which is still noticeable. As a far as I know Cpl. Booker was the only witness to this event but unfortunately he died in captivity.*
>
> *After the effects of the blow wore off my vision gradually returned to normal but I suffered frequent headaches. These also gradually reduced in frequency but never less than one or two a day. On being repatriated I did not declare this disability as I wanted to stay in the army and did not want to be regarded as anything other than A1."*

The consequences of this brutal assault would come back to threaten my father's life long after his liberation, and until the day he died he would run his hand over the ridge on the back of his skull. A permanent reminder of that day and of his time in captivity, as he points out in his own words in one of his regimental interviews;

> *"Every time I put my hand to the back my head I can feel a ridge that the Japanese had hit me with a log and the ridge is still there. Fortunately I get a pension for it, eventually, it took me a long time to convince the war pensions people that the headaches I suffered, and still suffer, have been suffering from for years and years, could be due to this blow to the back of the head. I take medication now, daily and nightly."*

I would dearly love to trace the relatives of his friend Lance Corporal David Booker who comforted him and showed the kind of comradeship that carried men through the most desperate times. The records show that David Booker died of enteritis at Kiu Yae camp on the 22nd June 1943 at the age of 33. He was originally buried in a common grave at Kuishi Cemetery before being moved to Kanchanaburi Cemetery after the war. Before joining up he was a clerk and lived in Saltash Road, Bexley. He was one of the many men from the East Surreys who embarked on the same journey to the Far East as my father but who never returned and remain forever thousands of miles from home in a Commonwealth War Grave. These men would never have the opportunity to rebuild their lives, start families and live again in freedom. It breaks my heart to think of them, and for the survivors they would never be forgotten.

The beating that my Dad took that day could easily have killed him, both on the railway and later on in his life when its legacy came back with a vengeance: but in the context of the forced labour camps in the jungle it was a daily reality. A "beat up" from the guards was just a routine fact of life, often for no reason at all and sometimes just for their own sport. My father only talked about this incident because he had to, he was giving evidence to the pensions tribunal. But I know that there was much else that happened to him that he never opened up about as it was just too painful to dredge up. He was also trying to protect us. The torture handed out for minor or imaginary misdemeanours would vary from camp to camp but the brutality and consequences didn't.

A man accused of not working hard enough would be picked out and forced to stand facing the sun holding a boulder, a sleeper or a heavy tool above his head until he collapsed when he would then be given a kicking with heavy boots or a beating with bamboo poles. Arguing with the guards, or standing up for yourself or your mates, would guarantee a "beat up" or worse being strung up by your thumbs from a tree with your toes barely touching the ground and being left like that in the sun for the day. It was not unusual for men to be tied with barbed wire to a tree for days on end for more serious perceived offences, or rammed in a tiny bamboo cage or box built by the guards. In some camps, what the guards called the "No Good House" was simply a hole in the ground with a corrugated iron sheet over it held down by heavy rocks with the full force of the sun beating down on it. The most sadistic of the captors invented their own favoured forms of torture and some of the examples reported after the war are a bench mark in horror. Holding a prisoner down, forcing a hose down his throat and pumping his stomach with water until he was bloated and then jumping up and down on him until he vomited the water up or his stomach ruptured, leading to certain death. The sheer inhumanity of these cowards masquerading as "warriors" should never be glossed over. I will never know the full extent of the brutality my father personally endured and survived. He took those secrets with him to his grave.

CHAPTER FOURTEEN

Death, Disease and Beatings

By April 1943 the medical condition of some of the men was so bad that the worst cases were now being evacuated back to the base camp hospitals although it would be a few months before my father's condition would deteriorate to that level. Men were now basically skin and bones and my own father's weight was under seven stone by this point. With your bones almost breaking through the skin it would be virtually impossible to get comfortable on the bug-infested bamboo slats that made up your bed and with your guts yearning for food it would only be sheer exhaustion that would send you off to sleep before you had to dive out to the latrines as dysentery and diarrhoea came to torment you over and over again.

The dreaded monsoon also came early in April 1943 but there was no respite and the work on the embankments, cuttings and bridges carried on regardless. The rains flooded the camps again and brought with them more disease and disgusting living conditions. The men could never get dry and whatever scraps of possessions they still had left rotted away. Death came every day and with all hope extinguished some just chose to embrace it as the only means of release from their living hell.

The bodies of the dead men had to be disposed of

swiftly to try and contain the on-going spread of disease; if burial wasn't possible the pals of the deceased had no choice but to heap the corpses into funeral pyres and torch them. I've seen reports that as the heat tightened the ligaments and muscles the blackened torso or an arm would suddenly spring upright from the flames. Truly an image of pure horror that would fuel your nightmares and live with you the rest of your days.

Come May and June 1943 the relentless and back breaking work continued and the section of the railway under construction was now taking shape but at a heavy toll on the prisoners slaving on it. It wasn't until the 22nd May 1943 that my father's military records list him as a "POW in Japanese hands" from information apparently smuggled out of one of the camps and eventually sent back by telegram, until then he had simply been listed as missing with no one knowing if he was dead or alive. I can appreciate how difficult it must have been to maintain any kind of meaningful records as the prisoners were divided up, transported from camp to camp and with so many dying along the way. Along with the challenge of getting accurate information out of the camps and back to London the reality was that his friends and family could only wait and hope.

Men were now shipped north again to work on railway bridges. The skeletal figures with their odds and sods of remaining kit began yet another march. Twelve kilometres the first day, an overnight stop at Rin Tin camp and then a much harder sixteen kilometre march on the second day over hilly and dense jungle terrain where the problem a lack of water en route was a major factor, again forcing the men to take the risk of drinking stagnant jungle water.

Eventually they arrived at a satellite of Hindato camp called Qui-ma where conditions were appalling but they only stayed for three days before being transported back to a new small camp near Rin Tin, which I believe was called Kui Yae, where work began again on building a base in yet another squalid jungle clearing. This amounted to nothing much more than some tattered old tents with twenty men under torn canvas designed for eight, with no end flaps and with the monsoon season approaching none of them were waterproof.

The starvation diet of boiled rice and the odd bit of stewed vegetable continued with no access to outside supplies this deep into the jungle. When the monsoon broke the camp was left under water and mud. After sleeping in the mud the men were sent out at dawn to work, again without boots or clothing other than a loin cloth, and to join the queue in the pouring rain for a scoop of rice in their mess tin. Day after day after day.

On the 11th June the men were moved out to a new camp to work on the construction of railway bridges. It was hard physical work for long hours in jungle heat that would be challenging to men in peak physical condition on a good diet with protection from disease let alone men who had been starved for over a year, racked with serious illness and beaten and brutalised by their captors. Gradually they moved north from camp to camp as the work progressed through locations including Kui Mang, Yongthi and Bangan. This was as far as my father got before his battered, starved and diseased body could be worked no more, he was physically ready to die but mentally, somehow, he remained strong enough to stay alive .

The Japanese and their Korean guards were now putting a limit on how many sick men could be excused from work with shocking cases being carried by their comrades to the bridges. Jungle ulcers were now becoming a major issue. A simple scratch would soon develop into a deep open and infected wound that exposed the bone, leaving the man in excruciating pain. Guards would kick and beat the wounds to punish men thought to be slacking regardless of their medical condition. The ulcers would often stretch from the knee down to the ankle. The only ways of trying to halt the spread was to scrape the rotten flesh out of the wound with the sharpened side of a spoon, inflicting horrific levels of pain, or grabbing a handful of maggots from the latrines and binding therm into the wounds with whatever scraps of fabric are available - hoping that they would eat the rotten flesh. The maggots sometimes bore in deeper, making the wound worse.

With no medicine or serious treatment available, amputation was for many men the only solution. My father told me that he offered to assist when one of his friends had to have his leg removed. With no anaesthesia in the remote jungle camps that meant holding the man down while the medics cut through his limb with whatever tools were available, usually a well-used butcher's saw. Often men would just pass out as the pain hit and some died of shock. The screams pierced through the heavy jungle air. It hardly bears thinking about, but the brilliance of these jungle surgeons, and those who made prosthetic limbs out of bamboo, tin and old bits of webbing, was just incredible. In some camps up to 24 ulcerated legs would be hacked off in a day in the most impossible conditions by the surgeons, a conveyor belt of pain and misery but for those strapped down to the table their only hope of survival. It was one hell of a choice that they were forced to make in the day to day battle for life or death.

Johnny Sherwood, in '*Lucky Johnny*', recalled his own experiences of the ulcers now affecting so many men in the jungle camps and the reality of amputation:

> *"Make no mistake, these men suffered, and sometimes gangrene set in, which meant certain death without quick action. Indeed, many lives were saved by immediate amputation, but remember this was nothing like a hospital operation under anaesthetic. It was a crude task, performed without the benefit of any kind of painkiller, so the poor victim was aware and in fearful agony throughout.*
>
> *There was one Australian medical officer who performed absolute miracles, with the most primitive of tools and utensils, while the poor orderlies held the screaming patients down. It used to send a chill through my spine every time, just watching these men having their limbs literally chopped or sawn off."*

Doctors who made representations to the Japanese on behalf of men clearly unfit to work were often subjected to horrific beatings themselves. The men were being told repeatedly that the railway was behind schedule - sick parades had become a mockery. The Japanese "honcho" or foreman made the decision even if some of the sick passed as fit to work had to be carried there on stretchers. By 1943 it had become Japanese policy that there would be no issue of rations for the non working sick, reducing available rations for the whole camp and weakening a workforce already dead on their feet. The stupidity of demanding more and more from these men while denying them basic food and medicines can only mean that there was a clear intention to work them until they dropped. None of this was an accident, it was deliberately calculated and pre-meditated, the view was that if you were too sick to work you were of no further use to the Imperialist project and there was no point feeding you.

In his post-war interim report on the experiences of POW's Lieutenant Colonel Dunlop of the Australian Medical Corps, explained how the sick were often picked out for the most brutal treatment:

> *"....exhausted men who fell out of working parties were beaten and maltreated. On one occasion a Sgt who was ordered out of hospital and manhandled for some hours died the next day. Blows and kicks and sadistic punishments were a routine measure. On occasion men with diarrhoea and dysentery were not permitted to leave their work. A special savagery was often shown to sick men."*

Stan Henderson sums up the conditions on Death Railway and the mentality of the captors at that time:

> *"The Japanese drove us to work with unrelenting savagery. Orders had been received by the commander of the Southern Railway that the railway had to be finished no matter what the cost to human life. If a man could stand, he was judged capable to work. If a man could not stand or walk then he would be carried to work. Prisoners stumbled on horrifying marches from camp to camp, some coming south, others going north. It was 'Speedo, speedo, hiako, hiako, you no beoki mei, you lazy mei,' and the bamboo pole would crash down on to bony shoulders and the blood would run down the emaciated bodies to mingle in the*

oozing mud that squelched warmly between our toes. The daily agony was never ending."

In everything I've read about the railway I have not come across a better written paragraph summing up the daily lives of the prisoners slaving under the hot Thai sun. Re-reading those words breaks my heart and brings me to tears every single time. It would be harrowing enough if you had no physical connection to Death Railway but knowing that this was the existence of my own flesh and blood, my own father, the man who gave me life, is hard to bear. His burnt and gaunt face and his haunted eyes come back to me and I just want to hug him and try to make it all better. But he was alone and other than the comradeship of his mates there was no one to offer him that love and comfort. It's beyond heartbreaking.

That comradeship, and the fine strand of hope that it must have helped to sustain, is worth another look. The POW and war artist Jack Chalker, who was in some of the same camps as my dad, tells a great story relayed in the oral histories "*Captive Memories*", published by the Liverpool School of Tropical Medicine, of a particularly brave fella, who before the war.....

"....was a cat burglar....he was a very dry little man, quiet little man, used to tell us about his jobs, used to say, 'I don't do jobs on people who can't afford it, see.' He was a cockney....and he was like Robin Hood. And he risked his neck, he used to go out at Nakhon Pathom over the wire, knowing very well that he would be battered to pieces and killed if caught. And he'd bring back 10 ducks' eggs, and a ducks egg will save your life. And he would give five to a bloke who's dying at the end of the hut. Now I just wonder whether I would do that, after risking my neck again and again?"

Time dragged on for the surviving prisoners left awaiting their fate. If they thought they'd seen it all in terms of the disease and sickness the jungle could throw at them, it got worse in July 1943 when the first outbreak of cholera hit the camp. This was the point at which my Dad's health and physical strength had collapsed to such a level that if he had contracted cholera there is no question that it would have finished him off. The arrival of cholera was a development that even the Japanese and Korean guards were forced to take seriously as this was one disease that was completely indiscriminate. Barely able to lift himself from the ground, my father's health, through a combination of dysentery, repeated bouts of malaria and black water fever, had deteriorated to the point that he was selected to be shipped back to the hospital at Kanchanaburi. It's impossible to overstate just how sick he must have been to be moved back from the work camp up country to the hospital and it would be another tortuous trip back along the river and hunger trail. Prisoners embarking on this journey weren't expected to come back.

In the pamphlet 'Comrades on the Kwai,' published by the Socialist History Society, Stan Henderson explains the limited treatment available in the camp hospitals:

> *"My treatment for dysentery was two meals a day, each consisting of boiled tapioca and as much boiled water as I could manage…I continued to lose weight. I was at this time visiting the slit trench latrines as many as fifty times in twenty four hours although it was frequently the case that my bowels were empty. Blood and mucus were all that one could pass and all the time ones bowels were writing in an agonised endeavour to discharge something."*

Although my father was reluctant to talk about the worst of times during his captivity I know that the period when he was so ill he classified as too sick to work was amongst them. He told me once that he was starving, riddled with pain and sickness and very clearly and understandably clinically depressed. Someone had stolen one of his most precious possessions while he was sick - an army jungle hat that had kept the burning sun off his head on the railway, of course there were selfish, greedy and desperate men amongst the ranks.

He told me of blokes who had ended it all at their lowest ebb by throwing themselves head first down the latrines and drowning in the filth, who on earth could blame them for taking the one route out that could end their suffering?

I will never know what inner strength kept my Dad and his pals going when it must have seemed like all hope had gone. I owe my existence to his courage, determination and resilience. It was that unfathomable level of determination and will power that drove men like my father beyond the usual barriers of human endurance but I cannot figure where he dredged it up from when he was at his lowest ebb.

The isolation from family and any contact with the outside world or news that may have given some glimmer of hope must have piled on that sense of absolute helplessness. As my father explains in another one of his interviews he never got a single letter, and although both his parents were dead his sister and the rest of his family got none of his POW cards until after the war. They didn't even know he was still alive....

> *"I did write cards and letters that were sent to my sister, I didn't have parents at the time, and she's kept them. They came after the war was finished when I was home.......but I've the letters I sent, or the cards and things. I never heard anything from my sister or my brothers, they'd written to me but I didn't get anything at all, I didn't find out anything until I got the first letter from my sister when I was in Manila waiting for repatriation to England."*

It's important to point out that although my father's health had deteriorated to such a point that he was shipped back to a base camp hospital at Kanchanaburi, known as Kanburi 3 Hospital, the facilities in the unit were still dire (although an improvement on the railway field camps up the line). The word 'hospital' creates the wrong impression. The sick men, most unable to move through weakness, were housed in bamboo huts with no beds, just bamboo platforms raised up from the dirt floor.

One special hut was reserved for men with ulcers where the stench of rotting flesh was overwhelming. There were other huts for men suffering from vitamin deficiency, where a bag of bones would suddenly be inflated overnight with beriberi, and dysentery huts where tortured souls would pass the remaining blood and mucus from their bodies as many as 70 times a day. All the huts were infested with lice and fleas and malaria-bearing mosquitos who would eat the men alive by night. Despite the brilliance and ingenuity of the medical officers, drugs and equipment remained in desperately short supply and the brutal truth is that many men were sent to Kanchanaburi to die, as the large graveyard at the camp confirms. The men must have been well aware of this.

A group of officers were deployed in the hospital huts overnight with the sole task of carrying out the corpses of those who died before those who survived the night awoke in the morning. Reginald Burton, an officer of the 4th Norfolks, recounts these duties in his book '*Railway of Hell:*

> *"Although I'd seen much of death I found this night a very harrowing one….This was something much more intimate, as though each body that I helped to carry from the arms was some relative. It was impossible to think of the burden as just another corpse. I was too conscious that this had been a man, that somewhere a wife or mother would mourn him, he had come out east with a determination to do his bit, that he had faced the defeat, despair and degradation to follow…..as I staggered through the dark wards with these pathetic dead I couldn't keep the tears from my eyes."*

Somehow my father was one of the lucky ones who survived, the soldier boy from Stepney who blagged his way into the army on that warm June day in 1937 had beaten death once again. The personal determination of the patient combined with the skilful deployment of their limited resources by the medics was the only way you came out of the Kanchanaburi hospital huts. But instead of that being the end of his pain and misery, as soon as he was regarded as being fit enough he was sent back up the river. The timeline of his movements runs a bit cold at this point but the records show he left the hospital in October 1943.

I believe that he would have rejoined his original work group operating out of Hindato Camp. With much of the work on the railway now completed the men were deployed on hut building and it would seem that conditions had improved compared to those endured by the work groups in the camps up river before my father was hospitalised. Food rations had increased and at Christmas 1943 the Japanese agreed to a full two days off and the prisoners did everything that they could to celebrate the occasion. If my Dad had been sent back from Kanchanaburi hospital to the working conditions on Death Railway I don't think he would have made it.

Come the New Year of 1944 the camp was seriously overcrowded and food rations had slipped back again to the usual diet of boiled rice and a small amount of vegetables and sickness rates were rising with malaria and blackwater fever both rife. More men were shipped back down south to the hospital camps, and for many this would be their final journey, but somehow my father had regained enough strength to avoid that fate. I don't think he would have survived another spell in the hospital huts any more than he could have survived a return to the railway conditions, every day and every new development had become a gamble between life and death , but somehow he kept winning .

By February 1944, and with the hard work of the men to make the best of their lot, the camp now even had a canteen and a library with a few very dilapidated books but the following month the men were on the move again to a camp called Nong Pladuk II near Banpong. The journey was made by train in the usual overcrowded trucks but the new camp was large, with better constructed huts, and a hospital with an operating theatre cobbled together with whatever materials and equipment the prisoners and medics had been able to salvage and scrounge.

A description of the sick arriving at Nong Pladuk a few months before my father arrived is recounted in Donald Smith's *And All The Trumpets* and is particularly graphic and moving;

> *"…..a working party was ordered to take stretchers to Ban Pong station. A train pulled in and it was full of Dutch, British and Australian prisoners. They lay mutely against the truck walls, their limbs were twisted, their bodies broken, their faces sunken and old, they were from Kinsaiyok …."*

CHAPTER FIFTEEN

Hell Ship to Moji

As the men settled into their new surroundings by April rumours were rife that a number of men were to be sent to Japan. By May the first drafts were being prepared. Word went around that every “fit” man was to be drafted for shipping to Japan. The captors were particularly looking out for prisoners with experience in the building trade or manual work, and as my Dad listed his pre-army occupation as labourer he came up on their radar. They were told that they were going to be working for the great imperial emperor and that they should be grateful. My father was now posted up on one of the lists and despite his long history of illness he left in May. The last Thai camp he was in prior to being transported south was Nong Pladuk. Piecing together his journey from here is difficult as I have no official records to work from but research from a number of online sources has enabled me to build a picture which I believe is accurate.

The selected men were transported back down to River Valley Camp/Havelock Road in Singapore and held for a few days before being lined up for their next and possibly toughest challenge so far. The journey back to Singapore was once again in the crammed, sealed and sweltering steel railway trucks with little food or water and the men were in a shocking state with many unable to stand as they were eventually released into the fresh air. For my Dad this would be a return to a camp that he was held in after the fall of the city and after more than two years of fighting to stay alive he must have been wondering what would come next. But if he thought there was to be any let up in the brutality, degradation and inhumanity that he had already survived the next few weeks would show that there were new depths his captors were prepared to subject him and his comrades to.

A British intelligence report from the time and dated May 1944 says:

> *"5.44 Rumours reach CHANGI of P.O.W.S arriving in Singapore by train ex Thailand.*
>
> *3.6.44. One RAAF and four Dutch to Changi ex SPE (Java 19). They report that P.O.W.S believed ex Thailand had that day marched out from H.V.R or HAVRd [Havelock Road] presumably to embark. This movement coincided with the departure of Java 20 [convoy number] (ovs 3.6.44) They also reported that coincident with this double departure other POWs marched into H.V.R or HAV Rd believed from the Railway St; ex Thailand - some were "D" Force. Number and composition of these parties not known."*

Before departure, on the 23rd of May 1944, my Dad sent another Imperial Japanese standard card home deleting some of the pre-printed words with pencil it left the message:

> *"My health is …usual…..*
>
> *I am working for pay…*
>
> *My best regards to ALL AT HOME*
>
> *Yours ever, Cliff."*

Despite the fact that it was essentially a pack of lies and nothing but a PR exercise by the Japanese authorities it would have at least confirmed to his sister and his family that he was still alive. However sadly it wasn't received until after the war and they were still left guessing.

I've concluded that my father was on a Hell Ship convoy that left Singapore on or around the 3rd to the 5th of June - unknown to those men who were being now forced into the holds of these rusting vessels back home on the south coast of England ships were also being loaded ready for the Operation Overlord D-day landings on the Normandy Coast. The war in Europe was moving towards its final and decisive phase but for the skeletal figures now gathered around my Dad on the harbour side the only thing that really mattered was surviving the next day and night. They could have little idea of what fresh hell now faced them.

I have an image locked firmly into my mind's eye of my father as he was sent down into the depths of that ship, terrified and traumatised all over again but trying to summon the inner resilience to put on a brave face and try and provide some sort of comradeship in the most impossible of circumstances. It leaves me shaking with emotion. I want to know how? How do you remain strong under those conditions when all logic is pointing to the fight for survival being well and truly up? I want to understand but I can't and that leaves me feeling troubled and wholly inadequate when measured against that benchmark and I carry that with me.

The comms confirming news of the Hell Ship convoys also suggest that prisoners at Changi were transmitting information back to intelligence at this time and that's another lesson in extreme individual bravery. It would take a huge amount of courage to be involved in this kind of operation as anyone caught could expect to be tortured and executed. I don't know for certain as there is no manifest available that I am aware of but it's possible he was on the Teia Maria, a 17,537-ton former French ship that had been captured in Saigon in April 1942, or another vessel in the same convoy, which set off for Moji on the 5th of June. That timeline would fit his movements.

This was not to be a short journey of course, and records show that of 62,000 prisoners who were moved by Hell Ship by the Japanese 22,000 died from either murder, starvation, sickness and neglect, or from being torpedoed or bombed by their own side. The Japanese failed to mark the ships with a Red Cross to denote that they were prisoner transport - in direct contravention of the Geneva Convention. Dad's convoy, like the other Hell Ships, was tracked by US submarines who assumed that they were part of a Japanese military or cargo transport and fair game.

The route to Japan followed by other ships I could find would take up to a month and would involve stopping at Miri in Borneo, Manila, Formosa and then across the East China Sea and finally Moji in Japan. It would be a long, tortuous and dangerous journey in the most appalling of conditions.

The prisoners were crammed into cargo holds with little air, ventilation, food or water for several weeks. The only way all the men could be squeezed in was to have them in rows in a sitting position jammed into the crotch of the man behind with another layer of men on top. The Japanese issued a series of regulations to prisoners on the Hell Ships which would mean summary execution including for speaking or moving without permission. Here's an extract of the rules handed out on one ship;

> "**Regulation for Prisoners**
>
> The prisoners disobeying the following orders will be punished with immediate death.
>
> Those disobeying orders and instructions.
>
> Those showing a motive of antagonism and raising a sign of opposition.
>
> Those disobeying the regulations by individualism, egoism.
>
> Those talking without permission and raising loud voices.
>
> Those walking and moving without order.
>
> Those carrying unnecessary baggage in embarking.
>
> Those resisting mutually.
>
> Those touching the boats materials, wires, electric lights, tools, switches etc.
>
> Those climbing ladder without order.

Those showing action of running away from the room or boat.

Those trying to take more meal than given to them.

Those using more than two blankets."

Many of these men were still sick and dysentery was rife leaving them starving and dehydrated in their own filth. On the high bar of appalling and inhumane treatment meted out to prisoners of war by the Japanese the Hell Ships are right up there. Some men, understandably, simply went mad. On some ships they were further tormented by guards lowering down buckets of "drinking water" which was really sea water contaminated with oil and urine.

There's a saying that you don't realise how important hope is until all hope has gone, and that's the line that these extraordinarily brave and resilient men were now crossing. Terrible and unimaginable things happened in the hold of those ships, some prisoners were crammed into them for up to seventy days of sheer and abject misery, Dads journey was mercifully shorter but the memory was stamped deep into the bank of his own personal trauma forever.

Holding it together as an individual in the face of such unthinkable degradation must have been hard enough but maintaining collective discipline as a leader of men dying in the dark in pools of their own shit and piss, with the corpses of their mates piled up around them, is just impossible to comprehend, but that's what Dad and others tried to do.

John Wyatt wasn't on the same ship as my father but he was another 2nd Battalion East Surrey soldier shipped out of Singapore on a different convoy a couple of weeks later. He writes of the experience of being loaded into the hold:

"I was horrified when the guards pushed us down a ladder into the stinking black hold and indeed my premonitions about what was to follow became very real. As I looked up towards the hatch all I could see were bodies falling down on top of us, legs and feet everywhere; the feeling of claustrophobia was frightening. The hold was low, not

much higher than twelve feet and had a wooden rack running right round. We were crammed in so tight that it was impossible to lie down so we had to squat on our haunches and any attempt to move around was an ordeal. The lack of air in the hold quickly became unbearable and I really felt that I was encased in a steel tomb….

"As I settled down in the stinking evil hold, the full reality of the situation hit me for the first time, especially when they battened down the hatches. Two out of every three of us we still suffering from dysentery, malaria, beri beri or jungle ulcers and there were emaciated bodies everywhere, lying around like rag dolls in a dark steel box. Rats were running across our faces and I felt doomed. Some of the boys began to panic. The heat was unbearable and many were screaming to be let out, but I knew that if we tried to rush the hatches we would be killed by the Japanese. We had no choice but to try and make ourselves as comfortable as possible in the wretched conditions. We were so hungry we would have eaten anything…."

I've seen reports that in these rammed out holds some men in complete despair, starving and dehydrated, would bite into the flesh of a man passed out or dead in front of them and draw their blood. I've seen nothing to corroborate this but what I do know is that, having been baptised after the war, my Dad refused to take Holy Communion. He told my sister that there was no way he could take part in the whole blood and body of Christ ceremony after what he had seen.

He never elaborated. Probably to protect us, but something triggered him. I've also seen reports that the Japanese practised cannibalism on some of their prisoners but, again, no evidence that Dad witnessed this. Maybe these were just things he'd heard about but it was enough for him to draw a line.

In an interview my father explained how on his ship they managed to agree with the Japanese on some toilet facilities and for some of the time to live on deck:

"Well I was recently asked by a lady, she said, "Well if you were confined in a hold where did you go to the toilet?"

and I had to explain to her that there were places like a cradle hung over the side of the ship. Two planks about six feet long with a gap in between and then joined at each end and this is what you did if you wanted to go, so many people wanted to, you had to slide out under the rails and crouch down, a foot on each of these planks.

Of course somebody got washed overboard eventually, I mean there was a freak wave because the Japanese were speeding along and so somebody thought of the idea of roping yourself on, sort of thing. It was the first mate of the ship who could speak a little English, a Japanese first mate, who got talking to us and saw the conditions we were in and finally got the Captain to agree to us living on the deck of the ship as it were, but only at certain times, but quite often we had to go in to the, can I just explain the hold. It was a hold and there were the platform of planks that they built and half of us went underneath the planks and the other half got on the top. So if anybody was sick or ill with diarrhoea or anything, it all came through to the people down below, and you were crushed into this hold, and that's about the only daylight you ever saw, the only air you could get in there."

He also highlighted the living conditions in the hold and preparations in case they were torpedoed:

"Then as we got nearer to Japan we were told to get up in the night, the Japanese would come round saying the Japanese word for danger, "kiken", and you all went up on deck, scrambled out of the hold, got up on to the deck and roped ourselves together in fives. Some of the officers with us said strong swimmers would support the weaker swimmers if you had to go over the side.

Well this first night we heard this clanging bell and "kiken" and we're standing there and all of a sudden there was light in the heavens, it was a dark night, and obviously one of the ships had been hit with a torpedo by an American submarine, they were attacking our convoy. This happened on quite a few occasions but fortunately my ship didn't get hit but quite a few people went down on those ships on that trip to a place called Moji in Japan, that's where we landed, Moji."

A small number of allied prisoners who were on the Hell Ships sunk by the submarines managed to survive, clinging to life belts and rafts, sometimes for days on end, and covered in oil they were pulled aboard by the Americans and were able to tell first hand the full story of the treatment that was being handed out to the prisoners. They became an important source of intelligence that for the first time shone a light deep into the darkest corners of the brutal FEPOW experience.

When my father's ship eventually docked at Moji on Kyushu Island, across the Straits of Shimonoseki from the main island of Honshu, the dead were carted off to be burnt, and the men who survived the crossing were herded into a warehouse, stripped and hosed down with disinfectant before being issued with some ill-fitting clothing. It's likely that this would have been second hand Dutch uniforms, captured from when the Japanese occupied Dutch IndoChina. They also would have been glass-rodded, lined up and then bent over while a glass rod was shoved up the anus to check for dysentery or cholera. This humiliation was conducted on the dock side in the open, in front of laughing civilians, as part of the continued dehumanising of the prisoners who had long been stripped of any shred of dignity by their captors. My Dad was a proud man and these sickening and degrading experiences must have lived in his head the rest of his days: but he never talked about it.

Writing 64 years later John Wyatt summed up the experience of the East Surreys and other men forced to make the Hell Ship journey in one powerful paragraph:

> *"The horrors of that trip from Singapore to Japan….will live in my mind until the day I die. Even today, I pray for the souls of those brave lads who survived the Malayan Campaign and horrors of the death railway, only to die in the dark, smelly, sweaty hold of a Japanese ship. During the fifty-six days of that voyage many men died. Many more arrived in a perilous state, hanging onto their lives by a thread. I have no idea, some sixty four years later, how my colleagues were affected by those two sea journeys to*

> *Japan, but I can tell you that even today when I close my eyes I can still see that filthy, stinking hold, smell the stale odours of sick, shit, urine and death. I can still hear the cries for help from my fellow POWs."*

Another survivor, Gordon Highlander Alistair Urquart in his memoir *The Forgotten Highlander*, painted an equally vivid picture:

> *"The noise was constant and deafening, an awful cacophony of throbbing engines, moaning, coughing and occasional panic-stricken screaming the background music for this latest torture. The chilling screams of the mad and insane would stop abruptly. I didn't know how they were dealt with but I could imagine. The smell inside the hold was indescribable, a repugnant stench. An overpowering mixture of excrement, urine, vomit, sweaty bodies, weeping ulcers and rotting flesh clogged the atmosphere. People died down in the holds from suffocation or heart attacks. The men who died were not taken away. Their bodies lay amongst us."*

It shocks me today how little public knowledge there is of the Hell Ships and how my father and his comrades suffered. Soon enough they will become little more than a footnote for those studying WW2 history and I think that's shameful. They weren't a footnote for my Dad. He relived the horrors daily, often in the dead of night when those smells, sights and screams would come back to taunt him and drag him back – to that stinking, foetid hold where he saw his friends die and suffer in utter misery.

For me, even writing about this specific episode forces me to sit back from the screen and take deep breaths. Typing the facts out is hard enough but trying to comprehend the reality I find almost impossible which is why I didn't want to for so long and also explains why my Dad shielded me and my sister from it for years. The spectre of my father's brutalisation deep in the bowels of the Hell Ship drags me along in its wake and forces me to confront the mystery of how trauma is channelled between generations and particularly how it impacts the children of FEPOW's.

It's another insult to the memory of those who survived them that the horror of the Hell Ships has been buried away like some dirty secret. An episode of the BBC series *'Who Do You Think You Are?'* on 15th August 2024 revealed that the actor Vicky McClure's great-grandfather had been transported on a Hell Ship, and the surprise at discovering the treatment of these men was a telling indictment of the lack of public awareness. I only hope that it helps to shine a light on the truth, but for those who suffered there will never be any justice. They are all dead. A quick search will show that there has been far more coverage of the Hell Ships in the US than there has been in the UK and the same applies to the subsequent war crimes trials where a number of those responsible for the appalling conditions were found guilty and punished by death or long terms of imprisonment.

But now my father was in Japan and a whole different world of brutality, back-breaking work, starvation, sickness and freezing cold awaited him.

CHAPTER SIXTEEN

Mitsushima - Byword for Brutality

There is no information on how the prisoners who eventually disembarked were transported to Tokyo 12-B Mitsushima but it was probably through a combination of train and marching. Other men making the same journey from Moji were shipped by ferry across the Straits of Shimonoeski, marched to the railway station and then taken by train overnight and for most of the following day to the city of Nagoya, picking up a connection for the second leg of the journey and a climb up through the "Japanese Alps" to Hiraoka, a dingy railway station high above the Tenryu River.

Finally they would have been marched down the mountain road to Mitsushima. His records show that my father eventually arrived in the camp, also known as Tokyo-02D, on the 28th June 1944. Thanks to the Gibbs Report on POW camps produced by the Americans shortly after the war we have some good information on the camp.

It was first established in November 1942 as Tokyo 3-B, and was located in Central Island Japan on the banks of the Tenryu River. The POWs were primarily put to work as stevedores and labourers building the Hiraoka Electricity Generation and Dam on behalf of the Kumagai-gumi Construction Company. By August 1944 there were 116 British prisoners, captured in Singapore and Java and 93 Americans captured in the Philippines. A number of the British prisoners had arrived in November 1942 including some from my father's regiment. The senior British officer when my Dad arrived at the camp was Lt. Rhys of the RAF.

Mitsushima became a by-word for brutality and was marked down as one of the worst camps in Japan. 59 men are recorded as having died in the camp. Random beatings and punishments by guards were commonplace for the most trivial and often invented reasons. As the Gibbs Report sets out:

> *"The military guards in this camp were very rough on the prisoners They invariably made their own rules at every change of the guard and would go out and look for someone to beat for infractions of rules that never existed officially.*
>
> *"Many times men were taken out of their barracks in the middle of a cold winter night and forced to stand at attention in front of the guards for not apparent reason other than to amuse them. The general description of the treatment could be boiled down to two words 'very severe'. Justice was a forgotten word at Mitsushima."*

One particularly brutal death sums up the regime at Mitsushima. A War Crimes deposition by RAF Squadron Leader David Grant deals with the death of American prisoner Pvt Robert Teas. Teas had been accused of stealing some tins of Red Cross food that had been hidden by Japanese guards in a store. Suffering from malnutrition and dysentery, Teas was dragged from his sick bed by guards, forced to stand on his bunk while he was whipped across the face with a knotted rope and jabbed in the stomach with a stick. With no confession forthcoming he was then forced to stand outside in the freezing cold in his underwear. His food rations were also cut off. He died three days later.

The guards at Mitsushima carried wooden swords made of oak and those were used to beat men on a regular basis. Other punishments included being whipped around the face with ropes soaked in ice cold water and "solitary confinement" which at this camp involved being put in a wooden box similar to a coffin, with a slot in one end to allow some air in which was inserted in a wall morgue-style for days on end with no food or water. It's fair to say that some of the outright sadism and viciousness at the camp had eased slightly by the time my father arrived in June 1944 but it was still a hellish place.

It is clear from my father's correspondence after the war that there was a strong bond and comradeship between the American and British POWs. A letter from his friend Thomas P. Tison from Florida in November 1946 references the brutality that they experienced in the camp and the consequences at the subsequent war trials:

> *"Well old glass-eye as we used to call him has served a few months at hard labour in Japan. He has just the rest of his natural life to do so I don't think he minds that so much, if he will think back to the times that he beat us around.*
>
> *Have seen Kirch, in fact I live only 215 miles from his home. Saw Jack Wilson, Mitchell, Steele and Ivy of prison camp days. Saw Piel's picture in the papers. He answered a letter from the Goon, asking for some help, so that he would not be sentenced to prison. Piel wrote him that he hated him, and would not help and that he stood by and let the other Nips beat up prisoners unmercifully. Piel sure got him told and got into the news besides."*

Sergeant George Piel who is mentioned in the letter was a mate of my Dad's in the camp and was later involved in the plot to kill the most brutal of the guards. When another of the worst of the guards, nicknamed The Goon, asked for him to send a testimony on his behalf to the later war crimes trials he wrote:

> *"You used to keep me standing from dawn until dusk trying to make me squeal on my fellow prisoners….."*

He also offered some pointed advice on exactly where his former tormentor should seek help from. George Piel was captured with the 31st Infantry Regiment in the Philippines and was in Mitsushima from 26th November 1942 until liberation. He survived some of the roughest times and toughest winters in the camp. After the war he lived in New Orleans and built a life. Before being shipped to Japan on a Hell Ship he had survived St Peter's Ward in a notorious camp called Cabantuan in the Philippines, a place where very sick men were basically sent to die. He was a tough and brave man and I'm glad that my father had blokes like him around.

Thomas Tison was a sergeant in the 27th Bomb Group of the US Airforce. He was also captured in the Philippines in 1942 and would have been one of the American servicemen who survived the infamous Death March out of Bataan when 75,000 American and Filipino soldiers were force-marched 65 miles after the surrender on the 9th April, enduring extreme brutality along the way with many deaths.

In Richard M. Gordon's memoir '*Horyo*' he suggests that there was some animosity between the American and British prisoners in Mitsushima but my father seems to have struck up strong friendships with a number of the thirteen Americans who had been left in the camp after most of their countrymen had been sent out to Kanose in April 1944, another Japanese POW camp in the Tokyo group. They would have had compelling stories of survival to share with each other on the journey that had led them to this final destination in their years of captivity.

There was also a clear connection: the American surrender in the Philippines mirrored that of the British at Singapore, in that it was their greatest single military capitulation and the American troops would also feel – as many of the British lads did – that they had been let down by poor leadership and preparation. Thomas Tyson, George Piel and my Dad would have had plenty to talk about as they supported each other in the long dark, cold hours of the Japanese winter.

The temperate climate in Japan was a major change from the jungle. The men were housed in wooden huts with dirt floors which would flood during the heavy rain and would be ice cold during the winter. A small fire pit in the middle of the huts was wholly inadequate to provide any real heat and the small ration of wood for burning would often be cut off by the guards for some minor or imagined infringement of the rules even in sub zero temperatures. With no flues or ventilation lighting the fire for the three hours allowed in the evening would fill the huts with dense smoke. It also provided very little warmth, barely taking the edge off the freezing cold, and the men would huddle together under their thin blankets, eyes streaming from the smoke, hoping to survive the night.

In his book *'Prisoners of the Japanese'*, Gavan Daws paints the picture as dawn broke:

> *"Before work they huddled in the snow like cattle, the men on the outside of the huddle trying to burrow in, and gradually the whole mass would start revolving in a slow, shivering circle. At night, huddling inside, they could see their breath in the air like frosty vapour in a cold store, clusters of shaved heads like so many chilled melons. And out at the benjo, shit stalagmites were forming under the squat latrines, frozen spires building up until they reached floor level and had to be chipped away with a crowbar."*

The Japanese winter of 1944 was one of the coldest on record. A press report from the Yokohama trials of the testimony of Major Walter J. Hewitt, one of the American officers at Mitsushima, records him telling the court that:

> *"...corpses of Allied prisoners of war were tied securely with the heads between the legs and thrown into a coffin saturated with filth.*
>
> *Hewitt was testifying against Sukeo Nakajimba, camp commander, and six subordinates at Mitsushima P.O.W camp.*
>
> *He said 50 deaths occurred there one winter when the Japanese had a stove burning 24 hours daily in their quarters while prisoners lay dying of cold in a bare shack."*

This was the story in the camp every winter. The figure on deaths appears to refer to the total number of prisoners who perished at Mitsushima during its time housing POWs. As Richard M. Gordon wrote in *Horyo*:

> *"Just getting through the day was a constant challenge to every prisoner at Mitsushima. Because of its location high in the "Japanese Alps" in Nagano Prefecture, about*

7000 feet above sea level, winters were especially brutal and lethal. Many men died in the winter months due to a mental state brought on by their low morale. Morale reached rock bottom during every winter there. Our greatest concern every second was how to stay warm."

It's worth trying to figure out just what information was reaching back home to my father and his fellow prisoners' friends and family around this time and the answer is very little. Of course the Japanese controlled any official communications from the men but a search of press coverage in the UK in 1944 suggests that the British authorities may well have been complicit in throwing a veil over the truth. I find it extraordinary that the most basic of offers to the Red Cross by the Japanese, to allow the POWs and internees to send one ten word telegram home in October 1944, was greeted with cheers in the House of Commons when it was announced by Mr Law, the Minister of State, even though he admitted that the pledge still had to be delivered as the Edinburgh Evening News reported:

"I feel bound to strike a note of caution. Having accepted the proposal, we look to Japan to carry it out, but as the large majority of prisoners of war are not in Japan itself, but in Japanese occupied territories in the south, everything depends on the messages being sent from that area through Japan."

The prisoners were also supposed to have received a message from their loved ones as part of the agreement but as my Dad points out in a heavily censored message back to his sister, that never happened and the Government were right to caution that the Japanese simply could not be trusted which makes the response of MPs even harder to comprehend.

We are lucky enough to have the original camp communication that my father sent to my Auntie May, just touching this yellowing fragment from over eight decades ago forms a physical bridge for me from the present back to the past and is one of the few surviving items that establish that link which is so important. It wasn't received until after the war but he would have desperately hoped that it would reach her and the rest of the family:

> *"DEAR MAY, ANOTHER CARD TO LET YOU KNOW I AM SAFE AND WELL. I HOPE YOU AND ALL AT HOME ARE SAFE AND WELL. HAD NO NEWS OF YOU YET. PLEASE DON'T WORRY, MY HEALTH IS GOOD. LET MY BROTHERS KNOW I AM OK. WISH FOR NEWS OF SOMEONE. MY LOVE TO THE GIRLS AND YOUNG GEORGE. HOPING TO SEE YOU ALL SOON. LOVE. CLIFF."*

May and my dads brothers were in the same position as the other friends and relatives of prisoners as post wasn't delivered and very little information was available on their sons, father's, brothers and husbands. And what information they were picking up was heavily filtered. A British press report in December 1944 on ***Japanese POW Camp Conditions*** is particularly hard to fathom unless there was a deliberate attempt to play down the truth, presumably in the interests of public morale and a lingering embarrassment over the humiliation of the fall of Singapore. That small group of men who had been rescued from the water after the torpedoing of a the Hell Ships had been debriefed as Sir James Grigg Secretary of State for War told the House of Commons:

> *"As relatively few men had got back, and as the Japanese camps were widely scattered, it was unlikely these men would have information about more than a small proportion of all the prisoners. "If the next of kin hear nothing, I am afraid it is because nothing new has been heard of the particular prisoner," he added.*

Major Keatings, Conservative MP for Bury St Edmunds, then told the House:

> *"....there is nothing to stop these men from talking to their neighbours, and the impression is getting abroad that the conditions are not quite so universally bad as recent statements might suggest."*

For friends and relatives desperate for news this would have registered. Although Sir James Grigg added the caveat that they may have been talking about a modest improvement after the work on the railway was completed where he accepted that the "***conditions were horrible,***" I believe that this approach to the "forgotten army" out in the Far East is significant. The British Authorities would have been well aware of the overall conditions and the incidence of death and disease amongst the prisoners. The brave men and women of the Thai resistance were in touch with the camps along the railway and would have reported back, and comms were coming out of the base camps including Changi as the men returned. Of course there was a war on, and of course maintaining morale was important: but the stage was already being set for the world of ignorance and silence that the men would eventually return to.

CHAPTER SEVENTEEN

Slaving for the Emperor

Sleeping arrangements at Mitsushima were on two decks with each man allocated a total living area of 30x73 inches. The huts, each of which housed 120 prisoners, were infested with fleas, bugs, lice and vermin. Latrines were in a separate wooden building and were simply a trench with no drainage that had to be dug out. The openings were not covered and the camp would become infested with flies and maggots. The latrines froze over in the long Japanese winter month.

The food and water situation in the camp was no real improvement from Thailand with a diet of boiled barley and rice with the occasional addition of a small amount of vegetables. Sometimes the men were able to get hold of the intestines and bones of cattle slaughtered in the area, the guards would steal any decent meat that might be supplied. Fish supplied by the Japanese would be rotten. The prisoners essentially existed on 400 grams of grain per day. Some of the men working on the docks risked their lives trying to steal whatever they could to augment the meagre rations. Water was supplied from the river which was also the outfall for the town's sewage and drainage, so remained dangerous and had to be boiled in a small tank for the whole camp.

The Barbed Wire Surgeon explains the food situation at Mitsushima:

> *"....meals came at seven o'clock, noon and six o'clock, and consisted of an almost indigestible rubbery mass of steamed barley, millet and a little rice. This combination gave me chronic diarrhoea as long as I was at Mitsushima. About twice a week we got a piece of dried fish, herring size, or some soybeans in our barley mix. This was our only source of protein..... When fresh fish came in it had deteriorated during transport. We buried it to prevent starving men from eating it....Once a month we got seventy pounds of meat and bones which came from a local slaughterhouse....the bones were covered with a green scum..."*

On these rations the men were forced to work long hard hours on building the dam. As with the railway they were expected to work regardless of their health as the contractors were promised a set number of men each day. It is worth pointing out here that the civilians as a whole were regarded as quite considerate of the men and my father told my wife how one civilian once gave him some ointment for his dried and cracked lips.

A small act of kindness like that in appalling circumstances had clearly meant a lot to him. Some of the contractors were also well regarded by the men as being fair-minded although under the constant watch of the camp guards. When they were eventually liberated the men rounded up whatever supplies they had that weren't being taken with them and handed them over to some of the local civilians in recognition of their humanity.

Tucked away with my Dad's small collection of mementoes we later found an envelope with a colourful collection of Japanese Imperial Government issued bank notes in various denominations and currencies. I suspect that this token currency, similar to Monopoly money in looks and status, was paid out as part of the illusion that the men weren't slaves, they were being rewarded for their labour. Another hoax of course as there would be nowhere to spend the money as far as I'm aware and if it did have any value Dad would have used it.

If there was one stroke of good fortune for the British prisoners at Mitsushima it was the presence of their Medical Officer, Dr Richard Whitfield who had been captured in Hong Kong. Trained at St Mary's Hospital in London he had been called up from the Naval Reserve and was one of the first Allied prisoners to be sent to Japan. A brilliant physician, he was also a brave and highly-respected leader of men who fought a relentless battle with the Japanese authorities in the Tokyo area for medicine, equipment, food and improved conditions for the prisoners under his care at Mitsushima - risking beatings and his own health and well-being in the process. He was also a genius at flattering and cajoling the guards into loosening their grip on supplies and his brilliance as a medic and a leader must have saved many lives in the camp.

When Al Weinstein, author of '*The Barbed Wire Surgeon*', arrived in the camp he asked Dr Whitfield if there was much sickness:

> *"Plenty. After they were captured in Singapore, the British prisoners now in camp worked for a year building a railroad through Thailand to Burma. More than twenty thousand of them died of cholera, malaria and starvation. The survivors all have recurrent malaria. Most of the Americans in camp have chronic dysentry, probably of the amoebic type."*

The post war Gibbs Report confirms that morale at the camp was surprisingly high during 1944 and 1945 despite everything, and it attributes this to the fact that men were able to steal or scrounge newspapers from outside the camp and keep up with developments in the war and the advance of American forces.

By May 1945 the arrival of new prisoners brought news of the fall of Germany. The war with Japan was now the priority. After years of isolation and despair the men suddenly had something that had been missing. Hope. The senior Allied officer in the camp who arrived at that time was now Captain Gordon, captured after the sinking of the *Exeter* in March 1942 in the second battle of the Java Sea. Along with his second in command, Lieutenant Commander Twiss, they organised and maintained a high level of military discipline and that made a big difference to overall conditions, because they had no hesitation in standing up to the camp commander.

Twiss later rose to the rank of Second Sea Lord of the Admiralty and and after retirement was appointed Black Rod in the Houses of Parliament; my father, as a sergeant, would have formed part of the chain of command through the ranks under him and Gordon. But although morale might have improved as more news of the progress of the war was deciphered and passed on, and discipline and camp organisation improved, sickness and brutality remained a daily fact of life and escalated as the allied troops advanced in the Pacific theatre.

The sheer spitefulness of the Japanese guards running the camp is amplified by the fact that they refused to issue Red Cross supplies to the men in any quantity. Despite the cold and wet conditions the POWs were forced to work either barefoot or in homemade straw shoes. On liberation it was found that there was a store full of leather boots supplied by the South African Red Cross that were never issued. These boots probably would have lasted the prisoners the duration of the war and would have made a huge difference.

Long after the war one of the surviving guards, Little Glass Eye, gave Richard M. Gordon two reasons why they weren't issued - firstly that the prisoners would have hurt themselves slipping on boulders along the river if they had decent footwear and secondly that they were being saved for when the men went home. Total nonsense of course. The boots and other supplies were withheld out of pure malice.

Even worse, when the Red Cross inspected the camp a fake canteen was set up to create the impression that food parcels, clothing and supplies were being regularly distributed to the prisoners as this press report into the later war crime trials illustrates:

"Fake Canteen To Deceive Red Cross Representative

YOKOHAMA, Friday - Japanese officers and guards at the Mitsushima prison camp, near Tokyo, attempted to mis-

> *lead the representatives of the International Red Cross into the belief that Red Cross supplies were freely distributed among Allied war prisoners by establishing a fake canteen, which disappeared half an hour after the representatives visit was concluded, according to evidence given at the trial of Tatsuo Tsuchiya.*
>
> *When a Red Cross representative named Pestalozzi visited the camp, the authorities established a canteen whose shelves were stocked with Red Cross supplies which had been sent to the prisoners, but which the guards diverted. The Japanese attempted to give the impression that it was regularly open to British and Americans.*
>
> *Cory's [American officer and POW] said prisoners were told before Pestalozzis visit: "You must answer all questions favourably to the Japanese." But instead the prisoners told him about bad food, lack of clothing, improper diet and and medical treatment, brutal beatings, filthy living conditions and misappropriation of Red Cross supplies.*
>
> *Pestalozzi told the prisoners it was a regrettable situation, but Japan was not a signatory to the Geneva Convention and prisoners were treated according to regulations laid down by the Japanese high command. Prisoners who gave evidence to Pestalozzi were subsequently punished."*

In the War Crimes trials there were further reports that in another plot to con the Red Cross, Mitsushima prisoners were issued with new clothing and sat round a table laden with food and ordered not to touch anything while pictures were taken. When the photographer had finished the men were handed their old rags back and sent away to their freezing cold huts and their diet of watery gruel. The guards ate the food. This was just pure torment for men who had faced years on a starvation diet.

A group of American prisoners in the camp decided that they would try to exact some revenge and hatched a plan to try and kill the very worst of the guards, the sadist known as The Bird, real name Watanabe. Infected blood was extracted from the mucous stools of dysentery patients, kept warm in a culture and mixed in with the guards' food by one of the cooks, George Piel, a friend of my Dad's mentioned earlier. Despite two goes at it, and despite The Bird falling seriously ill and losing a lot of weight, he survived the assassination attempt. It would have taken extraordinary courage by the men involved to make this audacious attempt on their tormentor's life: if their plot had been uncovered they would have faced torture and a brutal death.

The fact that despite everything men were prepared to take that risk in an attempt to fight back speaks volumes of their spirit and bravery after more than three years in captivity. George Piel who laced the food with the special "gravy" had taken the biggest risk of all. When Al Weinstein and the other plotters had asked him if he would get involved he just said "I'll take care of it," and when warned of the potential consequences he said "I'll take my chances." That's real guts. George, Thomas, my father and the rest of the men in Mitsushima must have been thoroughly hacked off that The Bird/Watanabe escaped before the camp was liberated and was never caught and brought to justice.

From a search of newspaper records it does seem that there was a lot more coverage of the Japanese War Crime Trials in the States than there was in the UK. Was this just another example of the forgotten army that surrendered at the humiliating surrender at Singapore being written out of the script? A post-war story in the *Sunday Mirror* on the 11th May 1947 would suggest so. Reporting that British prisoners had only found out about outcomes of the trials because an American witness present had written to them individually it says;

> *".....while microphones and news reel cameras went to Nuremberg and a score of correspondents covered lesser trials little is known in this country about the fate of the most inhuman criminals of all.*
>
> *So when Kunie Yoshizawa, interpreter, "Mushmouth" to his POW charges was sentenced a witness at the trial sat down and wrote to each of his former companions.*
>
> *From them other letters will go out. Soon all those who suf-*

> *fered at Mitsushima Camp Nagano - and the relatives of those who died - will know that "Mushmouth" has been hanged.*
>
> *All but one of the seven Japanese officials sentenced for atrocities at Mitsushima had nicknames. The exception was the Commandant. For there was no humour about him said one witness:*
>
> *"Nakajima weeded out the sick according to his own ideas, ignoring the doctor, and sending most of them out to work. Many returned to sick quarters shortly afterwards to die."*
>
> *Five of the seven Japanese accused were ordered to be hanged. The other two were sentenced to life imprisonment."*

My father was pictured in the camp in September 1944 wearing what appears to be battle dress but I believe this was only issued for the purpose of the photograph, along with a shave and a haircut, and was set up by the Japanese for the Red Cross to continue to peddle the lie that the men were being well looked after. My father's weight at this time was seven stone twelve pounds and the haunted look in his eyes tells its own story. I carry that image of him around in my mind at all times, it is the only picture I have of him in captivity.

Even more sinister, Grant McLachlan, in his book '*Sparrow - A Chronicle of Defiance*', a tribute to his own grandfather who served time in Mitsushima, reveals that the guards at the camp kept their own individual photographic record of the prisoners, solely because they expected every one of them to die. Out of some strange sense of obligation they wanted something to be able to send their relatives as a memento. Grant has managed to locate and archive all of these pictures. Flicking through them to find my Dad was like walking over these men's graves.

Eighty years on I am guessing they will all be dead now, but their sunken, tired, emaciated and tortured faces will forever be frozen in time in Japan in 1944. Dad managed to pull his picture from his file during the final days of the war, keeping it tucked away in his small box of memorabilia, and it makes for an appropriate cover for this book.

That winter of 1944 more than one in ten of the men in

the camp were classed as seriously ill on a daily basis with beriberi, dysentery, malaria and pneumonia and there were many accidents resulting in serious injuries for the men as they slaved on the construction projects. The medics would fight hard with little success to stop sick men being sent out on the work parties.

In December 1944 work on the dam had come to halt as the contractors ran out of reinforcing steel and cement and the starving men were sent out twice a day to climb up the mountains to fell trees and bring the logs back down. This hard and punishing back-breaking work on starvation rations led to most of the men suffering severe beriberi with its symptoms of swelling of the face, stomach and legs and partial paralysis, blindness and cardiac failure.

Nevertheless they were still sent back out, day after day, of the two hundred men in the camp 185 were classed as having beriberi, with forty of them showing a weakening of the heart as a result. Three men dropped dead in a week just before Christmas. Pneumonia was an added problem that winter and put a further strain on the limited medical resources.

Pressure from the medics led to a marginal but important increase in food rations and although the diet was still wholly inadequate for men involved in such hard physical work there is no doubt that more lives were saved.

Around this time, the back end of 1944 and early 1945, the Japanese once again showed themselves to be adept at playing the PR game through the press in the UK using the Red Cross as a convenient conduit through which to channel their lies and my father and his comrades in Mitsushima were very much pawns in this game as the later trials would reveal.

A report in the *Northern Daily Mail* of Friday 2nd February 1945 showed that since the previous December the Japanese Government had been using the promise of Red Cross visits to the camps to try and fend off attacks on conditions and treatment of prisoners by British Foreign Minister Anthony Eden:

> *"……the [Jap***anese Government]** *spokesman said. "In view of the generally tense war situation such a generous decision by the Japanese Government towards war prisoners and internees should be fully appreciated by the enemy.*
>
> *Earlier the spokesman was quoted as saying: "More than once the Japanese Government have declared their willingness to improve, if there is still room for improvement , the conditions of prisoners and, in fact, much improvement has already been effected to make the life of prisoners and internees as comfortable as war-time conditions permit."*

My Dad, freezing and starving in Mitsushima, and forced to take part in this fake pantomime of Red Cross visits, would have smiled at the sheer brass neck of this bunch of lying bastards.

When he died we found amongst my father's possessions a small, pink notebook. We believe that he would have acquired this during the later days of his captivity in Mitsushima. He had seen the punishment meted out to those keeping any form of written records in the railway camps and it's hard to believe that paper goods would have survived the flooded huts the Hell Ships. The small pencil written notes also convey an optimism about the future, and the things that he was looking forward to if and when he was released. I can imagine him reading and re-reading his lists as he clung to the hope that he would survive and make it home.

He lists books to read:

Testament to Youth

Captain Blood by Raphael Sabatini

by CS Forester:

The General

The Gun

The Good Earth (Pearl Buck)

How to win friends and influence people by Dale Carnegie

And now Goodbye - James Hilton

We are not alone - James Hilton

He lists presents that he will buy members of his family, chocolates for his sister and his nieces, cigars for male relatives and a belated wedding present of a china tea service for one of his brothers Gus.

It's these relatively small and everyday gestures, carefully noted down, that must have given him a sense of hope and a belief that it was worth carrying on to make them a reality.

More poignant after the long years of starvation and deprivation he sets out a list of foods that he is planning on eating:

Shredded wheat and cream

Golden cutlets

Poached egg on toast

Brown bread

Sausages

Roast chicken

Potato croquettes

Cauliflower

Wine trifle

Biscuits and cheese

Coffee

Beans on toast

Celery

Lyons fruit pies

Books written by other prisoners held by the Japanese report that one of the main topics of conversation amongst the men was food to the point of obsession. This is hardly surprising, but at times it must have felt like they were tormenting themselves further by spending so much time focused on something that was out of their reach. My father's notebook shows that it was giving him a real target to look forward to. The treats on his list remained firm favourites in the years to come.

Amongst other notes are some addresses, including those of American and Australian prisoners he was held with, and with whom he would later correspond. Intriguingly there are a couple of addresses in Penang, Malaysia, possibly of locals who gave him some help and whose details he had memorised. Another note that jumps out is simply Racecourse Road, Singapore - this was the site of an important battle on the 11th February 1942 in the final days of the fight to defend the island. I'm left to wonder what it was that led to my father making a specific reference in his little book some years later.

As well as some faded translation of key Japanese phrases that he would have needed outside the camp wires he also wrote a poem that tells his story and looks forward to freedom:

Ours was a common cause for this we've suffered long
But the wind that blows us all our woes
Tends to make us strong

In the days to come when we're safe back home
Just review the days gone by
We had a cause for which to fight
To protect we swore to die

But fate was cruel and we lost our duel
We were shipped to a foreign land
Flared and fought the reward was nought
We remained a stubborn band

But when we're free we'll plainly see
After mists of hate are banished
That a lasting friend is a friend in need
And a friend in need IS A FRIEND INDEED.

It's incredible to me that at this stage he was already thinking of banishing the mists of hate and celebrating the stubbornness of the men who had survived. That just reflects on his inner strength and his positive forward thinking when it would be perfectly natural to be consumed by hate, bitterness and anger. There was no self-pity in the few words that have survived his incarceration, despite everything that had happened his focus was on the comradeship and determination that had got him and his mates that far and which he was clearly convinced would get them over the line to freedom. He would be proved right but as the war raged on there would be plenty more threats and challenges to face up to and survive.

CHAPTER EIGHTEEN

Kill All Prisoners

In early 1945 the American bombing raids on Japan escalated and the March 9/10 firebombing of Tokyo was regarded as one of the most destructive acts of war in history - thought to have killed between 80 and 100 thousand and wiping out 16 square miles of the city. Squadrons of B29 bombers dropped thousands of seventy pound napalm bombs reducing the city to ashes. The prisoners must have been able to see the sky on fire from their camp, and with the Allies now commanding air supremacy over Japanese cities there would have been mixed emotions in Mitsushima and other camps - relief and hope that the war was heading towards an end, coupled with fear that the guards would seek retribution.

My Dad's military records show that in January 1945 the authorities back in London still thought he was in Thailand, they had no idea that he had been shipped back to Japan. The confusion and uncertainty doesn't surprise me as the lack of information and deliberate isolation was part of the psychological war against the prisoners. Denying contact with home wasn't just mean spirited and spiteful, it was designed to break the spirit and show the men that they were under the complete control of their captors and had no value beyond the prison camp fence other than as slave labourers for the Emperor. They had been dehumanised since their capture and that would last right through to the end.

On the 7th of March my father wrote another letter home, not knowing it was part of another callous stunt and wouldn't surface until after liberation but I like to think it would at least have given him some sense of hope. This was longer than the standard postcards but was written out in block capitals under close monitoring from the Japanese translator and intelligence.

Other than the signature I don't believe it was written in his hand, and although a few words are redacted, and it doesn't read well after it had been through his captors hands, along with his little note book it's the only contemporaneous record we have of what was going through his mind at that time and it shows him thinking of home, his family and the hope that soon he may be free now the bitter winter was over:

TOKIO No. CAMP

DATE 7th MARCH 1945

DEAR MAY AGAIN A CHANCE TO LET YOU ALL AT HOME KNOW I AM SAFE AND WELL MY SINCERE HOPE THAT EVERYONE IS O.K. RECEIVED RED CROSS FOOD PARCEL AT XMAS. MORE CHEERFUL NOW WINTER NEAR OVER ALWAYS THINKING HOME AND GOOD TIME TO COME HOPE ITS SOON [censored] MY LOVE TO YOU THE GIRLS BABY BOY AND ALL. Cliff

Clearly it tells only a small part of the story and is heavily loaded towards the message the Japanese want to sell the outside world, that their prisoners are safe and well and being looked after when nothing could be further from the truth. Dad never got a Red Cross parcel that Christmas, he got to share one with a number of other men: the guards had nicked the rest. "Always thinking home and good time to come..." it would be a while yet but beyond the camp fences things were moving at some pace.

By now the men in the camp had a good system in place for translating news on the progress of the war from Japanese newspapers and conversations with local civilians. News was carefully passed on by the officers to raise and maintain morale of the prisoners as it was clear that Japan was losing on all fronts, despite the spin.

However the cost to the Americans of every step of progress was incredibly high as the Japanese fought to the death, and their progress was much slower than expected, gradually they were achieving their objectives. But the military advance of the allies would bring its own terror as the word was that the Japanese would line up and shoot the prisoners rather than surrender. This is precisely what had happened to American POWs in the Philippines in December 1944. There was also a fear the starving prisoners would be "death marched" deeper into the country rather than be surrendered.

In fact a "kill all" order had been sent out to the camps across Japan in the event of a ground invasion. The order featured in the post war trials and couldn't be clearer:

> *"....at such time as the situation became urgent and it be extremely important, the POWs will be concentrated and confined in their present location and under heavy guard the preparation for the final disposition will be made.*
>
> *The time and method of the disposition are as follows:*
>
> *The Time*
>
> *Although the basic aim is to act under superior orders, individual disposition may be made in the following circumstances:*
>
> *When an uprising of large numbers cannot be suppressed without the use of firearms.*
>
> *When escapees from the camp may turn into a hostile fighting force.*
>
> *The Methods*

Whether they are destroyed individually or in groups or however it is done, with mass bombing, poisonous smoke, poisons, drowning, decapitations or what, dispose of them as the situation dictates.

In any case it is the aim not to allow the escape of a single one, to annihilate them all, and not to leave any traces."

Effectively, this was my father's final death warrant. There has been some debate about whether the order had come from the right department and whether it would ever have been actioned but I don't understand why anyone would dispute the stated intent. The plan was to murder all prisoners starting in September 1945 in line with the orders already followed in the Philippines:

"Policy of the Division Commander is to put all prisoners to death..."

The Japanese had mobilised massive numbers to resist an American ground invasion under the military and political strategy called Ketsu Go (Operation Decisive) and had made it clear that they would fight to the last man and woman and would never surrender, their prisoners of war would be caught in the middle of this scorched earth policy. The men in Mitsushima must have had mixed thoughts, cheering the allied military success but fearing they would be murdered as a consequence. Some prisoners had mentally accepted that execution would be their final fate and that they would never see freedom.

In fact at least one camp in Japan partially carried out the Kill All instruction. On the afternoon of the 15th August, hours after the emperor had announced Japan's surrender, more than a dozen American POWs held at the Fukuoka camp were taken to a mountainside execution site and beheaded. It's unclear what actually stopped the carnage but I suspect it was the Japanese guards trying to save their own skins as they realised the game was up.

At a camp associated with Mitsushima, Naoetsu, where the particularly brutal guard known as the Bird, survivor of the assassination attempt, split his time, August 22 1945 was set as the date for all prisoners to be killed according to the memoirs of American POW Louie Zamperini. The timeline fits, and the men's fate was left hanging by a string.

As Louie speculates:

> *"the great hope of an American victory also brings with it great fear: Will the impending doom of Japan mean freedom for the captives? Or will it mean death for the POWs under the standing "kill-all" order that's in force in Japanese camps?"*

The terrorising of the prisoners would continue right to the very end. By this point my father had adopted a pragmatic approach to his captivity, that each day he survived was a small victory and as long as he could still put one foot in front of the other there was hope that one day he might march out of the camp a free man. He carried exactly that same philosophy into his later life and it very clearly served him well.

In direct contradiction of the Japanese warrior principles and their "Bushido" creed, another order had been issued to camp guards involved in war crimes to run away. In Mitsushima this would probably have meant all the guards: but only one, Watanabe, known to the men as The Bird, the survivor of the carefully planned poisoning attempt as mentioned earlier, escaped and was never captured. The men in the camp gave the guards nicknames, not as a term of endearment of course but as a way of ridiculing their captors. The nicknames would prove useful in the later war crimes trials as a way of identifying the perpetrators.

The order was issued on the 20th August 1945, during the period between the Emperor's announcement of surrender and the official surrender document being signed which was clearly seen as a window of opportunity for those with blood on their hands to escape justice. Issued from the office of the Chief of Prisoner of War Camps in Tokyo and held in American archives it says:

> *"Personnel who mistreated prisoners of war and internees or who are held in extremely bad sentiment by them are permitted to take care of it by immediately transferring or*

by fleeing without trace. Moreover documents which would be unfavourable for us in the hands of the enemy are to be treated in the same way as secret documents and destroyed when finished with."

So huge amounts of important information was destroyed in the very final days of the war, impacting on our ability to build and research the full story. These panic measures also blow apart the myth of the great courage and professionalism of the Japanese "warriors." Come the crunch, they were cowards, cowards guilty of mass murder, gross inhumanity and sadism who when the writing was on the wall looked to cover their traces.

Inside Mitsushima, despite the encouraging news that was filtering through on the progress of the war after the German surrender in May 1945, the conditions were, if anything, worse. Beatings continued and escalated and the senior Allied officer, Captain Gordon, was badly knocked about for continuing to complain to the Japanese Commanding Officer about the treatment of his men. As Al Weinstein, the '*Barbed Wire Surgeon*' noted:

"Under constant nervous tension, hard labor, and inadequate food, the health of the prisoners deteriorated during the summer of 1945. Officers and men lost weight steadily - about ten pounds a month. The average weight of the camp was one hundred and twenty pounds. Much of the weight was water-logged beriberi tissue."

In May 1945 my father sent another heavily censored message home to his sister. It is a poignant and very moving reminder that he had still had no communication from home since capture, despite his family writing to him, and shows him keeping thoughts of England in the spring uppermost in his mind as he sat starving, clad in rags in his flea infested hut:

TOKIO No.......CAMP

DATE 15/5/45

DEAR MAY, AND ALL AT HOME, HOPE YOU ARE ALL SAFE AND WELL, AM O.K. MYSELF AND LOOKING FORWARD TO BEING HOME

SOON. HAD NO NEWS YET. NICE WEATHER HERE NOW, COUNTRY SIDE IN BLOOM. BEING WHITSUN REMINDS ME OF HOLIDAY TIME IN ENGLAND. KNOW THAT EVERY-BODY MUST BE ENJOYING THEMSELVES. MY LOVE TO EVERYBODY. Cliff

An end to the war couldn't come soon enough. The remaining men who had survived for so long against all the odds were starving to death. They had been made aware from translating local newspapers that the Japanese had refused the offer of unconditional surrender set out in the terms of the Potsdam Conference in late July 1945. How much longer could they hold out? With no meat on their bones and with the long freezing cold months of another winter looming on the horizon time was running out. The American prisoners even had a slogan for their plight as they trudged out of the camp for another gruelling day of hard graft:

"Frisco live in Forty-five or stiff as sticks in Forty-six…"

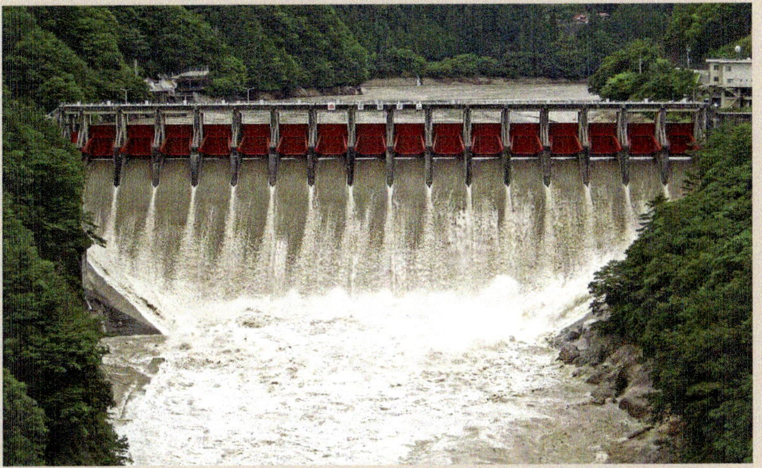

The Hiraoka dam at Mitsushima that my Dad worked on.

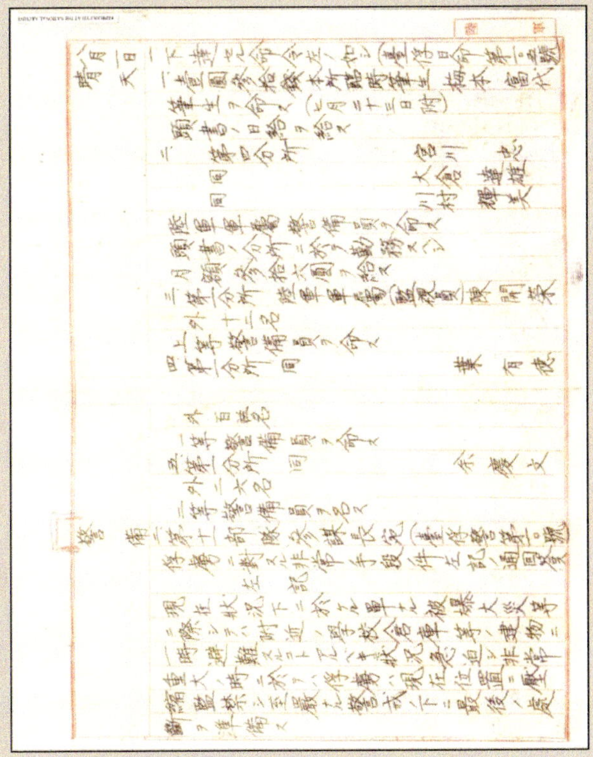

The Kill All Prisoners order sent out to Japanese POW camps

CHAPTER NINETEEN

Atomic Bombs and Surrender

On the 6th August 1945 an atomic bomb was dropped on Hiroshima, followed by a second bomb on Nagasaki three days later. It changed everything. The news reached Mitsushima as one of the British officers in the camp, Frank Twiss, explained:

> *"We got hold of a [Japanese] newspaper…and learned enough to know that a great bomb had been dropped on Hiroshima. This bomb…had disposed of Hiroshima in the twinkling of an eye…"*

Despite attempts by military hardliners to mount a coup to prevent surrender it was crushed, and at noon on 15th August Emperor Hirohito went on national radio announcing the Japanese surrender. These must have been confusing times as the report by Lt Downey of the US Navy says that the guards at the camp weren't disarmed until the 4th September, two days after the official surrender was signed on the USS Missouri in Tokyo harbour. The first indication that the war was at last over came when the Japanese Commanding Officer told the allied officers that there would be no work until further notice and for the first time the siren on the mountain peak calling the men to work failed to sound off.

For over a week men lay about the camp wondering what was going on as the Japanese guards who hadn't chosen to melt away in fear of prosecution refused to confirm the surrender. The Bird and other guards who feared that justice may soon be served had legged it. Eventually a group of men broke out of the camp and contacted one of the civilian contractors they had been working for, and he told them what they wanted to hear, and a newspaper was brought back as well and translated confirming officially at last that the surrender rumour was true. A party of men climbed onto the roofs of the hated barracks and painted the words POW CAMP in the biggest letters they could and the same message was staked out in old blankets on the parade ground.

Nearly two weeks after the official surrender had been declared the men spotted six black specks in the sky which eventually descended to follow the course of the river while the two hundred ragged men in the camp jumped up and down and shouted themselves hoarse. They knew that they were American Navy Grummans. The planes disappeared but turned around and headed back after what must have seemed like an age and began dropping supplies. It's hard to imagine the emotions unleashed by this first official contact with free men from your own side since the fall of Singapore and I know that my father would have been overwhelmed with tears of joy.

This was a day he must have doubted he would ever see, but something inside had kept him strong enough to embrace it at last. Notices dated the 28th August 1945 were dropped with the supplies into the known Japanese camp locations:

> *"TO ALL ALLIED PRISONERS OF WAR*
>
> *THE JAPANESE FORCES HAVE SURRENDERED UNCONDITIONALLY AND THE WAR IS OVER*
>
> *WE will get supplies to you as soon as humanly possible*

and will make arrangements to get you out but, owing to the distances involved, it may be some time before we can achieve this.

YOU will help us and yourselves if you act as follows:-

Stay in your camp until you get further orders from us.

Start preparing nominal rolls of men giving fullest particulars.

List your most urgent necessities

If you have been starved or underfed for long periods DO NOT eat large quantities of solid food, fruit or vegetables at first. It is dangerous for you to do so. Small quantities at frequent intervals are much safer and will strengthen you far more quickly. For those who are really ill or very weak, fluids such as broth and soup, making use of the water in which rice and other foods have been boiled are much the best. Gifts of food from the local population. Should be cooked. We want to get you back home quickly, safe and sound, and we do not want to risk your chances from diarrhoea, dysentery and cholera at this last stage.

Local authorities and/or Allied officers will take charge of your affairs in a very short time. Be guided by their advice."

So even after surrender, liberation was to prove another major logistical exercise, particularly for camps in remote areas like Mitsushima. The Americans mobilised Operation Swift Mercy, identifying the many camps, some of which were even more buried away than Mitsushima, and arranging air-drops of food, clothing and medical supplies.

As the supplies were from the US stores there was plenty of coffee, chocolate and cigarettes but no tea: it would be some time before Dad would get his hands on a proper strong cup of East End dockers' splosh. And new health risks had to be taken on board. Those risks were very real. Lessons had been learned from the liberation of concentration camps that sudden gorging after a long period of starvation diet can be a killer as the digestive system simply cannot cope. The temptation must have been high as bombers dropped 55 gallon steel drums packed with the kind of stuff these men hadn't seen in so long - cans of fruit, meat, milk, chocolate and cigarettes. Some of the canisters missed their targets and some buildings were damaged and a few men were injured by goodies falling from the skies. After the long and endless years of captivity the men would still have to be patient. One of the drums had a message attached as Richard M. Gordon reported:

> *"Hello folks. The crew of the USS Randolph send their best. Hope you enjoy the chow, keep your chin up. We'll be back."*

My father was one of the men charged with maintaining military discipline in the camp during this period. The temptation to exact retribution on those who had inflicted so much misery for so long must have been enormous. After three and a half years of being beaten, starved and tortured, while watching your mates die in their droves, they had their captors at their mercy now. But it would also take great courage and strength not to sink to their level. The dignified and respected presence of Captain Gordon was important as the senior ranking officer and he took control of the camp. In *'The Barbed Wire Surgeon'* Al Weinstein reports that he assembled the men in the camp parade yard and told them:

> *"The war is over. Japan has surrendered. Our forces haven't landed yet. I don't know when we shall leave the camp. Lieutenant Kubo will try to get us more food while we wait. We British and Americans don't believe in mob rule. These Japanese who have starved and tortured us will eventually get their just deserts. I beg of you not to take the law into your own hands. Some of these Japanese deserve to die. Be patient. After they are court-martialled many of them will be justly executed when our troops land. We must wait here for their arrival."*

The order was clear, remain in the camp until rescue was effected and await instructions. These must have been strange days indeed as the men waited, so close to freedom now, scanning the sky for more American planes and more information. Inevitably the former prisoners became restless and nervous as the days went by and they remained confined to the lice and flea-infested barrack huts that had been their home at Mitsushima for so long. As they played poker and sang songs to try and pass the time and keep morale up all they really wanted was to get out and get on their way home.

On the 4th of September the men were finally issued with orders to prepare to leave the valley at a moment's notice by Captain Gordon.

Lt Downey's report says:

> *'On 4 Sept 1945, after disarming the camp guards, the officers and men fell in and marched out of the camp along with the Japanese camp commander and proceeded to the railway station, arriving there 1120 and the train departed 1204. They travelled through small villages while proceeding to the sea coast, arriving at Toyohashi at Araimachi at 1630 and reported to the Americans there.*
>
> *The Mitsushima Prisoner of War camp was cleared of all Allied prisoners at exactly 1112 on 4 September 1945 and "taps" was blown by a bugler with a bugle that had been used by the United States troops in the Philippines."*

And so after more than three and a half years of sheer hell in captivity for my father and his comrades that grim period of their lives officially came to an end. It's impossible for me to imagine the emotions and feelings that would have been running through those carriages on that train with their first taste of freedom in so long as they rumbled on down to the coast. There were six other East Surreys on the Mitsushima liberation roster, all private soldiers, so Dad would have been the regiment's senior ranking man amongst them. Three of them, Privates Monteith, Nuttal and Shelley, had been there in Malaya in December 1941 with the 2nd Battalion when they first engaged the Japanese. Now, at last, they were free men again. It was an incredible feat of survival against all the odds.

In his book *Last Stop Nagasaki 1984* former POW Hugh Clarke attempts to summarise the experience:

> *"Being a POW was to become an involuntary subscriber to an extraordinary lottery. You could remain hungry and bored in Changi, but relatively undisturbed by your Japanese captors; you could work on the wharves and food dumps of Singapore and grow fat, if prepared to risk the inevitable bashings or worse; you could be shipped to Japan on the hell ships (allied subs permitting) and live in conditions worse than a Japanese miner or factory worker; or you could crack the bad luck jackpot and end up on the Burma-Siam railway."*

Other than growing fat on the food dumps, Dad pulled all these tickets out of the hat, including the jackpot of course, and had somehow survived to now begin his life again. Other than doing the football pools he never really gambled much as far as I know, maybe he just felt he had had his share of luck, both good and bad.

CHAPTER TWENTY

Liberation

On the 4th of September Sergeant Cliff Martin led his small group of surviving East Surreys as they marched out of the camp in military formation in good order and with their heads held high. Richard M. Gordon paints the picture;

> *"With everyone in a glorious mood at leaving, we Americans made our way up the winding road to the railroad station, and not in any military fashion. Looking down I witnessed an event that I recall with great pride for the British soldier. Assembled in the parade area were the British troops with their heads bowed. A Sergeant Major Maile, of the Surreys I believe, was leading his group in paying their respects to those who had died in the camp, while we Americans were practically running out of the place in our anxiety to leave. As I watched the British, they formed into a military unit and marched out as if on parade in England. A most impressive sight."*

After boarding a train at Hiraoka station the liberated prisoners travelled four hours down to Hamamatsu where they disembarked waiting to board one of the many landing craft that would have been used in any land invasion of Japan. Now they were taking the men to safety, men who almost certainly would have been shot if that land invasion had ever proved necessary. Just try to imagine the euphoria as they made that journey out to the deeper waters several miles off shore.

My father was received on board the USS Rescue, an American hospital ship, in Maisaka Bay for initial assessment. The stinking rags that the soldiers arrived in were chucked overboard and they were able to get the first hot shower and a shave before being de-loused and issued with some clean, fresh clobber.

They were looked after by the extraordinary American nurses. Confronted with the pitiful sight of men who had been beaten, starved and brutalised for so long my father told me that one of the nurses looked them up and down and said *"OK, which of you is going to be the first to kiss an American girl then?"* Some of the men reported that they fell in love with every single one of them.

It must have been harrowing work for the medical staff on board the ship as they began the long task of putting these broken men back together. My father told me that after so long on a watery diet his jaws couldn't chew properly but the nurses fed the men ice cream. They didn't need pity, they needed professional medical help: and the good planning that had sent the hospital ships into the theatre in good time must have saved the lives of a number of men whose health still hung by a thread.

There were a few even at this stage who were just too ill to make it, and that's just the ultimate sadness after coming so far. Many of the fitter men just wanted to be up on the deck savouring their freedom at last.

The rest bedded down on soft mattresses, in clean pyjamas taking in the waft of the nurses' perfume and the sound of the rustle of their starched uniforms and to so suddenly be safe after so long, in kind and caring hands without the fear of starvation and beatings, must have been a huge swing of the emotional pendulum.

I find these words from the American Lt. Henry G Lee who was captured at Bataan most poignant:

"I see no gleam of victory alluring
No chance of splendid booty or gain
If I endure - I must go on enduring
And my reward for bearing pain - is pain
Yet, though the thrill, the zest, the hope
Are gone
Something within me keeps fighting on"

In one beautifully-crafted verse that is the story of this disparate and ragged group of men who had survived to board the American hospital ships moored off Japan and begin the long journey home. Something had kept them fighting on when all hope had gone, and, with a huge dollop of luck thrown in, they had achieved the freedom that for so long must have seemed impossible.

On the 8th September the USS Rescue left for Yokohama where the former prisoners disembarked and joined the USS Benevolence to sail on to Manila. The Benevolence must have seemed like heaven to the former POWs. Just over a year old, it was a state of the art modern hospital ship with all the facilities, and had arrived in Japanese waters on the 20th August with the specific task of caring for the prisoners in the wake of the surrender.

Awaiting transport from Manila on to the UK my father was looked after by the 3rd Australian PW reception group which was part of the 5th American Replacement Depot.

It was here at last that he was able to send a telegram home confirming that he was alive and in safe hands, his family didn't even know at this point that he had actually survived the war, let alone been liberated. He also picked up the first letter from home he had seen since being captured and they confirmed that his family had also survived the war safe and well.

The telegram to his sister in Dagenham, wired via Melbourne by Cable and Wireless on the 21st September, more than a month after the official Japanese surrender, was short and very sweet:

"AM SAFE IN AUSTRALIAN HANDS HOPE TO BE HOME SOON."

Imagine receiving that message from a brother that for so long you may have assumed was dead. There would have been jubilation in that tiny front room of Auntie May's house in Dagenham and she would have passed the news on to the rest of the family that not only was Cliff alive he was now on his way back to England.

There was still some distance to go yet of course. The thousands of rescued prisoners were now in the hands of the RAPWI, the Recovery of Allied Prisoners of War and Internees organisation, and they had a massive logistical job on their hands.

While prisoners were classified A,B and C for repatriation depending on how fit they were for the journey, my Dad would have had some more time on his hands in Manila. With the so-called "Freedom Fiver" in local currency issued to all liberated prisoners in his pocket he could explore what was left of the city that had been devastated by a massive battle at the end of the war. I know that he bought a watch with the rising moon, stars and sun as the hands went through the 24 hour cycle and which he gave to me when I was a kid, but which I stupidly lost somewhere along the way. I wish I still had it.

It wasn't until the 21st September 1945 that my father's official military records show him as "recovered with allied forces", the same date as his first telegram home. The records also now record his rank as 'war sergeant', a temporary promotion that can be stripped away from him now that hostilities were over.

Eventually his number came up for the transport and so began the final leg of his long journey home on the Empress of Australia, which had left Hong Kong on the 12th of September, and my father boarded along with over 1600 other former prisoners.

They passed the time reading books and magazines, organising entertainment and discussing over and over again what they were going to do when they eventually got back to old Blighty. My Dad's ship sailed via Singapore to pick up liberated internees and it must have been an incredibly emotional experience for him to return to the place of his capture after more than three and a half years of the most abject misery and despair.

During this stopover Lady Mountbatten boarded the ship and asked the men if they had any complaints and as a result the living conditions were improved and more mattresses were loaded in. There had been issues with the sheer numbers now crowded on board the Empress of Australia, which put pressure on the sleeping accommodation and some petty rules and regulations imposed by the naval officers, but they were ironed out after the blokes made their views known.

After Singapore the journey continued via Colombo and Suez and a stop over in Port Said to refuel on the 17th October, where they must have disembarked because Dad took the opportunity to send another Cable and Wireless telegram back to Dagenham.

The small, buff wartime cable is a beautiful and precious thing, and I'm so glad that my Auntie kept it and that it has eventually found its way into our possession. As I read and reread it I think of my Dad in the hot Egyptian telegram office getting his message together and thinking about the last leg of his long journey. He was allowed three short lines but each one speaks volumes:

MANY THANKS FOR LETTER

DELIGHTED TO HEAR YOU ARE SAFE AND WELL

LOVE TO ALL THE FAMILY

And the men on board the ship slept - after so long trying to bed down in damp, uncomfortable, disease and flea-ridden hell holes, either in baking heat or freezing cold, they had some catching up to do. It must have been pure bliss to have a clean and comfortable bunk to retire to now that the accommodation issue had been sorted out. That level of comfort itself would prove a challenge for a few of the former prisoners who would take time to readjust.

Some men filled the days writing down notes on their experiences. The Empress of Australia arrived in Liverpool to great fanfare and an escort of tugboats on the

27th October 1945 with Dad sending another telegram to Auntie May saying:

"ARRIVED SAFELY SEE YOU SOON. CLIFF MARTIN"

Even this final journey was disrupted and delayed by bad weather at sea. However along the way my father's weight had increased to 10 stone and I remember him telling me that they spent time on board building up muscle mass and fitness with PT routines and games on deck. Quoits was a big favourite as they whiled away the hours. The length of the journey home may have tried the patience of the returning men but in some ways it may have actually done them a lot of good as it gave them time and space to put on weight, to rest and to exercise and possibly process to some extent what had happened to them. FEPOWs were issued with a liberation questionnaire, my father's is held at the National Archive at Kew and tells us very little, and another pamphlet called the Ministry of Defence Return Document containing detailed instructions on pay, leave, sickness and welfare.

Of real importance to my Dad's story from this point, and the FEPOW story in general, is the fact that the men were now presented with another very official and intimidating leaflet which basically told the prisoners not to talk about their time in captivity. There are a couple of examples of the document handed to returning FEPOWs, under the blunt title "**Guard Your Tongue**" and although I don't have the actual leaflet circulated on the Empress of Australia before its arrival I have seen a copy issued on other ships and it's fair to assume that the messaging would have been the same:

> *"This is a personal message from H.Q. ALFSEA* [Allied Land Forces South East Asia] *to all newly released Allied Prisoners of War*.
>
> *"You are news now and anything you say in public or to press reporters is liable to be published in the press of the whole world. ...*
>
> *"If you had not been lucky enough to have been recovered*

and had died any form of unpleasant death at the hands of the Japanese you would not have wished your family and friends to have been harrowed by lurid details of that death in the sensational press.

"That is just what will happen to the families of your comrades who died in that way if you start talking to all and sundry about your experiences...."

Although it is understandable that families and friends of those who died might not want to find out about the harrowing details from the press, I think that the message can be interpreted as going beyond that: it can be read as a blanket instruction to keep quiet. I suspect that that is how many of the men would have read it. My father was a regular soldier before the outbreak of war and remained in the army and reserves for many years afterwards. He would have taken orders and instructions very seriously and would have understood that there would be consequences for ignoring them. This leaflet had the military stamp all over it and really wasn't pulling any punches.

However, his own decision to keep quiet about what had happened to him and his comrades, and to bottle it up, was reinforced by personal experience. When he eventually made it back to the East End and was asked about the long hard years in captivity one of our relatives knocked him back on his heels and said that "we don't want to hear about all that, we've had it hard here as well mate". That stuck with him for years.

My father talked to me about this and although it was only one selfish comment I know that it left him hurt, bitter and angry and he told me that that was the moment when he decided that he would keep quiet. I imagine he would have had conversations with fellow survivors when they met up but until he met our Mum I believe he maintained his silence.

This was a man who would very clearly have been suffering from acute PTSD and whose mental and physical health was badly damaged by more than three and half years of brutality, starvation, sickness, slave labour and deprivation. Not only were there no support services for him, but he was being formally instructed to keep his mouth shut.

There was a much wider agenda in play here. The fall of Singapore was the biggest capitulation in British military history. Those who fell into enemy hands had been isolated and forgotten. Telling their story would be bad for morale on the home front. I've read about the wives of FEPOW's who were told by the military to assume that their husbands were dead and were given permission to remarry. This was truly the forgotten army. Even the coverage of the subsequent trials of their brutal and sadistic captors would be low key in Britain and there would be no political fight for compensation, not even from the Japanese corporations who benefited financially from the slave labour.

The cynic in me says that there were post war trade deals to be done and while it was convenient for some with short memories to preach "forgive and forget". But how could you, when the broken skull and pain from your beatings was there to remind you every minute of every hour of every day? And then there were the nightmares.

I know that after liberation my Dad thought a lot about his comrades who hadn't made it. They were always on his mind. John Wyatt estimates that of the 786 East Surreys who first experienced battle at the Japanese invasion of Malaya only around 125 returned home with over 500 killed in action and a further 125 dying in captivity. Those figures mirror my Dad's experience in his own close group of army friends. In our modern world you would need support and help to process that and the burden of guilt and grief that it would place on your shoulders. There was very little of that for the men told to keep quiet and move on.

So the hero's welcome home on the dockside in Liverpool soon melted away, and the men were cut adrift. The conscripts would be demobbed and would do their best to return to their families and civilian life, wracked with their pain and horrific memories - there are stories of men who struggled to hold a job down as the readjustment to Civvy Street was just too difficult. The years of deprivation impacted in some strange ways, with one fellow only able to sleep on the floor for years, as he could not get used to a bed. On the 27th October, the day he landed back in England, my father's Certificate of Service shows that he returned to his regiment - albeit with the 42 days leave granted in some sort of recognition of the long and brutal years since the surrender of Singapore.

During this period of leave Dad would have been required to appear before a medical board to decide if he was still fit for service, and he must have passed those tests, although he later admitted that he kept the recurrent headaches resulting from his beatings quiet as he didn't want to compromise his A1 medical status. He would also have been debriefed by MI9 and would have had an advance on the back pay owed to him of £8 and a travel warrant issued for the rail journey back to London.

He didn't have a wife, sweetheart or mother and father waiting for him. There was no little house with a gate for him to stride through with "welcome home" strung across the wall. What remained of his family had already been broken up and scattered in the great Cockney diaspora. Over seven years had passed since he left England and now he was very much on his own in a world that had changed completely that didn't really want to know about what had happened to him.

It must have been a bewildering time and it was no surprise that he went back to the certainty that the British Army offered him. Some of the returning men described a strange kind of melancholy descending on them as they disembarked and a feeling that they didn't really belong, I can understand that. What for so long had seemed like an impossible dream of freedom and a return to England was now a reality, but it came loaded with its own huge challenges and pressures that banked up like the dark clouds of the tropical storms the prisoners had endured. The country they were returning to must have seemed so very different, and probably quite daunting, compared to the one that Dad had left behind in 1938.

It's clear that the British authorities just weren't prepared or equipped to deal with the physical and psycho-

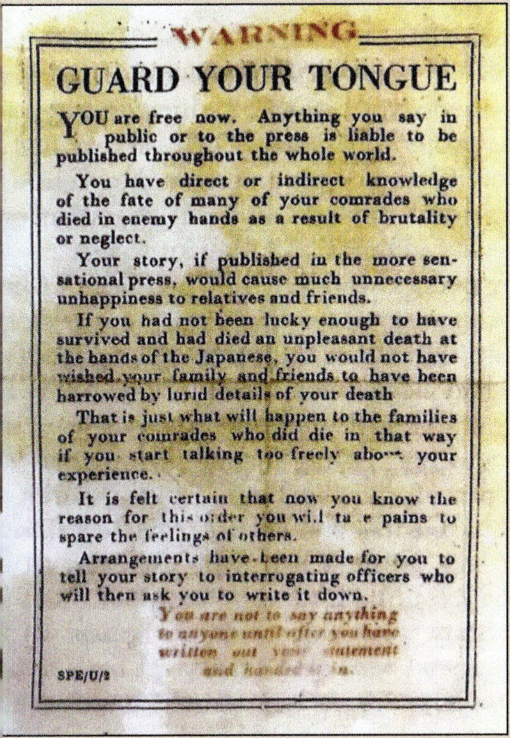

WARNING

GUARD YOUR TONGUE

YOU are free now. Anything you say in public or to the press is liable to be published throughout the whole world.

You have direct or indirect knowledge of the fate of many of your comrades who died in enemy hands as a result of brutality or neglect.

Your story, if published in the more sensational press, would cause much unnecessary unhappiness to relatives and friends.

If you had not been lucky enough to have survived and had died an unpleasant death at the hands of the Japanese, you would not have wished your family and friends to have been harrowed by lurid details of your death

That is just what will happen to the families of your comrades who did die in that way if you start talking too freely about your experience.

It is felt certain that now you know the reason for this order you will take pains to spare the feelings of others.

Arrangements have been made for you to tell your story to interrogating officers who will then ask you to write it down.

You are not to say anything to anyone until after you have written out your statement and handed it in.

SPE/U/3

The Guard Your Tongue leaflet issued to returning prisoners telling them not to talk.

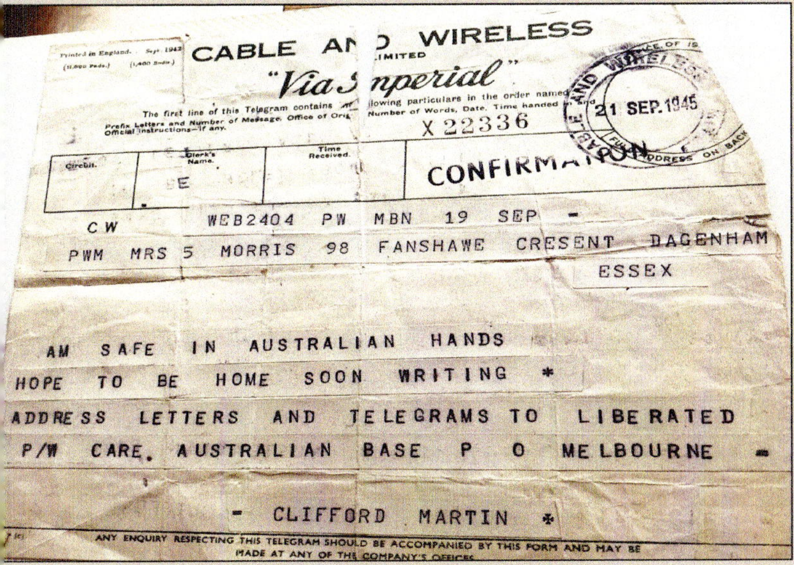

Printed in England. Sept 1943

CABLE AND WIRELESS LIMITED

"Via Imperial"

The first line of this Telegram contains the following particulars in the order named: Prefix Letters and Number of Message, Office of Origin, Number of Words, Date, Time handed in and Official Instructions—if any.

X 22336

21 SEP 1945

Circuit.	Clerk's Name.	Time Received.	
	E		CONFIRMATION

CW WEB2404 PW MBN 19 SEP -

PWM MRS S MORRIS 98 FANSHAWE CRESENT DAGENHAM ESSEX

AM SAFE IN AUSTRALIAN HANDS
HOPE TO BE HOME SOON WRITING *
ADDRESS LETTERS AND TELEGRAMS TO LIBERATED
P/W CARE. AUSTRALIAN BASE P O MELBOURNE -

- CLIFFORD MARTIN *

ANY ENQUIRY RESPECTING THIS TELEGRAM SHOULD BE ACCOMPANIED BY THIS FORM AND MAY BE MADE AT ANY OF THE COMPANY'S OFFICES

he first telegram home confirming Dad was still alive

logical scars of the men now returning in their thousands from the Far East. Simply organising the repatriation exercise itself had been a massive logistical headache and with the country skint, and with resources stretched to the limit, I can understand the difficulty in meeting the very specific needs of the FEPOW's. Much War Office thinking was still based on the post First World War experiences of trauma but some psychiatrists had been warning since 1944 of the very specific and lifetime problems that men like my Dad would face. As Billings wrote in the British Medical Journal in his piece "*The Prisoner Of War Mentality*";

> *"These are very slow wearing-down cruelties, the relief of which can result in no 'acute emotional reaction' but a chronic psychological stigma....There is only one class of man or woman who can experience all this (and much more) and who can be rehabilitated to fit into normal reconstructed society again and that is the 'superman'. The remainder will be a problem for their lifetime."*

Was my Dad a 'superman'? Well, he certainly was to me but that's just through the eyes of a son looking back at the horror he pulled himself through with sheer guts, inner-strength and no end of luck. But those men who slipped through the cracks and found it impossible to cope were no different to him, they had also survived the day to day torment but were facing an impossible struggle with its legacy.

Twenty two Civil Resettlement Units (CRU's) had been set up to try and bridge the gap between prisoner and civilian life, initially established to assist men returning from the European Theatre, they were voluntary but had a take up of 60% of those released from the European camps. Their take up from the 40,000 FEPOW's arriving home in the autumn of 1945 was just 12%. My Dad was one of those who swerved the offer, I don't know why: but if you've been instructed to Hold Your Tongue it would be hard to suddenly opt to start discussing your situation with someone you neither know nor trust. After everything that had happened since the Malaya campaign and the fall of Singapore I think trust had become a massive issue.

My father needed something solid and reassuring to hold on to and a few years later my he wrote some words about the pride in his regiment, the solidarity and the spirit that had helped carry him though the darkest days and it helps explain why he eventually decided to remain in the Colours despite having served out his time of engagement through the war years:

> *"And so to the POW days where again the qualities and spirit of the Regt were well to the fore. We had a pretty rough time as the whole world knows by now, but the mists of time are clouding the rough treatment that was meted out to us and we remember the good things that happened. The Espirit de Corps! The mucking in spirit as we like to call it. The helping of one another, without which many of us would never have survived. This has always been a great characteristic of our Regiment and I hope it never dies."*

My Dad was the master of understatement, describing his three and half years of hell as a prisoner as "a pretty rough time" is typical of the man he was. He didn't want to labour the point with new recruits to his Regiment, he wanted to be positive and instil in them an upbeat and collective approach to their soldiering, he was a born leader. He once referred to the disastrous Malaysian Campaign, where his Regiment was cut to ribbons and lost hundreds of men, as being "badly knocked about a bit".

I do wonder now if his approach was in part influenced by his decision not to talk in detail about what had happened to him and his comrades, hence playing down the brutal reality and skirting around the true horror. I think he would also have hated the idea that men under his command would have pitied him. He would have wanted to earn their respect on the basis of the soldier he now was, not on what had happened in the past.

CHAPTER TWENTY ONE

Back to the Colours

Back at the East Surreys Barracks in Kingston Dad immersed himself back into the army life he knew, and as he gradually regained his strength he threw himself back into sports and any training and education opportunities that presented themselves. But of course his post-trauma condition would never be far away. Although there was important work done on the condition of returning German POWs, notably by Dr Phillip Newman, these weren't easily applied to the men coming back from the Far East.

Newman warned that *"many returning prisoners would show anti-social and self-destructive behaviour,"* but although the War Office recognised that POWs would have psychological issues, the readjustment schemes they set up were orientated towards European prisoners, and weren't specific to the FEPOWs who the Government assumed would be in better emotional shape than prisoners of the Germans.

I just find this utterly bizarre, but it seems to be based on the assumption that they felt less guilt about being captured because they just accepted they'd been betrayed by their military leadership and it wasn't their fault, and they were less bored because the Japanese kept them busy! As far as I'm aware my father received no practical assistance and the only real support he got was from his own mates and comrades who remained in contact. That network would prove a lifesaver for many of these damaged men.

It wouldn't be until some years later that those few medics who made a study of the physical and mental condition of the men who had survived capture by the Japanese began to identify the earliest signs of what would become known as Post Traumatic Stress Disorder. We would now see that all of the main symptoms of PTSD were clearly present; reliving of the events with intense emotional reaction, difficulty sleeping and feeling irritable and angry, feelings of isolation, and guilt and in some cases resorting to destructive behaviour. The former prisoners would carry all of this with them for every day of what remained of their lives. The mental health of some would completely collapse under the weight. From the point of liberation, where they thought they had thrown the chains off, they were now engulfed by new ones which were invisible and carried in their own heads

Shortly after his return a reunion for the surviving East Surreys was held at Chelsea Town Hall. It must have been one hell of an emotional experience as it brought together both regular soldiers and conscripts who had shared the suffering of the years after the start of the battle for Malaya through to liberation. How many of the 125 who made it through attended I don't know, but as the regiment had been split up and fragmented in battle and captivity for most it would have been the first time they'd seen each other since the final days of the fight for Singapore and the early days as prisoners. But any joy would have been overshadowed as the numbers brought together would just have underlined how many of their old mates they had lost along the way.

The gathering was addressed by Colonel C.E. Morrison who confirmed what the men already suspected - that the instruction to kill all of the prisoners was real, and a copy of the official order had been found in a safe in one of the camps in Japan by the Americans.

John Wyatt, in his book *No Mercy From The Japanese* reports Colonel Morrison told the audience:

> *"This was to all intents and purposes a warrant for the massacre of all you men in this room along with many thousands of your comrades."*

I don't know whether this assembly, and the brutal reminder to the survivors of how right to the very end their lives had hung by a thread, would have helped the men process their feelings, but of course there would be a unique bond between them. I remember much later as a kid when Dad would get together with a few of his old comrades at the Regimental Association and they would talk quietly about Old Glass Eye and Hell Fire Pass. I thought it sounded incredibly exciting: it was only later that I realised the enormity of their experiences as young men and that what they were discussing as Hell Fire Pass was actually hell on earth and that Old Glass Eye was a murderous sadist.

While his Battalion took part in duties in Palestine, Egypt, Greece and Somalia between 1946 and 1950 his service record book shows that my father remained in Kingston and in fact had a break from regular service of four months from May 1946 to September 1946. His official military records held at the National Archive at Kew shed some more light on this period. Dad had now completed much more than the original seven years in the colours that he had signed up for in June 1937 with the register showing he had now racked up close to nine years and was entitled to release and during that period from the 21st May 1946 to the 18th September 1946 he was "relegated" to Section B of the army reserve in preparation for his discharge.

My father now stood at a crossroads. Documents for his "Class A" release with effect from the 21st May 1946 had been prepared and a glowing military testimonial for him to take forward into civilian life and been drafted:

"Conduct: Exemplary.

This NCO had the misfortune to be a prisoner in Japan for 3½ years. This makes it difficult to give a full account of his capabilities for civil employment. In normal circumstances he would undoubtedly have reached higher rank. He is an experienced driver and an intelligent and efficient worker who will give loyal service to a civilian employer. He is strongly recommended for a position of trust."

Although the testimony is strong and should have reassured any potential employer as to Dad's exceptional qualities it also confirms that the years of captivity would continue to cast a shadow over him. Instead of grabbing the chance to get out he chose instead to bide his time in the reserve and on the 19th of September 1946 he made the decision to rejoin the colours.

I have always assumed that FEPOWs returning to the regular army would have been excused an immediate return to international duties, they were certainly given an assurance that they wouldn't be returned to the Far East. You would hope that the forces would have shown some duty of care to these men, and my father's records show that maybe they did. He was given time to consider all of his options and ultimately concluded that he wasn't yet ready for Civvy Street and that his ambitions at this stage in his life could be best met within the ranks of the army.

The tattered remains of my Dad's Soldiers Service and Pay Book show that from 1947 he was grabbing every opportunity for training and personal development and he had an eye on promotion to the highest rank he could attain as a Non Commissioned Officer. Soon after his repatriation his war sergeant rank had been taken away and he had been returned to the substantive rank of corporal, a move that I would have found unnecessarily bureaucratic and insulting after all he had been through although I guess he probably took it in his stride, but by the end of 1947 he was back up to the rank of sergeant and cracking on.

That year news would have begun filtering back from the war crimes trials, and specifically the trial of guards from Mitsushima. Although the British press gave little priority to covering these trials my father would have been getting news from the States where it was a much bigger deal. However, I can find no evidence that he was ever asked to submit a statement. News that a number of his tormentors had been found guilty and hanged would have reached him. Dad was a supporter of the death penalty, certainly at that time and particularly within a military context, but I'm not convinced that the hanging of the Mitsushima guards and others found guilty of crimes on the railway and the Hell Ships would have brought him any real sense of closure. I have no doubt he would have welcomed it and would have seen it as purely a consequence of their actions, but it wouldn't erase his memories, relieve his constant pain or bring any of the dead men back.

As his son I have to confront my own feelings. On principle I've never been a supporter of the death penalty: but what about when it's directly related to those found guilty after due process of brutalising, starving and torturing my Dad, and systematically presiding over the deaths of so many of his mates? Then it all becomes raw and personal and my gut instinct is to want to kick the stool from under them.

On the political front in the immediate post-war years Britain was a very different place and there were huge structural changes underway, not least the creation of the Welfare State. The Far East prisoners would not have had a chance to vote in the decisive general election in July 1945 that delivered Attlee his Labour landslide. They would have still been fighting for survival in their various camps and wondering whether they would live or die. Although they may have had some news on the German surrender and the American military advances I doubt that they even knew there was an election on.

It seems strange to me looking back that an election was actually called before the war was over. Again the implication was that the only conflict that really mattered was across Europe and the forgotten troops still slaving, starving and languishing in the Far East could be pushed well out of public view. I'm not sure in the euphoria of their eventual liberation that the survivors would have felt slighted, but as a political animal I certainly would. However, there is no doubt that if my father had had the opportunity to vote, be it from Yokohama, Manila, Stepney, Dagenham or Kingston, that he would have voted Labour for a progressive future. I doubt he would have even known the election result until he was freed from Mitsushima. He would have noted that his old manor, Stepney, hadn't returned a Labour MP, but had voted for the Communist candidate, Phil Piratin, whose hard work campaigning for the community and against the fascists through the 1930s now saw him elected to the House of Commons.

It was the 1930s depression that had led to my father joining the army in 1937 and his experience of those grim years, and the class system that had shut off his education and employment opportunities, had shaped him and his views, and would have left him demanding something much better now he was back. In the prison camps, when the men had the time and the energy, they would fill the void in the darkness of their huts and tents discussing everything and anything and that would include politics and the kind of lives they hoped to return to one day. Now they were back and it was time to try to move forward into those lives.

It's a sad fact that the post-war Attlee Labour government didn't do a lot directly for the former Far East prisoners although the jewel in the crown of its achievements, the NHS, would benefit Dad in the long term and he would go on to work within it. Our family would also be beneficiaries of the health, education and welfare reforms of the post-war political settlement. Me and my sister and our kids have been afforded opportunities that had been closed off to our father.

Although rationing and the bomb sites would be a reminder to the returning FEPOWs that the impact of war would be with them for some time, the sports stadiums, dance halls and race tracks were packed out as the shackles and restrictions were thrown off. Being based in Kingston my father would have watched the local amateur football team, Kingstonians, at their Richmond Road ground, where his Regiment also paraded on occasion. The Oval and Surrey and international cricket was within easy reach and there would always be someone in the barracks who was good for a ticket. A bus ride away was Craven Cottage, Fulham, and that's where he watched most of his football, they remained his team through the rest of his life.

And he would have gone out dancing. It was at a dance held at the Raynes Park Tennis Club in 1947 that he got really lucky and met our Mum. Mum was born in 1926. She was no stranger to the military herself and as the daughter of an officer in the Artillery Regiment and in the REME she had been brought up in the barracks at Woolwich and at overseas postings.

As a child between the wars she would have seen soldiers from her father's regiment who had been physically and mentally damaged in WW1: her father was also away on active service for the duration of WW2. I think that would have given her a resilience and insight that she brought into the relationship with my Dad. The hard truth is that she would have needed it: as his confidant and closest friend she gave him the love and support he desperately needed to put him back together. She also gave him hope and a belief that he could now build the kind of future that must have seemed just a distant dream to him as he laboured - starved, battered, sick and broken - on Death Railway and in Mitsushima just a few years before.

My grandfather on Mum's side, Herbert Cecil Seall, was born in October 1900 and carved out a glittering military career for himself that defied the class structure. Although Mum was born in Woolwich the family had to be mobile and that had included a posting to Germany as part of the occupation forces, regulated and imposed by the Armistice Agreement, during the post-WW1 days of hyper-inflation. I remember my Nan telling me how shoppers used to queue up with wheelbarrows full of cash to try and buy a loaf of bread only to find that prices had risen again by the time they reached the counter. She gave me a billion mark note that she had kept from the time that they were there. The economic chaos in Germany at that time helped create the conditions a decade later for the rise of the Nazis. Nana also had roots embedded in East London and had been born in West Ham and I remember her telling me that her school sports day used to be held at the old Boleyn Ground, the home of the football club.

In the early 1930s the family were shipped to India when my mother was very young, such was the lot of the military family that she was born and brought up in. They were back in Britain in the run up to WW2 and my grandfather had what would probably have been described as a "good war". At the beginning of the conflict he was a Sergeant Major, before being promoted through the ranks in the battle field to Lieutenant Quarter Master in the Royal Regiment of Artillery, transferring to the Royal Army Ordnance Corps and finally the Royal Electrical and Mechanical Engineers (REME). There he was appointed as Temporary Captain: these were wartime appointments that reflected the shortage of commissioned officers who had been through the rigid military training process.

These men drawn from the ranks were referred to as "Temporary Gentlemen", implying that they were uncouth and unrefined compared to their upper-class Sandhurst counterparts and could only be trusted while the shells were flying. Absolute nonsense of course and Captain Seal proved himself beyond any doubt when he was mentioned in dispatches for bravery on the 6th April 1944 during a desert battle in the Middle East. My Mum told me he rescued some men from a burning tank, under enemy fire, at great personal risk to himself.

My grandmother, Mum and Uncle Frank were back at home while grandfather was away for the duration of the war, and like all families with Dads on active service they would have been worried that they would never see him again. Dealing with that would serve my mother well in later life as I think it gave her a very clear sense of perspective and understanding of what war could do to people. I suspect my grandfather came back a different man. Mum was part of that generation who had been kids at the start of the war and had gone through the Blitz, rationing, disrupted education and in her case a brief evacuation to Weymouth in the early days of the conflict with her brother Frank. She left Central Girls School in Central Road, St Helier Estate, Carshalton in March 1942 with a leaving certificate describing her as:

> *"...[a] steady reserved girl who should make a good reliable office worker."*

Almost immediately she landed her first full time job as a junior clerk in the transport department at the London Electric Supply Company in Morden, on a wage of one pound, two shillings and sixpence a week. By the war's end that generation, who were now coming of age, sought out any entertainment they could find to shake off the constraints of the previous six years - cinema, dance halls, and sports - and Mum was a regular in the packed-out stands at the Wimbledon Speedway down Plough Lane.

There was plenty going on in that part of south west London and a trip into town was an easy hop on the Northern Line and sometimes Mum would be called on to work at the company HQ in New Broad Street in the heart of the city. She also loved her tennis, and there are great pictures of her as a young woman on works outings, glammed up and just enjoying a lot of those freedoms that we now take for granted.

But Dad had got lucky in another way, as it was only by chance that Mum was around to dance with him in the first place. Her parents had relatives in the United States and as the bombs fell on London they offered to pay for Mum and her brother, my Uncle Frank, to be shipped across the Atlantic to safety. The arrangements had all been made but my Nana backed out of the plan right at the last moment before their ship was due to sail from Southampton. If Mum had gone that would likely have been that and she would have built a life the other side of the ocean and would never have met my father.

Dad was still training hard and planning for his future. He started attending night school classes, learning double entry book keeping and his service book shows that in

February 1949 he attended the "Officers Mess Stewards Course" at the army cookery school in Aldershot. He became the steward in the officers' mess in Kingston. If I'm being honest whatever cookery skills he attained were kept pretty well hidden in later life, maybe a fry up occasionally, but other than that Mum kept him well away from the stove. Dad's denial of a decent education as a kid due to pure family economics was a massive driving factor for him and he grabbed every opportunity that came his way. He never stopped learning, he saw it as the route to a better and more rewarding life.

CHAPTER TWENTY TWO

Love, Hope and More Soldiering

After a short engagement Dad married Mum in June 1949 at the St Lawrence church on London Road in Morden with the reception at the George just down the road where Auntie Daisy, my great aunt, was the landlady. Despite rationing still being in force the photos show that it was a great occasion with a fantastic spread and a proper tiered wedding cake, not one of the wartime cardboard jobs. Dad looked fit and sharp in his dress uniform and Mum just looked beautiful. They honeymooned in Lloret de Mar at a time when international travel was rare for a couple from their background but they must have saved hard to make it happen. Later, they named their first house together "Lloret" in memory of that trip.

Mum and Dad moved into a flat in the married quarters at the Kingston barracks and it wasn't long before they were sharing their new home with a number of cats, local strays that they rehomed. I remember Mum telling me that Dad used to stink the place out boiling up lights - guts - to feed the cats who gravitated to their digs. One cat, Sooty, was their favourite and Mum would slip him inside her coat and take him out and about on the bus and the tube. They'd remain cat lovers all their lives.

In 1951 the surviving FEPOWs were given another kick in the teeth that left my Dad and his comrades feeling bitter and dredging up old memories of how they had been forgotten and cut adrift by those in authority. Under the terms of the San Francisco Peace Treaty they were told that they were now getting the pitiful sum of £76 in reparations for their years of captivity and slave labour. Dad was one of those who renewed efforts through their regimental and prisoner associations to fight for some meaningful recognition and compensation while the private corporations who had benefited from their back-breaking work in Japan were rehabilitated as respectable businesses and were making serious money. But my father and his mates would see none of that.

Six years after liberation the survivors would have to fight again, and for my father that fight would go on well into his old age when he should have been putting his feet up. Successive governments, both Labour and Tory, seemed to be afraid of risking confrontation with the Japanese over the issue of the treatment of the prisoners as they now emerged as a post-war economic powerhouse. For my Dad I know that it was never about the money: how do you adequately financially compensate tens of thousands of men for living through hell? Dad and his mates just wanted some recognition and respect rather than seeing their file pushed to the bottom of the pile in the hope that they would eventually go away. But they wouldn't.

1952 marked the 250th anniversary of the East Surreys, my Dad often referred to them in Cockney rhyming slang as the Mutton Currys. Here are some words he wrote to mark this auspicious occasion, by now he was truly one of the old guard in the ranks and wanted to send a rallying call to the newer recruits who looked up to him:

"Hello you 'Mutton Curry's'

I'm an old 2nd Btn man myself, and when I say "old 2nd Btn", I mean the original 2nd Btn, as we knew it before the last war. We had a grand spirit in our Bn - Yes! We used to call it our Bn because there was a sort of friendly rivalry between the 1st and 2nd Bn then. But whatever the differences of opinion between the Bns we were united in the great pride we had in our Regt.

The Bns are amalgamated into the 1st Bn now, and I am sure that the spirit of pride handed on by the old Bns still exists throughout the East Surrey Regt today. I can imagine some of you listening to this and thinking that I am laying it on a bit thick, but any old "Surrey" among you will admit that what I have said is true…

…….the message I wanted to get over to you is "Keep that old mucking-in spirit and pride in the Regt going. It has been handed on to us since 1702, 250 years and it's good for another 250 yet."

On the 18th of May 1952 Dad left the UK as a regular soldier with the army for the last time with the First Battalion of the East Surreys. After completing an emergency tour in Tripoli and Dernia as part of a force assembled to meet an expected threat from Egypt after the overthrow of King Farouk in a coup d'état they were then shipped to the Canal Zone on HMT Devonshire - arriving in Tobruk in February 1953.

My Dad proudly kept a press cutting from the English language newspaper dated the 25th May 1952 publicising a big parade planned for the Queen's Birthday:

"The whole of the British community in Tripolitania will be en fete for the Birthday of Queen Elizabeth which is to be celebrated on Thursday 5th June, and already the 1st Battalion The East Surrey Regiment have held rehearsals for the Birthday Parade to be given on the Seaview parade ground."

The Battalion had originally been rushed out of England as part of massive airlift of troops - 45 fully equipped soldiers per Hastings aircraft. While in Tripoli in July 1952 my Dad completed his senior NCO's Cadre training, opening the door to further progression through the ranks and he was promoted to acting Colour Sergeant in September 1952 and Warrant Officer 2nd Class in November 1952 whilst with the Middle East Land Forces (MELF).

The British Army was a class-based organisation and the old division between commissioned officers (those who hold the King's or Queen's Commission and have been through the old-school-tie officer training) and warrant officers (enlisted and experienced soldiers who hold the King's Warrant and have progressed through the ranks) was key to the archaic structure.

Amongst his things I found a slip of paper from the Forces Broadcasting Service confirming that a special request for my Mum with both a message and tune would be broadcast at nine pm on the 17th August 1952, it was one of the few ways that he could send a signal from the Middle East that he was thinking about her and missing her.

The Suez base was seen as essential to Britain's strategic objectives not least as the Abu Sueir airfield, with its lengthened runways, would be capable of basing US Superfortress B-29 bombers within striking distance of Soviet targets that were beyond the reach of UK Strategic Air Command airfields.

Some 14 years after my Dad first sailed out on protectorate duties to Shanghai he now found himself pulled around on the whim of global politics once again, but he was a different man now to the lad who took those first steps as a young private. Now he was an experienced soldier and leader, carrying responsibility on his broad shoulders but also leaving a young wife behind. His records show that he completed drill course training early in 1953. It was his job now to bring the young lads up to scratch, for many this would be their first overseas tour.

The extension of the original tour, and the transfer from Tripoli to the base at Tel El Kebir (TEK), had not gone down particularly well. TEK had been painted as a bit of a fly-blown dump compared to Tripoli on the Mediterranean coast but with accommodation for some 13,000 troops it actually boasted a wide range of facilities and sports and educational opportunities.

After what he had experienced in Malaysia and Thailand it must have been tempting for my Dad to ask them what they were moaning about. I've got a picture of him as part of the fencing team, and by all accounts the sports facilities were excellent.

The Surreys had three main roles;

- Defend the Canal Zone border with Egypt and monitor the Egyptian Army close to the TEK base.

- Prevent sabotage

- Protect the base itself from thieves who would be after anything they could get their hands on, including the cables that served the massive garrison.

There were a lot of guard duties to organise and man, with patrols sent out to protect the huge 17 mile perimeter of the base round the clock in the heat and dust of the desert. It must have been a pretty tedious tour of duty and a challenge for my father and his officers to keep spirits up amongst the troops - many of whom were completing their national service. In September 1953 the Battalion was mobilised to defend one of the main Middle East ammunition depots at Abu Sultan, this was an arduous task and was also marked by a long return march to TEK through the desert at night. I wonder now if that had sown a seed in my Dad's mind that maybe his marching days were now coming to an end, maybe it also reminded him of the forced marches a few years earlier in the jungle heat of Thailand.

Time was passed training and organising desert exercises. Whilst he was in Egypt Dad took the slightly odd decision to get himself baptised into the Church Of England and I am not sure what motivated him to do this now he was in his mid thirties but maybe he thought it would be a nice surprise for Mum. When I talked with him about religion much later on he was pretty much agnostic and asked why, if there was an all-seeing and all-powerful god he hadn't intervened to stop his mates being killed in their droves on the railway, in the Hell Ships and in the Japanese camps. There is no evidence that religion played much of a part in his life growing up in Stepney other than benefitting from the charitable handouts linked to the church organisations. It's fair to say he trod lightly where religion was concerned but he would give short shrift to anyone who tried to ram their opinions down his throat.

Tensions were high in the Garrison at Christmas 1953 with an expectation that the Egyptian Army would try to exploit the festive season in the hope that the guard might be dropped, but in the end it passed off peacefully and the troops did their best to celebrate the arrival of another New Year.

Early in 1954 the British Government reached an agreement with the Egyptians to withdraw from the Canal Zone and the Surreys were scheduled to move back to a camp at Shorncliffe in Kent, but Dad had been separated from his sweetheart for 20 months now and must have been missing her badly. His mind was made up. It was time to leave as soon as he could.

He returned from MELF duties on the fourth of January 1954, and was discharged from the Regular Army the next day. His Certificate of Service marks his military conduct as "Exemplary" in the 16 years and 79 days he was in the colours. Not surprisingly his final testimonial was glowing:

> *"He has proved himself to be a very capable, efficient and reliable Warrant Officer.*
>
> *He is well above the average in intelligence and is a hard, accurate and conscientious worker.*
>
> *He is smart in his appearance and has a pleasant, cheerful personality. He gets on well with both his superiors and subordinates, but is nevertheless firm and a good disciplinarian.*
>
> *He is very loyal and completely trustworthy."*

The 17 year old unemployed cockney lad who had wandered into the recruiting office on Whitehall sixteen and a half years earlier, and lied about his age to enlist in the East Surrey Regiment, had been on one extraordinary journey in that time, a journey that had taken him to hell and back but which had also shaped him into the man he now was.

Dad agreed to sign up for the army reserves, but with his testimonial under his belt, and his night school qualification in double entry book keeping, he was ready to embark on a new chapter in his life on Civvy Street. I suspect that my Mum, who had been left alone for the best part of two years while Dad served out his tour in the Canal Zone, had decided that was enough and that despite her own family's military background it was now time for them to settle down properly away from the barracks and the parade ground.

CHAPTER TWENTY THREE

Cold War in Surrey

Mum and Dad moved in with my Nan at 23 Farm Road, Morden and my father landed himself a job as a clerk working in the accounts office at the nearby Merton Park Studios where they kept up with post-war cinema demand, churning out B movie features and classic series like 'Scotland Yard'.

Mum was now working as a secretary at Jarvis's, motor dealers and mechanics, whose Art Deco building was a real landmark on the section of the A24 London Road between Morden and South Wimbledon with its concrete tower. As kids, whenever we passed it in the car we would shout out "that's where Mum used to work!" Sadly, it has long gone, as has the fabulous Wimbledon Palais de Dance, another Art Deco masterpiece up the road where my parents used to go dancing. The Palais had opened in 1922 and boasting the largest sprung floor in Europe was a rival to its more famous namesake in Hammersmith. The pictures of the dance hall in its post war pomp show just what we have lost. I remember it when it was on its last legs as a furniture warehouse, but it was allowed to fall into a poor state of repair and was pulled down.

The St Helier Estate could be quite a lairy place post war, and the local Rose Hill Teds were a notorious handful at the time my parents lived up there. I've always thought they swerved the rock and roll explosion, possibly because they were a bit too old, but also because my Dad had a confrontation with a couple of Teds one evening outside the cinema on the Rose Hill roundabout. He wasn't a violent man, far from it, but he was no mug either and he was a trained soldier who had fought for his life time and time again and wasn't about to get pushed around by anyone, never mind a yobbo in a drape jacket. Dad and Mum were more big band, Matt Monroe and Perry Como, music they loved all their lives.

Dad's soldiering wasn't over yet though as a couple of yellowing and faded press cuttings from the local paper, the Croydon Advertiser of the 2nd August 1957, show that he had now been given a leading role, as Regimental Sergeant Major, in building the military reserve forces in Surrey - recruiting across the county for the 31 (Surrey) Battalion of the Mobile Defence Corp. There's a fabulous picture of him displaying vehicles and equipment out on the streets at a recruitment event in Wellesley Road, Croydon alongside the Civil Defence Corps, the Fire Service and the Special Constabulary. By now my father was talking to the press to promote his new unit:

> *"We are recruiting a very good calibre volunteer," said R.S.M. Clifford Martin, of Farm Road, Morden. "They come from all walks of life and have a varied service background, but we could do with a lot more of them." R.S.M. Martin was formerly a Regular company sergeant-major with the East Surrey Regiment.*

My father had made it to the most senior enlisted rank of the Warrant Officer Class 1 and was now preparing his men for a 15 day training camp at Millom, Cumberland. Weekends would be taken up with his work for the Emergency Reserve. Dad was a very calm and understated man and nothing like the cartoon version of the Sergeant Major you see in TV programmes from that post war/national service era. I remember him telling me that you get nothing out of your troops by shouting at them and bullying them: but on the other hand I know full well that he wouldn't have been a soft touch and would have instilled discipline and pride in his Regiment. There's no question he would have won their respect and loyalty in return, I would dearly have loved to see him in action drilling his men as it was a side of him that I never saw.

The Battalion of the Mobile Defence Corps covering Surrey was part of an intended national network of 48 battalions that had been set up in 1955. They had a specific and gruesome role and that was to provide support to the Civil Defence Forces in the event of a nuclear war. A strategic decision had been taken to establish the Battalions, each around 600 men strong, after the arrival of the hydrogen bomb to reinforce the civil forces in areas under nuclear attack with a "disciplined body under direct military control."

The Mobile Defence Corps was drawn from experienced reservists like Dad and men who had completed their national service. My father would have been selected by the top brass as the senior Non Commissioned Officer in the 31 (Surrey) Battalion. As well as being trained in firefighting, rescue and ambulance duties the men under his leadership would clearly have had a role in helping to protect centres of regional government and maintaining public order on the streets in the period after a nuclear attack. These would have been the early days of the Cold War, which had effectively begun in 1947 and had escalated by 1955 with the formation of the Warsaw Pact bloc and West Germany joining NATO.

The threat of a limited nuclear attack on London and the South East by this point was very real, and scenarios had been war-gamed and detailed plans to move the apparatus of Government into secret and well-defended bunkers had been developed. Food supplies would be stretched, medical facilities were expected to be swamped with casualties, transport and other key infra-structure would be seriously damaged and emergency legislation ready for immediate action had been drafted which would effectively declare martial law on the streets. The Mobile Defence Corps would form a key part of the military operation charged with delivering it. A British Government committee, led by Sir William Strath, reported to ministers on the expected consequences of a nuclear attack on Britain:

> *"Hydrogen bomb warfare would be total war in a sense not hitherto conceived. The entire nation would be in the front line. Life and property would be obliterated by blast and fire on a vast scale. An attack of the size assumed (10 bombs) would unleash an explosive force equivalent to 100 million tons of TNT. This is forty-five times as great as the total tonnage of bombs delivered by all the Allies over Germany, Italy and occupied France throughout the whole of the last war."*

The report of Strath's Committee would remain secret for fifty years. It predicted that the dropping of these ten H-bombs of 10 megatons each would result in ***".....a threat of utmost gravity to our survival as a nation"***. It forecast that the expected level of attack would lead to 12 million dead and 4 million other serious casualties - one third of the population. A further 13 million people would be confined to their damaged homes by fallout, and with food and water supplies contaminated malnutrition and disease would soon be rife.

Although the authorities tried to maintain a position of reassurance that they had plans in place to cope with World War Three, in private they accepted that civil defence measures would simply be unable to cope. There was a major PR exercise as part of that campaign of public reassurance, including the publication of the information pamphlet 'Nuclear Weapons' in 1956, and I'm convinced that the parading of my father, his colleagues and the Mobile Defence Corps equipment in town centres around Surrey at this time was part of that Government public relations initiative. By the mid to late fifties the prospects post a nuclear strike, particularly in London and the Home Counties, were so horrendous that it's almost impossible to see what the Corps could have achieved - assuming any of the men survived the blast and fall-out themselves. However, the Strath Committee believed that the country would have survived in some form and had plans to evacuate over a million people but warned of a total breakdown in civil society:

> *"......there might be complete chaos for a time and civil control would collapse. In such circumstances the local military commander would have to be prepared to take over from the civil authority responsible for the maintenance of law and order and for the administration of government. He would, if called upon, exercise his existing common law powers to take whatever steps, however drastic, he considered necessary to restore order. He would have to direct operations of the various civil agencies including the police, civil defence services and the fire service. In areas less badly hit the civil authorities might still be able to function, but only with the support of the armed services."*

This was martial law in everything but name. My father would have been briefed on these plans as a key player in their potential delivery at the local level and this was another grim and terrifying world outlook he would have to confront and process without breathing a word to anyone.

He never spoke to me or my sister about these times and it was only the faded old press cuttings that he had decided to keep that opened the door into this part of his life. He would have been sworn to secrecy under the Official Secrets Act and would have taken that responsibility extremely seriously. The Mobile Defence Corps were wound down and finally abolished by 1959, as the ending of National Service limited the pool of available men, and the rapidly changing nature of the Cold War and its weaponry called for a different approach. Dad remained in the reserves.

The winding up of the Mobile Defence Corps was debated in the House of Commons on the 3rd December 1958 with the Defence Minister setting out the reasons:

> *"....it has become clear that a Mobile Defence Corps consisting solely of volunteers will not be able to carry out its tasks. In these circumstances I have decided, with regret, that I should inform the Queen that the Corps should be*

> *disbanded at the end of February 1959……I know that the House will want to join me in paying tribute to the volunteer members of the Mobile Defence Corps. The methods which they have developed will be of great value to the Territorial Army units which take up the task. They have also engendered a spirit of close cooperation between the Army and Civil Defence authorities and this will be fostered and maintained under the new arrangements."*

So, another pat on the back for the old man. The immediate post war threat of another world war, this time fought with nuclear weapons, even while rationing and the damage, destruction and loss of life from WW2 were still clear and present across society must have felt like a weight that would never be lifted. It seems from contemporary reports that most people just put it out of their minds and got out there and enjoyed themselves.

While the sounds of rock and roll filled the dance halls and cinemas, hardened soldiers like my Dad were training and drilling men to deal with the next conflict. It must have seemed relentless, and knowing what the likely outcomes were, while the public simply got on with their lives, would have been another burden and responsibility that he carried with him on top of everything else. There must have been something within him that drove him to shoulder that responsibility when he could very easily have walked away and got on with his life as well. I suspect that Mum must have been thinking that enough was enough by now and that he had done more than his share for Queen and country and she would have been dead right.

CHAPTER TWENTY FOUR

Campaigning for Justice

If the FEPOWs thought that being forgotten, unrecognised and told to keep quiet about their experiences was bad enough they were about to have their lives as prisoners on Death Railway completely misrepresented through the release of the award-winning big screen feature 'The Bridge on the River Kwai'.

I didn't realise until quite late in his life just how much my Dad and his comrades despised and disliked that film and why. The film had been released in October 1957 and was an instant box office hit, a group of former prisoners had been invited to a private screening and came away feeling angry and betrayed.

The film was of course a work of fiction but that wasn't made clear and efforts by General Percival himself to persuade the producer Sam Spiegel to state that clearly on screen failed. As a result millions of film goers who flocked to the cinema would potentially come away thinking that this fictional account of life on Death Railway was historically accurate.

As a kid I was obsessed with the war, like most of my mates, and more than two decades after hostilities came to an end there were still air raid shelters and bomb sites to be explored and battles to be read about in comics and reenacted. There was also a regular diet of war movies to be watched in black and white on the telly. I would often watch these with Dad, but I remember him leaving the room when Bridge On The River Kwai came on. I have a recollection of asking him what the problem was and him telling me "it wasn't like that" but I now understand not only why he was angry but also how the film itself may well have triggered his own personal trauma. Not only does the movie create the impression that the POWs worked willingly and were focused on doing a good job but it also completely fails to represent the terrible condition of the men themselves.

It also portrays the central character, the British commander based on Colonel Toosey, as a collaborator, when nothing could be further from the truth. Everything I've read tells a different story, with Toosey widely respected by his men with his leadership putting himself at personal risk and subject to frequent beatings by the guards. My father never came under the command of Colonel Toosey, and was never in the camp at Tamarkan portrayed in the film, and I don't know if their paths ever crossed, but one of Dad's great mates from the East Surreys, Len Jelley, did know him. He set the record straight in an interview he gave for the Queens Royal Surrey Regimental Association:

> *"....the Colonel never wanted us to build the bridge. He taught us all ways to slow it down. Colonel Toosey, a great man, I've never met a man like him and I mean that, a wonderful man."*

I met Len and I know he wasn't the sort of man to lavish praise unless it was well and truly deserved. I hate the idea that many years later the film is still seen by many as an accurate historical account. Some of the brutality is there, but the men look too well fed and clothed. Of course it would be near impossible to find actors to represent the skeletal men in their cobbled together loin cloths riddled with disease and sickness, but I understand well now why Dad and his mates were pissed off. With so little representing their real experiences to the British people this blockbuster movie was now presented almost as if it were some kind of documentary.

David Lean's biographer later wrote that had the director *"shown the extreme brutalities of torture, starvation and suicides, the film would have been unbearable to all but an audience of psychopaths."* But for the former prisoners that in itself was just a reminder that their real story would rarely, if ever, be told. They would just have to put up with having their experiences sanitised and misrepresented for public consumption. 'Bridge on the River Kwai' may well have just been categorised as a 'drama movie' by those involved in its production, but such is the power of popular culture that for many it would lodge in their minds as the only representation of life for the Far East prisoners that they would recognise. That was the real problem for my father.

John Coast, a young British officer who wrote of his experiences as a prisoner in his book *'Railroad of Death'*, the original account of life and death on the railway, had this description of the film some years after its release:

> *"As nobody should ever have need telling, the picture is a load of high-toned codswallop."*

If you were struggling to prevent yourself being consumed by bitterness after the years of captivity, brutality and death there must have been times when it seemed like the world was conspiring against you. My father had a lot of other things to focus on, but if it hadn't been for his own ambition, the love of my Mum and the support of his pals it's quite possible that he could have lost his way under the weight of his own trauma and anger.

Often when I talk to people about my Dad they will recall that as kids they knew someone who'd come back from Death Railway and who never talked about it, painting a picture of reserved, quiet and broken men.

Many had decided early on not to talk about their experiences unless pressed, like my Dad, but they didn't need pity, they needed support, respect and someone to honestly tell their story.

Dad believed for many years that no one was really interested in what he had to say, and in some respects he was probably right. Sometimes he would meet people who did find out about his past and they would say knowingly that they had seen Bridge on the River Kwai as if it put them in the picture. He wouldn't bother putting them straight. His truth wouldn't start to emerge until much later.

A couple of years after leaving the colours Dad managed to get himself onto the career ladder and the job stability that he craved. Using the leverage of his work experience at the film studios, and the testimonial and qualifications picked up during his army years, he got himself in at the lower rungs of the clerical side in the civil service. He remained a government employee the rest of his working life. The regular work and salary meant that, with some support from my Nan's life savings, my parents were now able to scrape together enough to apply for a mortgage and move out of the rented house in Morden.

There was a post war speculative housing boom, with new developments springing up everywhere and they started hunting for a base to embark on the next chapter of their lives together. For my Dad these must have been exciting times, and times that he could only have dreamt of in his fitful and exhausted sleep in the ragged, fly blown camps of the death railway.

His demons and physical reminders hadn't left him, but that hope for a brighter future, supported by the love of my Mum, must have helped to keep them at bay. He now had a mortgage offer in principle from the Woolwich Building Society in his back pocket and it must have felt fantastic. Only a generation before a working class boy from Stepney wouldn't have been expected even to aspire to own his own home, let alone make it a reality, unless he had struck it lucky in business. But come the 1950s the world had changed, and my parents were embracing that.

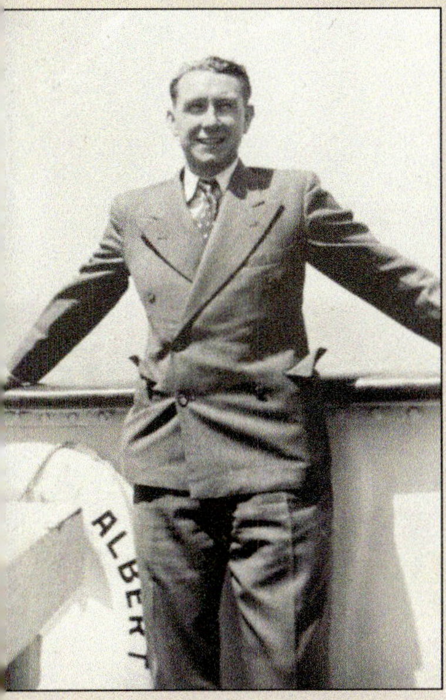

Dad looking fit and sharp 1951

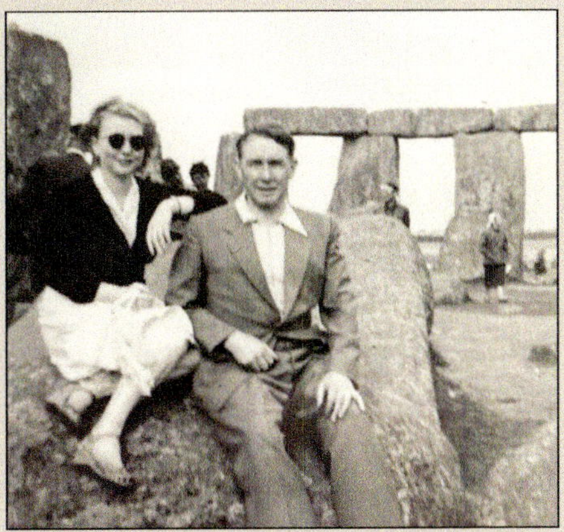

Mum and dad at Stonehenge 1954

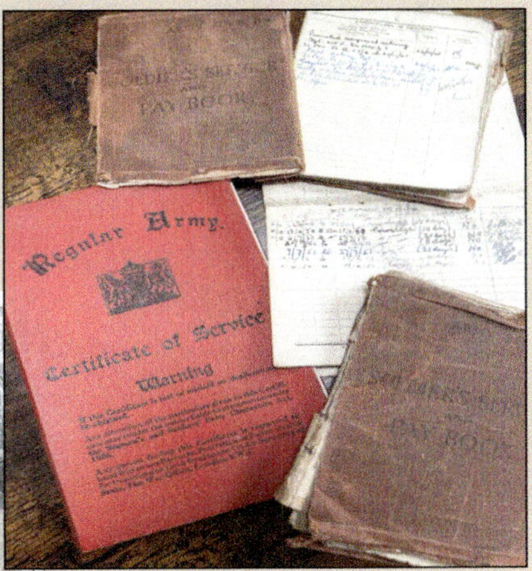

Dad's certificate of service and the battered remains of his pay books

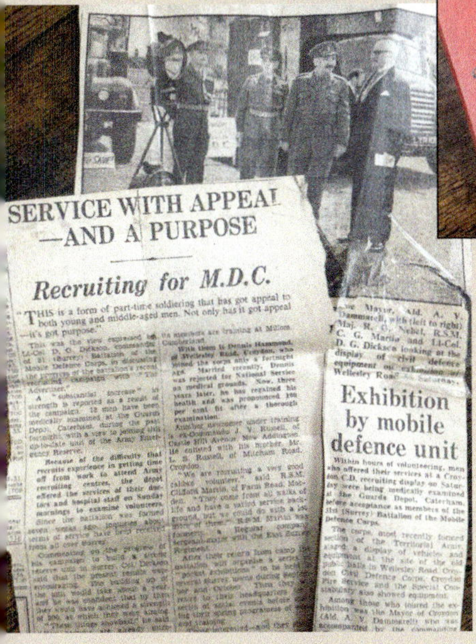

Press coverage of Dad recruiting post war for the Mobile Defence Corps

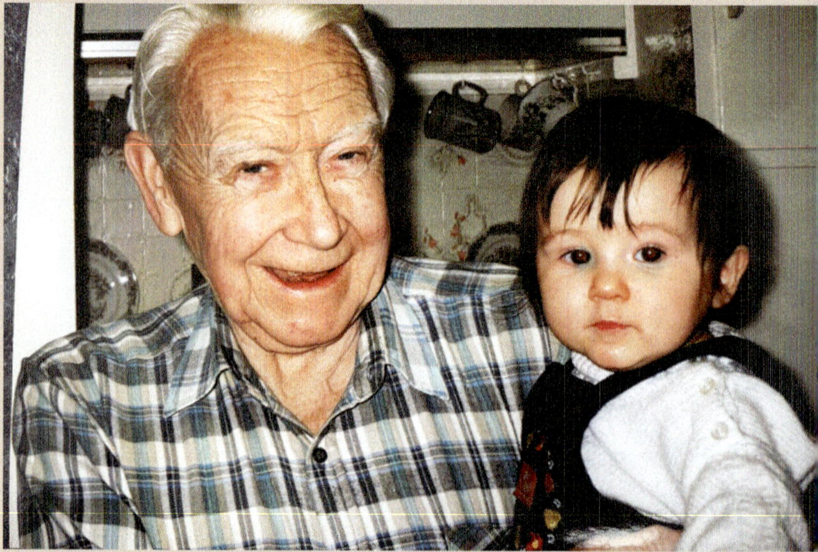

Dad later in life with my daughter Katie. His grandchildren were his pride and joy

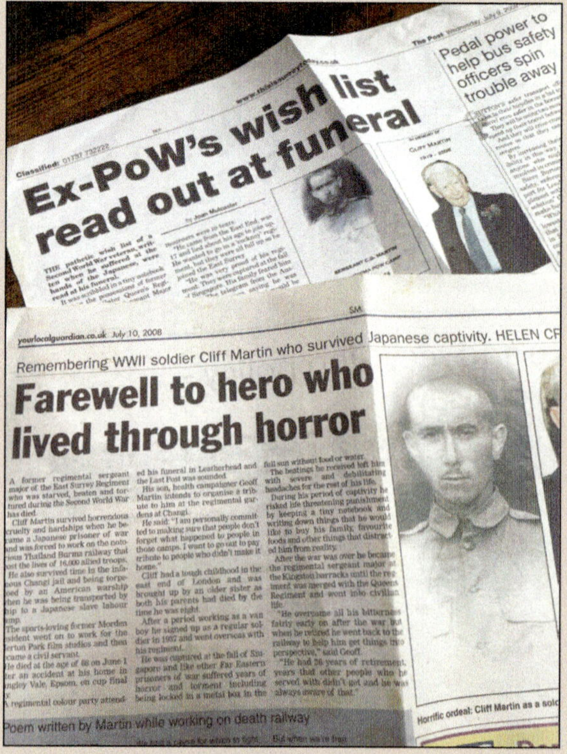

Local press coverage of Dad's funeral

Eventually they settled on a new housing development that was being built on Epsom Downs in a village called Langley Vale, almost a stone's throw from the start of the famous race course. It was to prove a brilliant choice as my parents remained there for the rest of their lives. For Dad this was his dream coming true, the roads and houses had been carved out of land that was formerly Langley Bottom Farm. To be at last surrounded by the open fields of the Downs must have done wonders for his mental well-being after a lifetime being hemmed in by the streets of the East End, the dense jungle of the prison camps and the brick walls of the barracks.

So in 1957 they collected the keys and moved into a small semi-detached house with a driveway and garden in Beaconsfield Road in Langley Vale. My Nan who had helped them get their deposit together came with them from Farm Road Morden and would stay in the house until the family grew and she moved out over to a council flat in Curtis Road on the Watersedge Estate in Ewell. My Mum and Dad threw themselves into getting their dream home in shape, it was pretty much a bare shell and the garden needed to be levelled. Dad developed a life-long love of gardening and DIY and with the help of Uncle Frank shifted tons of earth to get his little patch of land how he wanted it. Right up to his later years he would spend hours and hours out there, alone with his thoughts. I know it must have done him no end of good.

This was pretty much everything he had ever hoped for but there was one thing missing, the kids he craved. Those years of deprivation would have a long term impact on many aspects of a man's health, including fertility, and after nearly ten years of marriage I know that Mum and Dad would have been worried. I also know they at least considered the idea of adoption, but in the winter of 1958, a year or so after they moved into their new home, they got the news they wanted to hear.

My sister Janette was born on the 8th August 1959. She was a strong, healthy baby and her arrival would have brought huge joy to 42 Beaconsfield Road. She would prove to be a brilliant daughter and a great sister and we were lucky to be brought up in a loving home with parents who would have sacrificed anything for us. They may have gravitated away from their London roots but they instilled in us working class values and as time went on we came to appreciate more and more the back story that helped to make us the people that we are. Mum and Dad made great and lasting friendships amongst their new and growing community and would throw themselves into events and activities. I look back now and wonder how many really knew Dad's story. To him it didn't really matter, and to most to them he was just Cliff Martin who was always about to lend a hand when needed. That was exactly how he wanted it.

Dad was still in the military reserve, and less than a year after Jan was born he was off on an exercise again, possibly overseas as although I can find no records of his unit's movements at this time I do have a letter written to him by Mum on airmail paper. Clearly she was missing him badly, and talks about the progress in the garden and the baby's first teeth coming through, the letter is dated the 25th June 1960. I think this was Dad's last days with the military as with a new home, a young family and a career in the civil service taking up his time now it would be hard to maintain the level of commitment required.

Well over two decades after he first stepped through the doors of the central recruiting office in Whitehall, and after all that had happened to him since, he had done his time and I suspect that decision would have come as a huge relief to Mum. He was finally officially discharged from the Army Emergency Reserve on the 26th July 1961 with his papers showing *his services no longer being required on reorganisation of the AER.*

Of course the military would never leave him: his experiences, memories and personal trauma would not allow that. The black and white snaps of my father at this time in the early sixties show a strong, fit and healthy man usually with a broad smile on his face. But behind that smile were the persistent headaches and the physical reminder of his beatings from the unhealed ridge on his skull that he would constantly run his hand over. And the stuff in his head that he could never escape, the nightmares, the memories of his mates who he had watched die - starved, sick and beaten - and the residue of bitterness at the failures and incompetence that had stolen his youth from him. All this remained bottled up, the mental scars far outweighed the physical but the headaches, and his self-medication with aspirin to ease the pain, were storing up a time bomb.

I have no record of my father receiving any practical support from the authorities at this time. The Liverpool School of Tropical Medicine had set up a centre carrying out Tropical Disease Investigations (TDIs) with Far East prisoners with its work dating right back to the point of liberation. Many men had benefited from the LSTM work in the early months after their return to the UK but they tended to be from the North West. The Centre found that prisoners were still suffering relapses of amoebic dysentery and malaria years after release. By the sixties it had become the primary centre of investigations into the long term health effects of Far East captivity and along with physical health it also looked at the psychological impact and was recording symptoms associated with post-traumatic stress disorder (PTSD), years before it became a recognised condition. The LSTD was carrying out brilliant and innovative work, but access to its services seem to be random and geographical, and that was a real shame for men like my Dad who were ticking time bombs.

There was a service offered at the much closer Queen Mary's Hospital in Roehampton, and some East Surreys men were admitted there for treatment of residual medical conditions like malaria and dysentery on their return to England, but I don't think Dad ever sought the hospital's help. I suspect that was down to him trying to preserve his A1 army medical status, the same reason he never admitted to the chronic headaches from wartime beatings that still plagued him. He was in an impossible position, if he asked for help early on it could have meant him being discharged from the army and the regiment he had become such a part of. He should never have been left to face such a choice.

Dad's own work life, ironically, was now centred on the National Health Service and he was working his way up the career ladder. It must have been a wrench for him to sever his active involvement with the army but he still kept in touch with his old comrades through his Regimental Association and the FEPOW organisation Mum was a housewife although in time she would return to part time work as an assistant at the local play group. Mum also managed the household budget right to the nearest penny. My parents never took on any debt, other than the mortgage secured on their house, and if they wanted something they saved up and paid for it outright. Hire purchase was all the rage, but the whole idea was at odds with their pre war and wartime upbringing.

I was born on the 17th September 1962, in the run up to the Cuban Missile crisis. As the world held its breath and teetered on the brink of nuclear annihilation a premature and jaundiced baby was fighting for his life in an incubator at Epsom General Hospital while his Mum and Dad kept vigil. For my father, these would be traumatic days. Having cheated death himself so many times as a prisoner of war in Changi, on Death Railway, on the Hell Ships back to Japan and finally in the brutal Mitsushima Camp he now had to steel himself and stay strong again. He would have paced the floor, summoning up that power of hope that had sustained him in his darkest hours and doing whatever he could to give strength and succour to the son lying in a glass cot, plugged into pipes and wires in these early days of modern paediatric intensive care.

A few years later the same hospital would save his life when self-medication to alleviate the continuing pain directly linked to his years in captivity would see him rushed into emergency surgery. Much later still I was proud to march with him in protests to save the hospital that saved both our lives. I survived of course, and was carted home in our trusty Hillman Minx in that savage cold winter of 62/63. I still have the scars from the stitches around my belly button where blood transfusions were piped into my tiny, sick, frail body and my old man would later boast to people that "He's got none of his own blood you know!" as he bigged up the little medical miracle clinging to his strong hand.

Throughout the sixties Dad was working for the DHSS in the new Alexander Fleming House building at the Elephant and Castle and in 1969 he took on a role at the newly formed Hospital Advisory Service, an independent regulatory body set up to report to the Secretary of State for Social Services on hospitals in England, focussing on mental health and geriatric care. The objective of the service was to help hospitals improve the management of patient care by offering advice and spreading good practice. Inspections were carried out by a multi-disciplinary team of medical professionals and my father worked on organising the visits and drawing up the team's reports. The new role also meant a shift of office to a building in Sutton right by the railway station. He would drive over there from Epsom in his generally trusty old green Hillman minx, (reg MPE 46D), and on cold mornings he would be out there on the drive cursing as he tried to kick the engine into life with a turn of the starting handle.

CHAPTER TWENTY FIVE

Haunted by the Past

In 1971 Dad danced with death yet again. Feeling rough at work he was lucky that a consultant was in the building who took one long look at him and called an emergency ambulance. That decisive action saved his life, because little did he know internally it was ebbing away. Between 1964 and 1967 the headaches caused from the beating with a log by the guards while he was working on the railway with the elephants had got progressively worse and he was taking up to sixteen aspirins a day for relief. Dad eventually consulted his doctor who helped wean him off that level of self-medication but instead prescribed him the drug Equaprin.

He was referred to the neurological department at Guys Hospital and, unable to find any other solution for the headaches, the Equaprin was continued and it was this drug, subsequently banned, that had caused an ulcer and that ulcer had perforated and he was haemorrhaging and losing blood rapidly. The ambulance rushed him into Epsom Hospital where the team got to work and immediately opened him up. Dad told me that he remembered being rushed on a trolley semi-conscious and into theatres but as he drifted away he saw a light at the end of a corridor and someone beckoning him forwards but he was protesting that it wasn't his time yet and he had a young family. I know that this kind of recollection is common with people who have been through a near-death experience and may be related to the medication and the general trauma – but Dad was not one to spin a line, and he believed till the day he died that something stopped him getting dragged over the edge. I would put it down to the brilliance of the medical team and maybe his own strength and resilience but whatever, the surgeons pulled him through, and he lived to tell the tale.

I was only eight years old when this crisis rocked our little world but I can remember Mum crying and us as a family visiting Dad in intensive care with wires and tubes everywhere as he began his recovery. Eventually he came home and all I knew then was that something very serious had happened and that the strong Dad that I had got used to was much weaker and had a long vertical scar and bulge on his stomach where they had opened him up which he had to dress every day. I couldn't jump on his lap like I used to, and he needed to get his rest but over time he was back to fighting fitness and getting on with his life and earning a living.

The scarring from his surgery would be another permanent reminder of how he had swerved death yet again. 28 years after being beaten with in an inch of his life by a Japanese guard in the steaming Thai jungle, the events of that day had chased him down over nearly three decades. The drugs that had rotted a hole through his guts had only been prescribed to alleviate the legacy of pain that he carried with him through the years since liberation. It was a reminder that he could never be truly free from his past no matter how hard he tried.

As my sister and I grew up Dad kept much of what had happened to him from us, this would have been a conscious decision. All he really wanted was for us to have normal and happy childhoods: and that is exactly what we enjoyed in the warm and loving family home our parents had brought us into. Looking back now, I realise that the long shadow his experiences cast was never far away.

I got used to his nightmares, the shouts and screams in the night, but over time medication helped him to sleep better and maybe the demons who were always lurking in the dead of night waiting to taunt him once again started to fade as well. I've read that those suffering from acute Post Traumatic Stress Disorder can be afraid of sleep itself because they know what is coming and through the eyes of my father I can understand that. Dad seemed most content when he nodded off on the settee after a day's work and his dinner with the TV on and his family around him. That was when he was at his most relaxed, and that makes perfect sense.

I cannot remember when I first began to have any understanding at all of what my father had actually been through but it may well have been when the epic 'World At War' documentary series dealt with the theatre in the Far East. Although the episode only dealt briefly with the fall of Singapore, and Death Railway, the grainy images of skeletal men in their loin cloths and the statistics on deaths and sickness on the railway must have struck a nerve with me - that was my Dad. After that I did ask him questions, I was a kid, I wanted to know stuff and the war was a subject that fascinated me and my mates as part of that baby boomer generation. Dad told me a few self-censored bits and pieces, I think he would have wanted us to know about his life in broad brush terms but I suspect that he would have had a discussion with Mum very early on and that they had agreed that he wouldn't overwhelm us.

Gradually, over time, I would get to know more but it wasn't until I retired myself that I would eventually spend time piecing the whole story together as best I can. It would also take me time to realise that telling my father's story is part of my own quest for identity and finding some personal meaning and closure from unearthing as much of the truth of what happened to him more than eighty years ago as I can. I have come to understand that I am by no means alone as a child of a FEPOW in taking this journey later in my own life as Terry Smyth points out in his important study *Captive Fathers, Captive Children.*

Looking back now there were tell tale signs that the years of captivity never really loosened their grip on him. If Dad ate a piece of cake he would hold it over a newspaper and then carefully lick his finger and pick up every last crumb until the paper was clear. He absolutely detested food waste. A rare family treat would be a trip to the Wimpy Bar in Morden, and if you didn't eat the lot you wouldn't be going again in a hurry. To be honest I didn't need much incentive to polish off a Bender Brunch.

As a kid I thought it was a pain that we weren't allowed to leave the table until we had finished our dinner but I didn't factor in that the man sitting opposite me had spent three and half years close to death from starvation and before the war had grown up in abject poverty. And if you were feeling a bit peckish and said you were starving he would raise an eyebrow at you quite understandably, sometimes he didn't need to say much.

I have a hazy memory as a kid of Dad taking me to the Imperial War Museum in South London. The huge naval guns outside took my breath away and I was fascinated and quite scared by the atmospheric reconstruction of First World War trenches. But there was also a small area with some artefacts from the Japanese camps and Death Railway. I can recall as I write these words some hand-made surgeons instruments and one of the false legs built out of scraps for the amputees. I'm ashamed to say that I wasn't very interested. It had none of the drama of the D-Day exhibits in the next hall.

We passed through quickly and I think my father would have had tears in his eyes, not from my schoolboy ignorance but as his own memories were triggered by these fragments of war that were all too real for him. He said nothing, but did the sight of that scratch-built saw that had been used to hack off countless ulcerated legs in a squalid bamboo hut while men screamed out in pain invite those nightmares back in that evening? I will never know but suddenly being confronted with his past as we turned that corner rocked him back on his heels and I just wish I'd understood more and been able to help him in some way.

Dad very rarely lost his temper. I've read reports that some of the men who came back from the Far East were so angry and damaged they became violent and abusive in their later relationships, and I thank our lucky stars that despite everything our father carried with him, physically and in his head, he remained a kind, gentle and loving man to whom family was everything. My parents made a decision before Jan and I were born that Mum would be in charge of discipline, and she was not to be messed with. I don't recall my father ever lifting a hand to me despite some extreme provocation on my part as I was growing up. This was a time when giving your kids a slap to keep them in line was perfectly normal, Dad had seen enough causal violence to know that it was never a solution.

Apart from his family Dad's pride and joy was his house and his garden. A keen and meticulous DIYer, he would have a go at most things around the house and was particularly proud of his wallpapering skills. This was in the days before the DIY superstore and if he needed any paint, paper or other materials we would pile into the old Hillman and whiz down to the hardware store just under the bridge by Epsom station and be served by a chatty geezer in a brown coat smoking a pipe. Dad would engage in a long discussion about knotting or sandpaper grades while I poked around fascinated by the array of goods on display. I loved the smell and feel of those places, and we would come away with various bits and pieces like original wooden Rawlplugs packed carefully in brown paper bags and tied up with string. These were such lovely vivid memories: I can't imagine my kids reminiscing in years ahead about the times I took them to Wickes.

But his garden was his real oasis. He had carved it out himself from a bare patch of builders' rubble and would spend hours out there spraying for pests and fungus with a brass pump, pruning and taking cuttings, sharpening the blades on his old cylinder lawn mower and watering and nurturing his plants. This was therapy for him, alone with nature and his thoughts and I understand it totally. I've got a press cutting from the local paper where Cliff Martin of 42 Beaconsfield Road won first prize for his gooseberries in a flower show at the church hall. He would have been absolutely chuffed to bits. Fruit and vegetables were very much his speciality and when Mum cooked up a rhubarb crumble from sticks he had pulled from the garden that morning it would have tasted like the best grub ever. He would pick her some roses to thank her for everything.

If he wasn't out in the garden or doing a bit of DIY he would be out in the garage fiddling around with his motor. These were the years when most blokes were expected to turn their hands to car maintenance and repairs. Bits of rusting bodywork on the Hillman Minx would be repaired with patches of fibreglass and filler and he would do his own servicing. I loved helping him out, passing him spanners out of his old tool box.

The smell of Dad's garage lives on with me and I have an old Morris Minor in mine from that same era that I tinker with and have accumulated many of the same tools that he used to use, it just takes me back to a more primitive and hands-on time that has been lost. But Dad had no real love of old cars, this was 'needs must' more than a hobby.

One family trip back from a day out to Frensham Ponds when a wheel sheared off and went rolling off down the hill was laughed about later, but not at the time. As soon as he managed to scrape together enough cash he went out and bought a new motor, under warranty, and paid someone else to service it. That was another aspiration chalked off.

Dad welcomed the dawn of every new day, I think he understandably saw each one as a bonus that he was lucky to be able to enjoy and I also realise now that the daylight would release him from the nightmares that pursued him right to the very end.

Up early, he would do his army PT exercises, stick on the radio, feed the cat and take Mum a cup of tea in bed before getting his gear together to have a shave - always a proper old bladed razor, soap and a brush. It was an important daily ritual, even in the worst camps up the north on Death Railway the men would try to retain some dignity by shaving by whatever means possible and keeping their hair cut.

My Dad always took his tea strong and a pot, using leaves not bags, would be brewed up early and kept stewing with a tea cosy to keep it warm. He passed that love of strong tea on to me. I always thought it was an old Cockney thing, but in fact it was another legacy of the camps. The prisoners would get an occasional tea ration and the leaves would be reused over and over until the tea was, in his words "weak as piss," so a good strong cuppa, with just a splash of milk, was a lifetime joy for him. I remember fondly cold winter mornings as a boy when he would wake me early with a steaming cup and we would listen to Lindsey Hasset and Richie Benaud commentating on Ashes test matches on his old wireless live from Australia, just some of the best father and son times.

In his youth Dad had been a fine sportsman both pre and post war, playing football, cricket, hockey and tennis and I even have pictures of him from the early fifties as a member of the regimental fencing team. By the time I came along he was no longer playing sports himself although every morning he would get up early and do a set of military exercises, press ups and stretches - he kept himself in shape. We watched sport on the TV, and although I can't remember the 1966 World Cup I do have the vaguest recollections of the FA Cup final in 1967 with Spurs beating Chelsea.

Around that time me and my oldest mate Robbie Poacher had declared ourselves as Chelsea fans - Epsom was very much blue territory in many ways. So that meant relentlessly nagging my Dad to take me to Stamford Bridge. The first professional team he had seen was Millwall in the early thirties although he became a Fulham supporter after liberation as it was convenient for the East Surreys barracks, him and Mum would bus it from Kingston to Putney, watch the game at Craven Cottage and then head up the West End for a night out.

I must have nagged him for years about going to the football, and he would come up with all sorts of excuses (one of the best was that I wouldn't be able to stand up for ninety minutes). He held the line, although I do remember he landed a couple of tickets for a test match at the Oval and we went along to that together. I must have been about ten years old and it was just the best thing hanging onto Dad's hand as we wound our way through the crowds on the Harleyford Road, eventually emerging into that huge open arena for the first time. We would go to quite a few test matches together after that, and they were the best of times.

In 1974 I surprised everyone, not least my teachers and myself, and passed the 11-plus which meant entry to the local grammar school, Glyn in Ewell. The head teacher at St Martin's CofE called my Mum and Dad in and advised them that the pass must have been some sort of mistake and they should decline the offer of the grammar place. Dad rarely got angry, but he was absolutely bloody furious. He had been denied a scholarship and a decent education himself due to cost and class and now his boy was having opportunity snatched away from him – and so the papers were signed taking up the place and that was the end of it.

I didn't want to go to Glyn, I wanted to go to either of the local secondary modern schools in Epsom or Leatherhead with my mates, none of whom passed the 11 plus, but the decision was made and I decided to get my head down and graft to prove the teachers wrong. I'd like to say it was to make my parents proud, but although there may have been some of that going on it was really down to my own stubbornness and personal pride.

Dad had promised that if I passed the 11-plus he would take me to Chelsea, and now he was lumbered as he was a man of his word. So we headed off to the railway station for the rattler to Wimbledon to pick up the District Line on a lovely September morning. By the time the tube train had reached Parsons Green a large group of boot boys had pretty much taken it apart. My Dad shoved back one of them who had bounced into him on his DMs, and as he stood his ground I realise now that he could very easily have had the shit kicked out of him, but he had no fear at all, other than for my safety. That was the last time we went to Stamford Bridge.

A couple of weeks later we headed down to Gander Green Lane, the home of Sutton United, and for a season or two we went to games together, including some of the away grounds, and I loved it. A special treat before home matches would be lunch at the greasy spoon at the old covered market in Sutton. Although Dad enjoyed these trips, and we had found a football experience we could both appreciate, I recognise now that he was giving up a chunk of his precious weekends primarily to make me happy. On the way home we would tune in to Sports Report as the old medium wave signal faded in and out and discuss the afternoon's entertainment and the Chelsea and Fulham results. These are more magic father and son memories that I treasure. Of course, by the time I hit my teens I didn't want to go to the match with the old man anymore. He went back to his vegetable patch and I acquired a pair of Dr Martens and it wasn't long before I was bouncing up and down in tube trains and on the terraces with my mates.

As far as I remember Dad never went back to the East End after he had gravitated out to the suburbs. He didn't have much reason to. Apart from one of his much older brothers, Albert, who had moved to Hackney the rest of the family had been part of the great pre and post war cockney exodus. The two siblings he remained closest to were Uncle Gus and Auntie May. Before the M25 was built the only way out to the giant Becontree LCC estate to see May was up and over Tower Bridge and on through the streets of East London: the same with Gus who now lived in Harold Wood. Dad would call out the names of the pubs and other buildings and landmarks as we rolled past.

After he retired I asked him if he wanted to go with me back to the old manor and retrace his early roots, but he wasn't interested. I realise now that his memories weren't that great. The death of his parents while he was still a child, poverty, unemployment and homelessness had driven him away and although he was undoubtedly a proud cockney he hated the idea of romanticising the grim reality of Stepney in the 1920s and 1930s. He had no desire to dredge all that up.

Auntie May, who had brought Dad up when he was orphaned, died when I was a child and that must have hit him hard. All of his attempts to write home from the POW camps had gone to her, she was listed as his next of kin and he also used her home at 98 Fanshawe Crescent, Dagenham as his address on all of his Japanese records, even though he never lived there. I remember her as a warm and kind woman with a diamond-edged cockney accent, but it appears from my research that May was a nickname that stuck from childhood. Her real birth name before she was married was Helen Martin - my wife's name. That was a bolt out of the blue when I first saw it on a couple of documents. What goes around comes around.

Dad lost contact with some of his older brothers, maybe the odd phone call and a Christmas card, but he maintained a strong relationship with Uncle Gus who was a truly lovely man and me and Jan always looked forward to trips across London to their house. We would be given a bag of chocolate bars and Auntie Muriel would put on a superb spread for tea - it was the first place I had salt beef. Before we left, a bottle of Johnnie Walker black label would be produced on a silver tray with a small jug of water, and Gus and Dad would have a couple of nips before we headed home.

Martin family legend has it that Uncle Gus had been captured by the Italians during the war but after Mussolini was hung from a lamp post by the partisans the prison camp gates were opened up. Despite orders from the officers to stay put, Gus and thousands of other British soldiers decided they weren't going to hang about waiting for the Germans to turn up, and had it on their toes. He apparently made it to Switzerland where he holed up on a cattle farm, sleeping in a barn and helping out until he was eventually repatriated. His story couldn't have been much different from his younger brother's, and Dad was cool enough to laugh about that.

Gus was also an absolute ringer for sixties and seventies comedian and entertainer Harry Worth, to such an extent that he would often get pestered for autographs while out shopping in Romford and eventually decided that it was easier to just sign them rather than trying to explain that it was a case of mistaken identity. Uncle Gus made it well into his nineties, but when I took Dad to see him in a nursing home shortly before he died it upset my father enormously - they were piping Vera Lynn and other WW2 tunes through speakers on a loop and the place smelt of death and piss and had that grim finality of a waiting room. Dad was in tears as we sat in my car and he asked me to promise him that I'd never allow him to end up in a place like that. It was a promise I couldn't make him but I'm glad he never did.

CHAPTER TWENTY SIX

The Fight for a War Pension

By his 65th birthday in 1984 my father had retired from work and was collecting the occupational and old age pensions that he deserved and had worked for. But his request for a war pension based on the health issues attributable to his army service had been knocked back in 1981, a decision he appealed and lost despite the fact that the War Pensions Agency accepted that a number of medical conditions were clearly service related.

It's hard to believe that any official giving my Dad's records even the most cursory of examinations could conclude that he wasn't worthy of a full pension, never mind a "nil award", but that's what happened. So when he should have been kicking back and taking it easy he had to stand up and fight all over again. And that's exactly what he did with the support of the London Branch of the Far East Prisoner Of War Association.

It's clear that he didn't find it easy to cast his mind back and dredge up memories that would refuel his lasting trauma as he points out in a letter to the Agency:

> *"I also return the questionnaire you sent which I have tried to complete to the best of my ability but it was difficult to cast my mind back through the years.*

Also with my army service I have found it difficult trying to fathom what it is you require. I have opted to tick "High Noise Level" as I have recalled the cacophony of sound during our battles with the Japanese due to the explosions from their shells and mortar bombs falling around our positions and the return fire from our own artillery…."

It took him 12 years but eventually I remember him being admitted to the Queen Elizabeth Military Hospital in Woolwich for a week of tests and assessments, and it was the report from these examinations that eventually landed him some of what he deserved based on the following being attributable to service:

Basal cell carcinoma

Contusion of occiput

Malaria

Dysentery

Malnutrition and privation (including beri-beri) with associated nervous features

Dengue fever

Ringworm

Scabies

Bilateral sensorineural hearing loss

The basal cell carcinoma was the early signs of skin cancer and the contusion of the occiput was the lasting damage to his skull and his brain from the beatings by Japanese guards. A letter from the Agency in June 1993, confirming his award of a pension at last, also makes a passing and clumsily written reference to his ongoing trauma:

"Our doctors have told us that the conditions nightmares and bad dreams are part and parcel of your accepted condition malnutrition and privation (including beri-beri) with associated nervous features and any disablement from it is included in the assessment."

That is the only recognition by the authorities of the mental or psychological impact of the suffering related to his war time service.

When I first introduced my wife to my Dad and told him she was a nurse he shot upstairs to bring out his medical file and, despite a career in intensive care, she was stunned to see the catalogue of conditions this beaming and happy fella had survived. But despite all the evidence my father still didn't get a full war pension. His skin cancer, attributable to years of exposure to the jungle sun on the railway, worsened, and although it proved to be treatable, in January 2003 the Veterans Agency agreed to bump his pension up a bit to 90% - just a few years before he died.

Dad wasn't a cynical man, although he clearly had good reasons to be, but I do remember him thinking that the Agency had only relented on his war pension case and others because they knew the remaining FEPOWs wouldn't be around much longer. I think he was absolutely right. By now he was profoundly deaf: old age and the battering his body had taken was catching up with him. He could no longer drive, and that was difficult for him as he had lost some of the independence he so valued.

My Dad also felt that he had been treated like some sort of scrounger and he hated that, he was a proud man who had fought for King and Country and who had worked all his life. The war pension made a big difference to him and my Mum in their later years. It meant that they could live in some comfort and didn't really need to worry about money any more. And that's exactly as it should have been after all he had been through.

It was wrong that he had had to argue his case line by line when it was so clear cut, and it was wrong that despite the mountain of evidence he had had his entitlement chiselled away as time rolled on. I've heard it said that you can judge a nation by the way it treats its veterans and in the case of my Dad this country failed him and only really made partial amends when it was very late in the day. Campaigners are still fighting for justice for military veterans today, notably those who witnessed the post-war nuclear tests, and my father would have been proud to march alongside them in solidarity.

I really wouldn't want to give the impression that my Dad was totally consumed with fighting for personal and collective recognition for the FEPOWs. Important though it was to him he had other things to be getting on with and that included living life to the full. My parents would stick aside money for holidays and at Pontins holiday camps they would always be one of the first couples up on the dance floor. Dad wasn't a big drinker, but he loved a beer or a gin and tonic and he was great company and never happier than when he was out and about with friends who shared some of his background.

I would often go to his Regimental reunions at the TA barracks in Kingston and listen in as he chatted with men like Dave Boorer, a fellow East Surreys sergeant who had been with him since the early days of the war and survived a similar journey. When checking Dave's records I found that the little house in Garth Road, Morden that he had grown up in was the same house he returned to after the war and where he eventually saw out the rest of his days. I lived in Garth Road for a while and popped in and saw Dave occasionally and I dearly wish I had recorded our conversations as we chatted over a glass of Famous Grouse.

One of the other old 2nd Battalion East Surrey comrades Dad would spend a lot of time chatting with was Len Jelley. Like Dave Boorer they shared the bond that only men who have been to hell and back together can know. Len had been with Dad all the way from Shanghai to the battles down Malaysia and the eventual fall of Singapore. They also would have shared that first nightmare journey up through the jungle to Bon Pang as they joined some of the first groups of prisoners slaving on Death Railway until sickness and different work details eventually separated them. Len was another East Surrey man who had had a miraculous escape from the Japanese massacre at the Alexandra Hospital, mentioned earlier in the lead up to the fall of Singapore, where he was an eyewitness to the bayoneting of patients and staff. He survived by jumping out of his bed and laying on the floor but out of the corner of his eye he saw another East Surrey man Private Deakin being murdered on a stretcher by the rampaging troops. Len, who like my father stayed in the colours and rose to the rank of Company Sergeant Major, also gave an interview to the Regimental museum where he talked about the working conditions at Kin Sai Yok:

> *"....we were building a railway cutting. As soon as you took the top soil off there were big granite stones so they all had to be blasted out and there is nothing worse than walking over blasted granite after it has been blasted with dynamite with no shoes on your feet. We suffered there, believe me, very much so."*

Len remained in Thailand for the rest of the war and was eventually liberated from a place called Ubon near the Laos border where he was part of a crew digging a runway for an aerodrome, labouring right to the very end. He would have made a different journey back to the UK than Dad but it must have been an extraordinary thing when these last surviving fragments of the 2nd Battalion East Surreys were eventually reunited. None of them knew who had lived and who had died as they were split up along the route of their individual journeys. It's no wonder they kept in touch and leaned on each other for support. Few other people would have been able to understand the horrors that they shared. Their network was crucial and lasted for the rest of their lives.

Like Dad, Len was one of the driving forces in the regimental association and they ran the annual Christmas draw together, and that was always one of the top nights of the year when I was growing up. I am just eternally glad that this special band of men had each other or the story might have been very different, effectively they were their own support group although I doubt that they would have seen it quite like that, they were just old mates doing what old mates do.

Another 2nd Battalion East Surrey man Fred Cox wrote in his memoir, *'Faith, Hope and Rice'*:

> *".....many former prisoners of war still carry not only the physical scars from those years of captivity, but also the kind of scars which cannot be seen. Some have felt unable to*

talk about what they experienced, ever, to anyone. Back in 1945, when we met people from what we then thought of as the outside world for the first time in three and a half years, I know I wasn't the only one who felt that perhaps the only people who could really understand what those years had been like were those of us who had been there. Amongst ourselves there was no need to try to explain anything, but with other people it was hard to try to describe the awful things we had seen or the things we had sometimes had to do in order to survive. It had been our own hell and sharing it with others was difficult."

Johnny Sherwood, in his book *'Lucky Johnny'*, recalled how over a few beers in London he would talk with fellow survivors about the very worst of their experiences, conversations they wouldn't have with anyone else:

"I have met up with several of my old POW friends since the war and we've talked about our terrible times together in the death camps. It seems to help us to go back over our worst memories together, as if it somehow lessens our trauma and pain.

'Do you remember those cages? I asked Reg one time when we met up in London.

'I'll never forget them,' he said, with the emphasis on the 'never'.......

It was a punishment that used to happen in most of the camps and it still makes me shudder when I remember it now. These brutal Japanese and Korean guards used to build very small bamboo cages, and when anyone did anything that displeased them, he was thrown into one of them, just like you might do with an animal.....

A man would be caged like that, not even able to stretch his back, for several days at a time, and when he was finally released he could no longer stand up."

These were the kind of memories that shaped the men's repeated nightmares and for those who carried them in their head all the time the only chance they would get to share them was with those who knew and understood. It must have been a huge relief and comfort for men like

Johnny and my Dad to know that they at least had that outlet but the sheer scale and complexities of the Post Traumatic Stress that sat on their shoulders, undiagnosed, required far more . Although these fellas may have ended up on different journeys and in different camps after the Allied surrender, they were bound together by the common experiences of starvation, brutality, death, disease and the psychological torture of no contact with home, no predictable end point to their nightmare and the long term burden that all of those factors left them with for the rest of their lives.

Access to the kind of modern support available for PTSD may have helped them to live better and more rewarding lives, but it's another measure of their courage that so many found their own way of coping. They should not have been cut adrift and left to muddle through on their own or within the ranks of their own networks. So much more could have been done. But this was the Forgotten Army and in so many aspects of their post war lives that was where they would always remain. It is no surprise that some of the men were just left to retreat into their own worlds of pain, torment, bitterness and hatred and lived grim lives but I'm forever grateful that my Dad and most of his mates found a way to move forwards. My Mum played a massive part in that, instinctively providing the support and encouragement when it was needed most.

CHAPTER TWENTY SEVEN
Return to Singapore

It must have been a big decision for him when my Dad agreed to go back to Singapore in 1995 on a pilgrimage to mark the fiftieth anniversary of liberation. Supportive as ever, Mum, went with him, and I know that he never regretted it. The fear of stirring up grim memories was far outweighed by the prospect of confronting those demons head on and putting them behind him. I think the timing was right as well.

Dad was now 75 and it was very much a case of now or never. He had written to the Commonwealth War Graves Commission before the trip, to see if they had any information on some of his mates who had died alongside him as young, brave men more than five decades before, including Lance Corporal Dave Booker, his close friend who had helped him and comforted him when he was badly beaten by a guard and when he was at his lowest ebb. The reply was:

> *"....Private John McDonald McLeary, 6140746, serving with the 2nd Battalion, the East Surrey Regiment, died on the 5th February 1942, aged 25. Sadly, he has no known grave and is therefore commemorated by name, on the Singapore Memorial Singapore. Members of the East Surrey Regiment are commemorated on Column 70 of the Memorial.*
>
> *We also hold the additional information that he was the son of*

John and Catherine McLeary of Cambuslang, Lanarkshire.

The Singapore Memorial stands in Kranji War Cemetery, 22 kilometres north of the city of Singapore on the north side of Singapore Island, overlooking the Straits of Jahore.

Lance Corporal David William Booker, 6150586, serving with the 2nd Battalion, The East Surrey Regiment, died on the 22nd June 1943, aged 33, and is buried in Plot 6, Row F, Joint Grave 68-69, in Kanchanaburi War Cemetery, Thailand.

We do not hold any additional information on our records in respect of Lance Corporal Booker's next of kin details."

Half a century on, his mates who never made it back were uppermost in Dad's mind. He must have carried the memory of their young faces, forever frozen in time, every day of his life. I don't know whether he also carried the survivor guilt of the man lucky enough to come through. He never talked about that, but it would be a perfectly natural reaction.

I've come to believe that Lance Corporal Dave Booker quite possibly saved my Dad's life just months before he himself succumbed to the same weight of pain, starvation and sickness. Ten years older, he must have been like a big brother figure, and I'm certain he was instrumental in pulling Dad through when he was beaten, tortured and when the important currency of hope was ebbing away. Dave Booker's story is just one of many thousands that will never be told, and my Dad would have wanted him to get some sort of recognition at last.

2000 veterans, widows and relatives headed over to Singapore in September 1995, with my Mum and Dad amongst them for a ceremony at the Kranji war cemetery.

There was a full report in the *Daily Telegraph* on Wednesday 13th September:

"On a hilltop overlooking the spot where the Japanese invaded the Island in February 1942, the haunting lament from the bagpipes of two young Gurkhas filled the humid dawn air as the Duke of Kent joined veterans and dignitaries in laying wreaths at the memorial.....

John Griffiths, a private in the 2nd Bn East Surrey Regiment when he was captured in 1942, wiped away tears as buglers played Last Post. After a year on the Siam-Burma "death railway" he was sent to Japan and ended the war in a labour camp outside Nagasaki when the atom bomb was dropped on the city.

"I've got friends buried here, friends I enlisted with back in 1937. I know there have to be survivors but I always ask myself what I did to deserve it. Why me?" Said Mr Griffiths, now 76.....

Singapore fell in just seven days in one of the great debacles of the war. Most of the prisoners were sent to toil on the death railway.

Disease, starvation and torture claimed the lives of about 16,000 Allied prisoners and 100,000 Asian slave labourers. The survivors also paid heavy penalties, physically and mentally.

Les Emery, now 83, a former sergeant in the Manchester Regiment, has been hard of hearing since Japanese guards repeatedly ducked him under water and then slapped his ears, damaging his eardrums. And he walks with two sticks, the legacy of severe beatings.

"But I guess I was one of the lucky ones as I am here to talk about it. And it is not just the ex-prisoners who suffer. I still have nightmares and my wife is the one who has to calm me down and cope with that," said Mr Emery, who was held until September 21, 1945."

I am struck my how closely John and Les's stories mirror my Dad's - enlisting to the East Surreys in 1937, the guilt, the permanent and physical legacy of the beatings, and the wife who calmed and soothed them on the long, dark nights when the demons returned to torture and haunt the men all over again. It must have been an extraordinary thing for these elderly survivors to come together one last time at 7.30am on Tuesday the 12th September 1995 at Kranji Cemetery to remember. It was followed by a thanksgiving service later that day at the St Andrew's Cathedral in Singapore.

I'm still not sure what they were giving thanks for - their own survival, the ending of the war, or something else that I may have missed? The remaining men and women certainly didn't have much to thank the authorities for, as many of them were still fighting for war pensions, and collectively they still hadn't received any sort of meaningful compensation or recognition. I'm sure the old soldiers would have talked about those things, but I'm also sure they would have raised a glass to their fallen comrades.

I know that the trip, tough as it was, did Dad no end of good, and he talked about it a lot. It certainly helped him to open up a lot more at last, and something had changed in him, no longer was he reluctant to chat about his experiences, I think he started to realise that it was important people understood what had happened after the fall of Singapore and that he was part of telling that story. He was interviewed by the Regimental museum and those videos are precious to me, I just wish I'd sat down in his garden at this point with a tape recorder in front of him and allowed him to tell the whole story no matter how long it took. But I delayed doing that until it was too late and I bitterly regret it.

It was the fiftieth anniversary of VJ Day that seemed to be the catalyst for a welcome surge in interest in the campaign for justice for the Far East prisoners with some politicians and sections of the media at last taking up their case. A group of FEPOWs, including John Neale from the London branch who Dad knew, secured a special reception with the then Prince of Wales as the momentum grew. My Dad wasn't the only survivor who now decided that this was the time to start telling the world the truth. I don't know whether it was a collective and instinctive feeling that this would probably be the last chance, but I do remember Dad telling me that he was scared of answering the phone around this time as he guessed it would be news of another one of the boys who had slipped away. They were all old men, with complex health conditions often related to their captivity, and they couldn't cheat death forever. Through their local FEPOW organisations, Dad would attend meetings of the London branch at the Union Jack Club at Waterloo, they stepped up their campaigning.

In a article in the *Barnsley Express* in July 1994, Arthur Robinson, President of the Burnley and District Far East Prisoner of War Association told how he had been found in possession of a jack knife that had been used by another prisoner to lever open a food store. Arthur was badly beaten and was imprisoned in a five foot square bamboo cage in full glare of the hot sun with just a ball of rice three times a day and little water to stave off dehydration. When he was eventually released he had to be carried out of the cage too weak to walk. His story mirrors those of the few who were still left to tell it:

> *"Stricken with Malaria 11 times over the war years and after suffering with beri-beri while at home, Arthur was so weak that his wife had to push him upstairs to bed.*
>
> *Horrific memories of imprisonment and war recurred - Arthur recalls diving under a sink at home when he heard something dropping on the floor. He thought he was being machine gunned."*

Jack Shuttle, another man my Dad knew, was from Staines and told of his continuing anger in an interview with the Walton and Weybridge Informer on the 11th of August 1995:

> *"The Japanese refused to be bound by the Geneva Conventions, POWs were starved, they had no clothes, nor medicines, and were made to do the work of slaves.*
>
> *"Red Cross parcels were plundered and the Japanese could not accept that people were too ill to work," Jack said. "I would never go back and I can't forgive. I think of friends of mine who died purely from being mistreated."*
>
> *Jack was picked to join the work gangs being used as slave labour to construct the Thailand to Burma railway.*
>
> *"We had no tools. We had to hack our way through bamboo jungle. The thorns were two inches long and the conditions were terrible."*

Another man, Bob Hawke, had risked death and torture to keep a diary on the railway. Speaking to the Cornwall

Advertiser in March 1996 Bob revealed that his diaries would at last be finding a permanent home at last at the Imperial War Museum - adding another important resource for anyone looking to explore first hand accounts of the treatment meted out to the prisoners.

One diary entry reads:

> *"I pray God with all my heart that some of us will survive to tell this awful tale to the world, so that this war for civilisation be not fought in vain."*

The fact that it had taken over fifty years for that tale to at last be told is shameful. Politicians had paid lip service to the prisoners and internees for more than a half a century. Sergeant Bill Lawson of the 125 anti-tank regiment who was captured at the fall of Singapore puts the lasting feelings of my father and many others brilliantly in an interview with the *Sunderland Echo* on the 24th April 1998:

> *"Those who were not there will never be able to comprehend what it was like, says Bill - and only those who were there can truly understand what survivors can neither forgive or forget.*
>
> *"Hatred is a word that I hesitate to use generally speaking but I am very near to it," he says.*
>
> *"People have said that time is a great healer, that if we cannot forget, we should at least forgive. I will never forgive the Japanese for the treatment I received during the 3 ½ years I was in their hands.*
>
> *"And as far as forgetting is concerned, the experience is so indelibly written on my mind that no way can I ever forget.*
>
> *"No one can understand. My wife and daughter can't understand. They try but they can't. Because they did not experience this, it is impossible for them to do so.*
>
> *"This is not a burning hatred, festering inside me. I am fortunate to be able to put it aside in my day to day life - but it will never go away."*
>
> *"I was one of the fortunate ones, in as much as I came back."*

Bill's words are almost a mirror of how my Dad felt.

I remember vividly a conversation with him around the whole "forgive and forget" issue. How could he forget when he bore the mental cars, the post-trauma and the repeating nightmares that would never allow him even if he had wanted to. He also had the physical reminders of the ridge along the back of his skull that he would run his hand across and the long term health issues associated directly with his captivity.

How on earth do you forgive sadists and psychopaths who have not only ground you into the jungle dirt but have been responsible for the deaths of so many of your young mates whose lingering, painful and tortured end you have watched day in and day out? I stand fully with my Dad on this. His tormentors weren't soldiers following some mythical Japanese warrior code - they were a bunch of cowards and animals directed by the forces of Japanese imperialism who saw no value in the lives of the prisoners they had captured.

In 1998 Japan's Emperor Akihito made a state visit to the UK. The former prisoners saw this as an opportunity to force their case into the headlines. These were brave and patriotic men who had made huge sacrifices for their country and many, like my Dad, were proud professional soldiers. But they had had enough of being ignored. Protests were held in London and Cardiff where a line of elderly veterans, wearing their medals and berets, turned their backs on the state procession and some booed and others whistled Colonel Bogey.

It must have been a difficult decision to make to bring their campaign into public view in such a direct and pointed way. They wanted both an official apology and serious compensation. Taking that hard decision to go for direct action that they knew would embarrass both the Japanese and the British state proved to be a sound one, and to some extent it worked. Although the Emperor said he could "never forget" the suffering during the war his spokesperson said that he could not apologise further because of "constitutional restrictions".

The spokesman did say in terms of the brutality to

British soldiers and internees...."*Those individuals who engaged in such acts...it was beastly. I am very sorry about it.*" Half-baked to say the least, and a refusal to accept any collective responsibility, but clearly the Japanese were embarrassed, and that would in itself put pressure on the British Government to take note. But these men should never have been forced to go to such lengths.

CHAPTER TWENTY EIGHT

Some Recognition at Last

On the 7th November 2000 my father eventually got some good news as a 55 year battle for some serious compensation and recognition of his years in captivity as a POW was at last resolved. Blair's Labour Government had earlier agreed that the prisoners and internees should have their suffering acknowledged and compensated, and they were true to their word. Lewis Moonie, the then defence minister, confirmed that all former FEPOWs and the wives of those that had died would receive a tax-free, ex-gratia payment of £10,000 in what he described as a "debt of honour." The cost, £167 million, was met from the public purse, with the government making it clear that they wouldn't pursue the Japanese for the money. It was very much a political solution but despite that it was a step forward and should be viewed as just that.

Arthur Titherington, chairman of the Japanese Labour Camps Survivors Association said:

> *"Today is a great day. The British Government has shown that it has fully understood the importance of these issues to today's society.*
>
> *"My only disappointment is that the real culprit, that is the Japanese government has got away scot-free. The least that it can do is recognise the gross errors of its past which it can do by providing a full, unequivocal apology."*

By this time my father was eighty years old and his remaining comrades would have been of a similar vintage. They could certainly have done with proper compensation and recognition much sooner as they attempted to rebuild their lives rather than the £76 they were awarded under the terms of the San Francisco peace treaty in 1951. That treaty also included a clause that if Japan agreed to better terms with other countries, British POWs could demand the same. In 1955 former Swiss POWs received £2000 but documents later released by the Public Record Office show that the Government never pursued this at the time, for fear of upsetting the Japanese. Lord Reading, a foreign office minister at the time, made that clear in the newly uncovered files:

> *"....we are at present unpopular enough with the Japanese without having to exert further pressure which would be likely to cause the maximum of resentment for the minimum of advantage."*

For over five decades British politicians had seen the former Japanese prisoners as an inconvenience who at best should be paid lip service. The stepping up of the campaign around the 50th anniversary of VJ Day, some decent press coverage, the protest at the Emperor's state visit and the support of a core group of MPs had been crucial. A group of prisoners had met Blair soon after his landslide victory in 1997, and he had listened to them and taken their case seriously, I know that my Dad respected him for that and for delivering on his promises a couple of years later. He had nothing but contempt for those of all political stripes who had failed to act for decades. Perhaps it was easier for a government in 2000 so many years down the line, but I'm not so sure. I think they should be given the credit that they deserve.

My Dad didn't spend a lot of time talking about politics but I know he followed political developments closely in the newspaper and on the TV. He generally had a pretty low opinion of politicians even at a time before they became the circus that they are today, and the series of betrayals and cock ups by the British Establishment which dragged him all the way down the Malayan Peninsula to the humiliation of Singapore would have understandably coloured his views. His trust needed to be earned.

But he never forgot where he came from. His experiences as a Non Commissioned Officer and as a public servant in the NHS left him perfectly capable of holding his own in any company but he was never happier than when he was sipping a glass of stout with those who shared his own experiences and background. I remember being in a pub with him and his mate Freddie Jenkins who was a local official on the post with the Communications Workers Union and we were talking about a current dispute. Freddie said to Dad, you don't talk much about your politics Cliff do you? I remember so clearly Dad's reply… *.."you don't come from where I've come from and see what I've seen without ending up a socialist mate."*

If there's a politician he did have time for it would be Dennis Healy. Dad and I would watch Mike Yarwood lampooning members of the Government and although he never made it to the top job Healy was quite possibly the best-known politician in the seventies, and was mimicked from workplace to pub to school playground. Healy played that media game brilliantly and came across as self-deprecating and, most importantly, a genuinely well-grounded human being.

For Dad there was another important factor - Healy had been a beach captain during the allied landings at Anzio. This stuff mattered to him. At the time Dennis Healy was regarded as being on the right of the Labour Party, but he represented a kind of meat and potatoes, traditional socialism that my Dad identified with. We would argue about this, particularly when Tony Benn challenged Healy for the Labour deputy leadership and I had all that idealism and conviction of youth to throw into the debate. Today Healy himself would be regarded as being on the left of the modern Labour Party, and now I'm able to step back and understand why Dad respected him.

Whenever the New Year or Queen's Birthday honours lists came out, Dad would give them a cursory glance. I know it hacked him off that entertainers, politicians and business leaders would land various top-notch gongs while he kept his five very basic medals for all his years of service and suffering tucked away in a box in his wardrobe. Well connected people who weren't fit to lace the boots of my Dad and his old comrades would be in the news turning up at the Palace and waving around their glittering awards. He called it 'the old boys' network', and it certainly stirred the class warrior within him, but he would put the kettle on and put it out of his mind. The thing is he knew that the honours system, like so much else, was loaded against the likes of him and he didn't need to be reminded of it two or three times a year.

During those post war years, when Dad very rarely talked to people about his background and his wartime experiences, he became used to being patronised and would just shrug it off. I remember when I was at junior school a firework event was being organised and Dad volunteered to help out. I went along with him in the afternoon when the fireworks were being set up, including some fairly heavy duty stuff. A quite obnoxious man a good few years younger than Dad had assumed control and as some fuses were being laid he asked my father if he had any military and ordnance experience - "a bit", he said.

It turned out the bloke had been a captain in the Territorials and had never fired a shot in anger, but was very happy to dish out the orders. Dad just laughed it off, he was used to dealing with Captain Mainwaring type figures, Dads' Army was another programme we watched together and I remember a school holiday trip with him to see the film and we laughed our heads off, but I'm not sure I would have been so relaxed dealing with pompous fools. I think over the years my father had learnt to erect barriers around parts of his life and had also worked out that it wasn't worth expending energy and time challenging or explaining himself to people he clearly viewed as idiots. I wonder to this day how many people he encountered in civilian life had the slightest idea what he had been through and I suspect it was very few and I think he was just fine with that. It bears repeating that he was a proud man and the last thing he would have wanted was to be pitied, that is such a central pillar of his post-war story.

Dad had decided quite early on that he wasn't going to allow himself to become consumed with hate and anger, I think that he realised that that tightening ball of negative energy could easily consume you and would just cause you more pain in the long term. I'm sure that he thought that through for himself, he could never "forgive and forget" of course and he had contempt for anyone who suggested he should but over time he developed a finely tuned sense of perspective. He had seen first hand enough hate to last many lifetimes.

He told of how when he was working in London in the sixties if he saw a Japanese man walking towards him he would cross the street, that wasn't because he was a racist, it was because he was bloody scared! His own internal trauma could be easily triggered and he had to deal with that, and over time he did. Those intense feelings passed and I remember Dad talking to one of my mates' Japanese girlfriend in the pub using bits and pieces of phrases he remembered from the camps, and when she asked him where he learnt the language, he just told her he had travelled a bit.

He didn't blame her generation for what had happened to him, but of course it would have annoyed him that she probably would have known very little about what had happened to the POWs. When one former American prisoner went back to Mitsushima the local mayor denied that there had ever even been a camp there.

I think it's that denial, and the airbrushing out of history the truth of what happened to my Dad and thousands of others like him, that aggrieved him the most. I still feel that bitterness today, it's in my DNA, and it's one of the reasons I want his story to be told. He wasn't narrow minded in any way, he broadened his horizons at every opportunity, believed passionately in education and he never wanted his life to be defined by what had happened to him over those three and a half years in captivity but of course it would always cast a long shadow.

I know that a lot of former prisoners refused to buy any Japanese products for the rest of their lives. A number of the companies that went on to become household names had been built on the slave labour of the POWs, the dam that my Dad helped construct was still generating electricity to power these booming industries outside Tokyo. That angered him, while he had been left to struggle on with little or no recognition others were getting rich on the back of the hard and brutal work he had been forced into while starving, sick and exhausted. Those companies never compensated the men they had been allocated by the camps and their disgust is wholly justified.

When I was a young child I remember Mum and Dad being reluctant to buy Japanese toys, but I never really understood why. By the time I was a teenager in the seventies my first motorbike was a Honda. I know Dad was uneasy but he realised by then that there was no real alternative: the British motorcycle industry had been wiped out by cheap imports and he couldn't personally hold back the tide of the Japanese economy. So despite his reservations his pragmatism won out. He helped me buy the motorbike the 16 year old me so desperately wanted, I now hope that decision wasn't too painful for him and maybe I should have been more sensitive, but he put me first, as was his way.

It's a hard reality for the child of any prisoner held in Japan as the war drew to a close that they owe their life to the dropping of the atom bombs on Hiroshima and Nagasaki. A ground invasion would have almost certainly have meant that the "Kill All Prisoners" order would have been actioned and even if it hadn't I'm not sure my father and his mates would have survived another freezing winter, starving in the mountains outside Tokyo as the Japanese fought to the death for every inch of territory. That final land battle would have gone on for months and probably years and I suspect the meagre rations made available to the POW camps would have been diverted to the war effort.

Some military analysts suggest that the war would have gone on until 1948 with apocalyptic levels of casualties.

My Dad would have died one way or another - through starvation, sickness, execution or being death-marched deeper into the country - and not only would I not be writing this here in my kitchen right now but my kids and future generations of our family would never have seen the light of day. When I watched the movie Oppenheimer it was much more than a historical document to me, it was a fact of life.

But I'm conflicted, I've read the reports of the mass loss of life, destruction and legacy of sickness unleashed by the atom bombs. It breaks my heart that those men, women and children had to suffer in such numbers to bring the war to an end and secure the release from captivity of my Dad and thousands of other surviving prisoners and internees. The military and civilian casualties from any ground invasion would have been horrendous by any account as plans to throw women and children into the front line had already been drafted before Hiroshima and Nagasaki.

It's also a fact that the Japanese were racing to develop their own atom bomb, and there's no question if they had got there first they would have used it. For my father this was just about pure pragmatism. He knew full well that he owed his life to Dr Robert Oppenheimer and the Manhattan Project, and despite the lingering traces of my own youthful idealism I know that he was right. I may want to see a world free from nuclear weapons but I cannot rewrite my own family's history and that pivots on my Dad's survival and eventual liberation.

CHAPTER TWENTY NINE

The Last Post

As the years clicked by there were fewer and fewer survivors of the camps left and the dwindling numbers, and the serious health issues confronting those who remained, meant that it became impossible to keep the FEPOW Associations functioning. Dad dropped back as well and I know that he also found the constant barrage of funerals exhausting and distressing and became selective in those that he would summon up the physical energy and mental resources to attend.

On Remembrance Sunday he would get up early as usual, have a shave, comb his snow-white hair back over his broken skull, pull on his beret and wait for me to show up to take him and Mum over to the annual parade in Kingston. He still marched with pride and purpose and if the autumn sun shone through a crack in the clouds it would glint off the cap badge he had polished the evening before.

He was a soldier and those soldiering instincts never left him but we both knew that his time was running out, as I used to watch him from the crowd no son had ever loved a father more but the words of the great Eric Bogle song ***The Band Played Waltzing Matilda*** would run through my head:

"And the band plays Waltzing Matilda
And the old men still answer the call
But year after year, their numbers get fewer
Someday no one will march there at all"

My father had nothing but the utmost respect for the brave men of the Allied forces who had landed on the Normandy beaches on D-Day in June 1944. He knew some of them after the war, and he also knew that their sacrifice and success had helped free up the resources and materials needed to fight the war in the Pacific theatre.

But the regular anniversaries of D-Day, and the focus on VE Day that conveyed the impression it had marked the end of the war, was another reminder that the men who had fought and been captured in the Far East were so often written out of the script.

The casualty rate sustained by the 2nd Battalion East Surreys from the point of the Japanese invasion of Malaya up to their surrender in August 1945 is one of the worst to befall any regiment during WW2 but you hear very little of it. I fully understand the media concentration on D-Day, and Dad was proud to march alongside its ageing survivors in the annual remembrance parade in Kingston, but like many FEPOWs he would have resented the fact that his story of bravery and courage was so rarely told alongside theirs.

It wasn't his fault he was part of the retreat down the Malaysian peninsular or the humiliating surrender at Singapore: far from it, he and his comrades fought like lions and so many paid the ultimate price. But there was no liberation of Paris or hero's welcome for them, just the bitter years as slave labourers - starved, diseased and brutalised - to be pushed out of the public view. That really is the scandal of the Forgotten Army and it's shameful that it still persists.

But life wasn't all about doom and gloom and staring death in the face in Dad's later years. In January 1986 my sister and her husband Martin had made another dream come true for him and Mum when they presented him with a granddaughter, my niece Christina, and some years later he had two other grandchildren to dote on - our daughters Katie and Joanna. None of those kids would have drawn their first breath or seen their first dawn if he hadn't struggled and survived against all the odds in those long hard years of captivity.

I, my sister and our children owe everything to him and in writing this tribute I want them, their children and any future generations of our family to have a permanent record that can help them understand their history and the foundations their lives are built on. Every family has a story and my father's fight for survival is a big part of theirs. My eldest also gave him an opportunity to wheel out one of his favourite Irish tunes - *I'll Take You Home Kathleen* - and he would well up as he serenaded her with that emotionally charged belter.

I don't think I ever saw him sing a song without a tear in the corner of his eye. And he laughed a lot as well, roaring away at the classic TV comedies we grew up with, he always shared a joke with my mates when they came round the house and that's how they like to remember him. He would also give them good advice and one of his old favourites was to 'never turn down the opportunity for a cup of tea, a sit down and a piss': that one had been learnt from hard and bitter experience over the years and it was wise counsel.

On the 30th May 2002 the London FEPOW Association held their last ever service of remembrance at St Martin's-in-the-Fields, they had gathered in the same place every year since 1957 but as age and the cycle of life and death motored its way through their ranks it was decided that after 45 years it was right to call time.

A report by Brian McArthur in *The Times* paints the picture:

> *"After 45 years the Last Post sounded at St Martin's-in-the-Fields on Tuesday as members of the London's Far East Prisoners of War Association laid up their standard at their final service of remembrance. The service has been held by the FEPOWs at St Martin's every year since 1957 but most of the surviving FEPOWs are now in their eighties and they are becoming frail.*
>
> *'The years are passing and our members are ageing,' said Fred Ryall, their chairman, who was a prisoner in Java, the island of Haruku and Singapore. 'It's better to end our tradition while we can still act with dignity and are capable of organising this fitting conclusion.'*

> *Each year, as the Rev. Nicholas Holtam said in his address, there have been fewer in the congregation. Those who were left grew older and age did not weary them. It seemed characteristically realistic and courageously straightforward, he said, that they had decided that this service should be the last service.*
>
> *It was a poignant afternoon for the congregation of about three hundred, all with memories of their three and a half years of captivity under the Japanese and the cruelty and brutality they suffered at the hands of their guards. The FEPOWs are from an age when men wore suits and ties and held themselves erect whatever their infirmities...."*

My father was there, and it would be the last time he would see many of his old comrades.

Death didn't scare my Dad, he had stared it in the face often enough and as a young man from the point that the Japanese invaded at the top end of Malaya on the 8th December 1941 he had spent years where it came fast, sudden and often. It stalked the trenches he dug, the rotten huts he was held in, the death marches he embarked upon, the hospital camps he was never expected to survive and the Hell Ship hold he was rammed into.

He wrapped, buried or burnt the corpses of many of his mates who were cut down in the prime of their life and he had battled through to make it to old bones and he always knew just how fortunate he was. Everything he could have hoped for on liberation and repatriation he had achieved.

He had built a life and a family and had seen his kids grow up and go on to have their own children, he got to enjoy time with his grandkids. That was the ultimate victory for him. The only thing that ever bothered him about death was leaving Mum on her own, and Jan and I promised him on numerous occasions that whatever happened we would make sure that Mum was looked after.

Dad remained active through his later years and would still walk up and down the hill to the corner shop to pick up his morning paper for as long as he could, never without having a shave and putting a collar and tie on.

Often he would bump into my old mate Keith who still lived on the same road and unprompted Dad would open up and talk to him about the war, he trusted him. Keith told me that Dad recounted a tale of how he was on patrol in Malaya when they spotted a group of Japanese soldiers on bicycles.... "we machine-gunned them, killed the lot, they would have done the same to us," he said matter of factly and with that he was off to finish his constitutional.

The incident must have been on his mind for some reason but he wasn't bragging, he never did, and in fact he rarely talked about the war at all, even by this stage, unless it was with someone he felt comfortable with, he despised those ten-bob hard men who boast about how tough they are.

He talked with my wife Helen about some of his experiences, she's a nurse and trade union activist and he respected and adored her. Profoundly deaf by this stage, thanks to the machine gun training in a corrugated iron shed in Essex as a squaddie and the beatings in the jungle camps, Dad had taught himself to lip read and Helen was one of the first to notice this. It was another measure of his determination to cope with whatever adversity was thrown at him.

But time was catching up with Dad now and soon he was unable to manage the hill back from the paper shop and had to have "the coggage", as he called it, delivered. It annoyed him because I think he felt it was another sign that the sands of time were now slipping through his fingers and of course he was right.

I took him to see an old regimental mate of his at the Star and Garter Home up on Richmond Hill, a care establishment for ex-military personnel similar to the Chelsea Hospital with its famous Pensioners.

He was impressed, the Star and Garter was run on military lines and Dad asked me to promise that if it ever came to it I would try and get him in there. I told him not to be so daft and reassured him that he was still punching his weight and had plenty of gas in the tank, but I made a mental note of his request. If in his final years he had to rely on permanent care and support it should be somewhere he felt comfortable with: but it would never come to that.

The 2008 Cup Final was played at Wembley on 17th May with Cardiff City and Portsmouth competing for the trophy. I knew my Dad would be watching it, we always watched the FA Cup Final, and I also knew he was pleased that two less fashionable but historic clubs would be battling it out. As a bloke who loved the traditional pomp of the occasion he would be looking forward to it.

I rang him on the morning of the game and told him I'd pop over to mow his lawn, on the way I picked him up four cans of Mackeson milk stout - his favourite tipple. I'd made arrangements to watch the game later with some of my mates at The Plough in Sutton. It was a bright, dry morning and the old man seemed to be on good form and as Mum put the kettle on for a cup of tea I set to work with the lawnmower. Radio Two was on the wireless and it couldn't have been a more normal start to the day.

Dad was 88 years old now and although he was slower on his pegs and a bit shaky at times he remained with it and remarkably sharp. As I ploughed on with the small patch of grass at the back of the house I heard a loud, pained cry from upstairs. I knew it was my Dad and I legged it into the house and up to his bedroom and found him tangled on the floor where he had fallen.

It was clear he was in some real pain so we didn't try to move him and I dialled an ambulance while Mum stayed with him. Forever the soldier, he remained remarkably calm but couldn't understand why we wouldn't let him try to pull himself up. The paramedics arrived swiftly and took control.

It turned up that Dad had been trying to get his strides on, lost his balance and toppled over. We didn't know it then but in the process he had fractured his hip. The ambulance crew instinctively seemed to have picked this up as the likely scenario. As they did some tests and started manoeuvring Dad to get him down the stairs he began serenading the female crew member with one of his favourite tunes:

"Once I built a railway, made it run.....
Made it race against time
Once I built a railway, now it's done
Buddy can you spare a dime...."

It was no wonder that people fell in love with this beautiful old character, even people who knew nothing about the life that he had lived. Of course he didn't want to go to hospital, and told the medics that if they could just get him up on his feet he would be grand. But of course he wouldn't, and somehow we managed to get him on the stretcher and out of the house and into the ambulance, he must have been in agony but didn't show it.

Mum remained a tower of strength and went with him while I made a few calls and followed on in the car with stuff that I thought Dad would need thrown into a bag, knowing that this was going to be a long day.

He was admitted, taken down to X-ray and they confirmed the worst, a compound fracture of the hip. The nurses made him as comfortable as possible on the ward after I had helped him into his pyjamas and although he was now on analgesia I could see the pain in his eyes and he winced as he moved.

As I left the hospital that night I still didn't realise that my father was fighting his last battle. I remembered a conversation I'd had with him just a few weeks before when he asked me if I thought he would make it to ninety, I told him he'd go way beyond that as he'd proved time and time again that he was indestructible.

But that time was now running out. Dad was moved to St Helier Hospital. I had a holiday booked with the family, and Dad, Mum and my sister were all adamant that we should go, I went to see him just before we left and his appearance troubled me, he was the frailest and weakest he had been since the day of his liberation from Mitsushima POW camp on the 4th September 1945.

I made sure he got shaved, brought up a decent strong cup of tea from the canteen, got a nurse to sort a bed pan as he was "busting for a crap" and said goodbye for the last time.

I didn't realise it was to be the last time, and if I had I would have stayed and I would have talked to him and I would have told him just how much I loved him.

Dad contracted pneumonia. I got a call from my sister saying that he was very poorly, but by the time I had managed to get a flight back from Alicante my father had died. My Mum and my sister had been with him at the end but I can't help but feel that I had let him down, I don't think my mother ever recovered from being there as the love of her life slipped away from her. I know that there's nothing I could have done by then, but I owed it to him to be there, I made it back just too late.

For my Mum the grief and sense of loss was overwhelming. She had been with Dad for over sixty years and married for 59 of them. She had been the rock on which he had anchored and built a life after the years of trauma in captivity. In return he had showered her with a love, respect and loyalty that was incalculable. We rallied around her while dealing with our own grief. My mate, my hero and the rock solid geezer who had always been there for me had gone and we had to do what was right by him now.

Dad died on the 1st of June 2008 in Mary Moore Ward at St Helier. I registered his death the following day with the cause being recorded as myocardial infarction, atrial fibrillation and bronchopneumonia. The hip fracture is listed as a secondary cause. The death certificate just defines him as being born in Stepney in 1919 and dying in Carshalton in 2008, it would fall to me much later to tell the story as best I can of what happened in his life in between.

Dad's funeral was held at Randalls Park Crematorium just outside Leatherhead on the 12th June. We knew that he wouldn't have wanted a religious service so I decided that I would take on responsibility for conducting the ceremony. A Regimental Colour Party was in attendance, along with as many of his old mates who could make it, proceedings opened up with Nessun Dorma and my best mate Keith Connor read out the poem "Ours Was A Common Cause" that my father had written in captivity.

There was a nod to his Irish roots with Danny Boy, a song he was fond of singing, and which would have reminded him of his own father, and my wife Helen paid a glowing tribute to just what an inspirational figure Dad really was.

At the committal, a bugler piped the Last Post and the crematorium emptied to the tune of Unforgettable by the great Nat King Cole. The wake was held at my sister's house in Cheam where as much memorabilia from Dad's life as we could find was out on display.

I had contacted the local press and the *Post*, *Guardian* and *Comet* all wrote up lovely tributes with the *Epsom Guardian* running the headline:

> *"Farewell to hero who lived through horror.*
>
> *A former regimental sergeant major of the East Surrey Regiment who was starved, beaten and tortured during the Second World War has died.*
>
> *Cliff Martin survived horrendous cruelty and hardships when he became a Japanese prisoner of war and was forced to work on the notorious Thailand Burma railway that cost the lives of 16,000 allied troops."*

I know my father would have been surprised at this coverage, as he had long thought that few people, if any, would be interested in his story. I remember him welling up when some kids at the local school who were studying the war popped a handmade card through the door thanking him for his service and saying how sorry they were that he had suffered - one of the teachers had heard about him.

He would have been pleased though, not on a personal level but because his death at a ripe old age helped shine a light into the suffering of his comrades during a period of Second World War that is too easily forgotten. Shortly afterwards I received a letter from the local MP, the Conservative Chris Grayling, and although it's been mislaid down the years I remember clearly that he said that although he didn't share my Dad's politics he wanted to pay tribute to a brave and heroic Epsom man. I really appreciated that and thanked him for taking the trouble to pay his respects.

A massive hole had been left in all of our lives. I don't think Mum ever really recovered from the loss, and sadly she died in St Helier Hospital in November the following the year, bringing an end to an era of the Martin family. Some fifteen years later I still think about my parents every day. My Dad's story is my Mum's story as well: getting myself together to write up that story has truly been a labour of love.

EPILOGUE

Janette Moore - Cliff's daughter.

Firstly I want to say thank you to Geoff for writing our Dad's story. What an incredible story it is.

Through Geoff's extensive research I have learnt things about Dad that I didn't know. What is especially surprising for me is the fact that he was sent on an army reserve exercise after I was born. This was something that was never spoken of. I would love to know where he was sent at that time.

I was very interested to read about Intergenerational Trauma, something that I had never heard of before. I realise that I have always felt very conflicted when people talk about the horrors of war. They would often refer to Hiroshima and Nagasaki. I wouldn't know whether I should tell them that without the dropping of the atom bombs my family would not exist.

Dad would spend hours helping me to revise for exams. I realise now that he loved doing this because he also loved learning new things, and by revising with me he was extending his own knowledge.

Dad was so proud when my daughter Christina went to university. He would tell everyone that she was the first person in our family to go to university. It was heartbreaking that he died just months before she graduated. He would have been overjoyed at the achievements of all three of his granddaughters.

Our Dad loved reading. If I left a book downstairs when I went out or went to bed, Dad would start reading it. He would then talk to me about the book and usually he had enjoyed it. In fact he was the most unlikely fan of Danielle Steel! Not so keen on Stephen King though.

Mum and Dad loved their garden. I can remember as a child being in bed in the summer evenings and hearing Mum and Dad working and chatting in the garden. It's when I am working in my garden that I feel closest to them both. When Mum and I returned to my home on the Sunday afternoon after Dad had died, after making phone calls there wasn't anything more we could do until Monday morning. It was a beautiful sunny early summer's day and I had already got my bedding plants ready to pot up. We decided that Dad would hate us to be sitting around, so together we spent the afternoon planting flowers and chatting about Dad.

One memory that stays with me is that the day before Dad died, Mum and I were visiting him. I noticed that he was clinging on so tightly to the safety bars around his bed. I took hold of one of his hands and told him that he didn't need to hold on and that he was safe. He looked deep into my eyes and said "so I can let go?" I replied "yes Dad, you don't need to hold on."

My final memory is of Dad's funeral. As the final notes from the bugle faded there was one massive clap of thunder. I believe that was our Dad's last farewell.

Sources

Ancestry *ancestry.co.uk*
Anzac Portal *www.anzacportal.dva.gov.au*
Barnard, Captain John T. *The Endless Years*, Chantry Publications, 1950
Booth, Charles Inquiry into the Life and Labour of the People of London, Museum of London, *www.londonmuseum.org.uk*
Bridge Over The River Kwai, Columbia Pictures 1957
Britain at War *www.britain-at-war.org*
British Newspaper Archive *www.britishnewspaperarchive.co.uk*
Burton, Reginald *Railway Of Hell*. Pen and Sword 2010
Chye Kooi Loong *The British Battalion Malaya 1941-1942*. Privately printed 1984
Clarke, Hugh V, *A Life For Every Sleeper* Allen And Unwin 1986
Clarkson, Wensley *Hit 'Em Hard*. Harper Collins 2002
Coast, John, *Railroad Of Death*. Hyperion 1946
Daws, Gavan *Prisoners Of The Japanese*. Simon & Schuster 2006
Dunlop, Sir Edward *The War Diaries Of*...Penguin 2010
English, Jeffery *One For Every Sleeper*. Robert Hale 1989
Exploring Surrey's Past *www.exploringsurreyspast.org.uk*
Fepow History *www.fepowhistory.wordpress.com*
Gavin, Denis, *Quiet Jungle Angry Sea*, Lennard Publishing 1989
Gordon, Richard M *Horyo*. Paragon House 1999
Hansard UK *www.hansard.parliament.uk*
Henderson, Stan *Comrades on the Kwai*. Open Door Publications (no date)

Historic uk ***www.historic-uk.com***
Imperial War Museum ***www.iwm.org.uk***
Jackson, Bob. *A Doctor's Sword.* Collins Press 2017
Jacobs, Joe, *Out Of The Ghetto.* Phoenix Press 1991
Linehan, Thomas P, *East London For Mosley.* Frank Cass 1996
Liverpool School of Tropical Medicine ***www.lstmed.com***
Living in Stepney ***www.alondoninheritance.com***
London, Jack, *People of the Abyss.* Tangerine Press Reissue 2021
Lost Pubs Project ***www.closedpubs.co.uk***
Lowry, Cecil *Last Post On The River Kwai*. Pen and Sword 2018
Macarthur, Brian *Surviving The Sword.* Abacus 2006
Mansell, Roger ***www.mansell.com***
Mclachlan, Grant, *A Chronicle Of Defiance* ***www.sparrowbook.net***
Me, My Dad and The Atomic Bomb ***www.timshistoryhack.wordpress.com***
National Archives Kew ***www.nationalarchives.gov.uk***
National Army Museum ***www.nam.ac.uk***
National WWII Museum ***www.nationalww2museum.org***
Parkes, Meg & Gill, Geoff *Captive Memories* Palatine Books 2015
Percival, Arthur *The War In Malaya.* Eyre and Spottiswoode 1949
Reed Bill, with Mitch Peeke *Lost Souls Of The River Kwai.* Pen and Sword 2004
Regimental History 2nd Battalion East Surreys ***www.passeyfamilytree.org.uk***
Queen's Royal Surrey Regiment ***www.queensroyalsurreys.org.uk***
Sandler, Stanley. *World War II In The Pacific.* Garland Publishing 2001
Searle, Ronald *To The Kwai And Back.* Collins/Imperial War Museum 1986
Sherwood, Johnny *Lucky Johnny.* Hodder and Stoughton 2014
Shuttle, Jack. *Destination Kwai.* Tucann 1994
Smith, Donald *And All The Trumpets.* Panther 1960

Smyth, Terry. *Captive Fathers, Captive Children.* Bloomsbury Academic 2023
Solidarity and Suspicion; Irish Catholic and Jewish Radical Politics in East London ***www.liverpooluniversitypress.blog***
Spalding, bill. *Speedo! Speedo!* Majik Ink 2001
Stepney Reconstruction Group. *Living In Stepney.* Toynbee Hall 1945
Summers, Julie. *The Colonel Of Tamarkan.* Simon & Schuster 2005
Taylor, Ellie *Faith Hope And Rice.* Pen And Sword 2015
Taylor, Ronnie ***www.fepow-community.org.uk & www.roll-of-honour.org.uk***
The Changi Cross ***www.thechangicross.co.uk***
The Real Story Behind The 'Bridge On The River Kwai' ***www.coffeeordie.com***
Thompson, Peter *The Battle For Singapore.* Portrait 2005
Troubled Waters ***www.keymilitary.com***
Trove ***www.trove.nla.gov.au***
Urquhart, Alistair *The Forgotten Highlander* Abacus 2011
War Gen ***www.wargen.org***
Weinstein, Alfred *A Barbed Wire Surgeon* Brian Weinstein 2014
Wellcome Library ***www.wellcomelibrary.org***
Wolveridge, Jim *Ain't It Grand (This Was Stepney).* Stepney Books 1976
World at War. ITV 1973
Wyatt, John with Lowry, Cecil *No Mercy From The Japanese.* Pen and Sword 2008